Studies in Childhood and Family in Canada

Studies in Childhood and Family in Canada is a multidisciplinary series devoted to new perspectives on these subjects as they evolve. The series features studies that focus on the intersections of age, class, race, gender, and region as they contribute to a Canadian understanding of childhood and family, both historically and currently.

Series Editor
Cynthia Comacchio
Department of History
Wilfrid Laurier University

Manuscripts to be sent to
Brian Henderson, Director
Wilfrid Laurier University Press
75 University Avenue West
Waterloo, Ontario, Canada, N2L 3C5

Evangelical Balance Sheet

Character, Family, and Business
in Mid-Victorian Nova Scotia

B. Anne Wood

Wilfrid Laurier University Press

We acknowledge the financial support of the Government of Canada through the Book Publishing Industry Development Program for our publishing activities.

Library and Archives Canada Cataloguing in Publication

Wood, B. Anne (Beatrice Anne), 1937–
    Evangelical balance sheet : character, family, and business in mid-Victorian Nova Scotia / B. Anne Wood.

(Studies in childhood and family in Canada)
Includes bibliographical references and index.
ISBN-13: 978-0-88920-500-0
ISBN-10: 0-88920-500-0

    1. Rudolf, W. Norman, 1835–1886—Diaries. 2. Rudolf, W. Norman, 1835–1886—Religion. 3. Rudolf, W. Norman, 1835–1886—Family. 4. Nova Scotia—Social life and customs—19th century. 5. Nova Scotia—History—1784–1867. 6. Nova Scotia—History—1867–1918. 7. Nova Scotia—Economic conditions—19th century. 8. Merchants—Nova Scotia—Diaries. I. Title. II. Series.

FC2322.1.R83W65 2006   971.6'02092   C2006-902838-9

© 2006 Wilfrid Laurier University Press
Waterloo, Ontario, Canada
www.wlupress.wlu.ca

Cover design by Sandra Friesen, using a photograph by J. Kennedy, courtesy of Margo (Rudolf) Coleman. Background image is a page from "A Collection of Gaelic Poetry by Dr. Hector Maclean in Mull" from the Gaelic Collection of the Nova Scotia Archives and Record Management. Text design by Catharine Bonas-Taylor.

Printed in Canada

To the memory of Mum, whose idealism was always
balanced by respect for "de l'ordinaire"

We have two natures, or lives—
one our natural one, which is not always
allowed to develop or have fair play,
and the other the worldly—the "struggle-for-life"
—the business hard-sided one.

— W. Norman Rudolf, Journal,
vol. 3, 17 September 1875

W. Norman Rudolf, 30 January 1878. Notman Collection #36090,
Nova Scotia Archives and Records Management, N-8837

Mrs. W. Norman Rudolf (Cassie), 3 November 1906.
Courtesy of Margo (Rudolf) Coleman, Toronto

CONTENTS

ACKNOWLEDGMENTS

T his ship has been on a long journey. At the start, two family descendants of Norman Rudolf, Robert Weld and Margo (Rudolf) Coleman, loaned me the original journals and searched for family photographs. The Right Reverend A.G. Peters, Bishop of Nova Scotia, and the Reverend Dale Cuffe, Rector of St. James Anglican Church, Pictou, granted me permission to examine the church records of St. James Church. The staff at the Nova Scotia Archives and Records Management (NSARM), especially Barry Cahill, were very helpful in assisting me to locate the limited family-source materials. As we were in the process of moving from Pictou to Victoria, BC, I appreciated the excellent photocopying work done by Ginny Clarke of the microfilm copies of Rudolf's journals housed at NSARM. I thank all for helping me launch this vessel.

During the voyage, many people guided me. A number offered me valuable navigational tips and professional advice, and suggested further sources to explore—Peter Clarke and Maria Tippett, Faith Gildenhuys, Lynne Marks, John Money, Eric Sager, and Ann West. Several anonymous readers provided constructive criticism. I thank all of them for their assistance. I also greatly appreciated the encouragement and support of my husband, Connla Wood, over the many years of my Pictou research and writing. During rough storms and long doldrums, he proved a steadying hand at the tiller. Finally, I thank Wilfrid Laurier University Press for piloting this vessel to a safe haven, especially Lisa LaFramboise for her excellent editorial work.

LIST OF PERSONS

Archibald, George	Pictou tanner, owner of house purchased by Rudolf
Bayne, Rev. George	minister of Prince Street Church, Pictou
Binney, Bishop Hibbert	Anglican bishop of Nova Scotia
Burchell, Captain	co-owner and master of *Henquist*
Carré, Henry	brother of Rachel Primrose
Christie, Dr. George	physician at Pictou, Pictou delegate YMCA Halifax conference
Clark, Captain	master of *Duart Castle* 1863
Crerar, John	Pictou merchant, neighbour of Norman Rudolf, shipbuilder
Crow, George	Liverpool merchant, brother-in-law of Rudolf, partner in Crow, Bogart, and Rudolf
Crow, Jane	wife of George, daughter of Robert Dawson
Davies, Wm. H.	iron founder, owner of Pictou Foundry and Machine Co.
Dawson, J. William	Nova Scotia superintendent of Education(1850–1853), principal of McGill University (1855–1893)
Dawson, John Adam	Pictou merchant, son of Robert Dawson
Dawson, Robert	Pictou merchant, father of Jane Crow, Maggie Scott, Cassie Rudolf, John Adam Dawson, and Smith Dawson
Dawson, Smith	Pictou clerk and merchant, son of Robert
Douglas, Alex	co-owner with James Porter of Riversdale property
Douglas, Hugh	nephew of James Primrose, Wine Harbour bank agent
Doull, J.W.	Halifax merchant and director of Bank of Nova Scotia
Doull, Robert	Pictou merchant, Conservative, lt. col. in Pictou militia

Dunlop, C.H.	manager of Riversdale spool mill
Dwyer, Cornelius	Pictou auctioneer
Elliott, Rev. Charles	rector, St. James Anglican Church, Pictou
Elliott, George	Pictou lawyer, son of Charles Elliott
Fleming, Sandford	chief engineer of eastern extension of Intercolonial Railway
Fogo, James	Pictou lawyer
Forbes, Captain	co-owner of *Henquist* and of *W.W. Lord;* master of latter (1866)
Forrester, Rev. Alexander	2nd Nova Scotia superintendent of Education; principal Normal School
Fraser, Christiana	wife of J.D.B. Fraser
Fraser, J.D.B.	Pictou pharmacist, entrepreneur, Liberal, temperance leader
Fraser, Kate	daughter of Christiana and J.D.B. Fraser, friend of Cassie, engaged to Rev. McPhee
Fraser, Dr. Thomas	brother of J.D.B. Fraser, mesmerist, entrepreneur
Fraser, Capt. W.A.	master of *Magnet* and of *Dayspring* (Pictou mission ship to Aneityum)
Gaetz, Rev. Leonard	Pictou Wesleyan Methodist minister, temperance activist
Geddie, Charlotte	daughter of Rev. John Geddie, friend of Rudolfs
Geddie, Rev. John	1st Presbyterian foreign missionary from Nova Scotia (to Aneityum)
Genever, Rev. Henry	2nd curate, St. James Anglican Church, Pictou
Gordon, Rev. James D.	Pictou missionary, martyred at New Hebrides
Gordon, Joseph	Pictou merchant, partner of Smith Dawson
Grant, George M.	Presbyterian minister, St. Matthew's Church, Halifax
Hamilton, George	owner Hamilton Biscuit Co., Pictou
Harris, Minnie	adopted daughter of Mrs. Robert Dawson
Herdman, Rev. A.H.	minister of St. Andrew's (Kirk) Church, Pictou
Hockin, Daniel	Pictou merchant, County custos, member of St. James Parish Council
Hockin, John	Pictou merchant, replaced Rudolf as warden of St. James Church and as commission agent in Scotland
Holmes, Simon	Pictou lawyer, Conservative appointee at post office in Pictou
Howe, Joseph	journalist, politician, premier of Nova Scotia (1859–1863)
Ives, James	Pictou merchant, officer in Pictou militia
Ives, John T.	Pictou merchant, member of House of Assembly
Johnston, Dr. George	medical surgeon, Pictou militia marksman
Johnston, J.W.	premier of Nova Scotia 1863–1864, Conservative
Kaulbach, Rev. Albert	Church of England missionary at River John

Lauder, Capt. — master of *Lord Chancellor* and *Rothiemay*

Laurie, Col. John Wimburn — Capt. of the Fourth Regiment, NS, provincial militia inspector

Lippincott, Aubrey — principal of Pictou Academy, Dalhousie medical student

Macdonald, E. M. — publisher of *Halifax Citizen,* Liberal member of House of Assembly (MHA)

McArthur, Rev. — Evangelical Union minister, Pictou

McCullagh, Rev. William — Presbyterian missionary to Aneityum after Rev. Geddie

McDonald, Capt. Daniel — master and co-owner of *Lord Chancellor* and *Rothiemay*

McDonald, James — Pictou lawyer; Conservative MHA and financial secretary

McKenzie, Daniel — clerk for Messrs. Yorston; owner of Arnison's store and rum shop

McKimmie, Sandy — planer at Clarence Mills; manager of Howard Mills, Riversdale

McKinlay, John — Pictou lawyer, lt. col. Pictou Town Militia Artillery

McLean, John S. — son of Rev. John McLean, husband of Mary Fox, Halifax merchant, YMCA leader for Nova Scotia

McLean, Mary (Fox) — wife of John McLean, fellow boarder with Rudolf at Mrs. George Smith's

McPhail, Alexander — Pictou trader, post officer, member of Society of Friends

McPhail, Anna — daughter of Alexander and Jane McPhail

McPhail, Jane — wife of Alexander McPhail, ran dressmaking shop

McPhee, Rev. — minister of Pictou's Evangelical Union Church, engaged to Kate Fraser

McPherson, Murdoch — Pictou bookshop dealer and printer, member of Pictou militia

Monaghan, Patrick — editor of *Abstainer,* temperance magazine

Morrison, Rev. Donald — Presbyterian missionary to New Hebrides

Narraway, Henry — Pictou brass founder, in Pictou Artillery Co.

Odiorne — Boston agent of Jas. Primrose and Sons

O'Neil, Mike — geologist exploring for Primrose firm

Oxner, Ephraim — sailor, brother of Anna Rudolf and mortgage holder of her house in Lunenburg

Patterson, A.J. — Pictou merchant, owner of tobacco factory

Patterson, Rev. Geo. — Presbyterian minister Green Hill, Pictou County, antiquarian and historian

Patterson, Jim — co-editor with Rudolf of temperance magazine *Oriental Budget;* YMCA board member and temperance activist in Pictou

Porter, James — co-owner with Alex Douglas of Riversdale property

Primrose, Alexander — Halifax barrister, brother of James Primrose

Primrose, Clarence — son of James Primrose, Pictou merchant, partner in Primrose and Rudolf

Primrose, Helen   daughter of William Primrose, niece of James Primrose

Primrose, Howard   son of James Primrose, Pictou merchant, partner in
                              Primrose and Rudolf

Primrose, James   founder of Primrose Sons, Pictou agent Bank of Nova
                              Scotia

Primrose, Olidia   wife of Howard Primrose, sister of Archy Campbell and
                              Hannah McLean

Primrose, Rachel   wife of Clarence Primrose, sister of Henry Carré

Pryor, Rev. W. Ferdinand   first curate of St. James Church, Pictou

Purves, James   Pictou merchant

Rigby, Samuel G.   Pictou lawyer

Ross, Rev. Alexander   Presbyterian minister of Prince Street Church

Ross, Alexander Peter   Pictou merchant and post office commissioner until
                              1864, Liberal

Ross, Clara   daughter of A.P. Ross, friend of Cassie

Ross, James   son of A.P. Ross, died Nfld. 1866

Rudolf, Anna   wife of Wm. Rudolf, 4 surviving children (see below)

Rudolf, Catherine (Cassie)   daughter of Robert Dawson, wife of Norman Rudolf;
                              children Ida (b. 1861), Edith (b. 1862), William (b. 1864),
                              Robert (b. 1865), Prim (b. 1868), Norman (b. 1872),
                              and George (b. 1876)

Rudolf, James   son of William and Anna Rudolf, clerk Eisenhaur firm,
                              Lunenburg

Rudolf, Louisa   daughter of William and Anna Rudolf, telegraph oper-
                              ator, Lunenburg

Rudolf, Moyle   son of William and Anna Rudolf, sailor aboard *Rothiemay*

Rudolf, Norman   son of William and Anna Rudolf, partner in Primrose
                              and Rudolf

Rudolf, Hon. William   merchant, lt. col. First Battalion, Lunenburg, MHA and
                              councillor of Legislative Council, justice of the peace,
                              registrar of deeds, postmaster

Scott, Alexander   Glasgow merchant, partner in Scott, Rudolf and Co.

Scott, Margaret   daughter of Robert Dawson, wife of Alex Scott

Scott, George   son of Col. Scott, manager of General Mining Associa-
                              tion, New Glasgow

Sullivan, John   straw-mill paper entrepreneur

Swan, Mary E.   Bible Society tract distributor, teacher of "ragged school"

Tanner, Richard   Pictou shoemaker, warden St. James Church, justice of
                              the peace

Wilkins, Hon. M.I.   Pictou lawyer, Conservative MHA

Wilson, Charles   Pictou cabinetmaker

INTRODUCTION

Before leaving Pictou, Nova Scotia, for a new position in Scotland, Norman Rudolf considered that his chief asset after seventeen years' work as a clerk and as a junior merchant was his character. His partners, Howard and Clarence Primrose, would retain "the bulk of the Capital, or their father [James Primrose] for them, would as a matter of course retain the business whatever it might be on the ground of capital as well as the fact of its being founded by their father—the business premises theirs and all that would give a standing to the concern, while I would merely have my character, my ability whatever that may be, and a little money to start anew wherever I could find an opening" (N. Rudolf, Journal, vol. 2, 22 April 1870).[1] What did Rudolf mean by "character"? How did he acquire it? Like many other mid-Victorians, Rudolf's ideal of character, in the words of Stefan Collini, "enjoyed a prominence...that it had apparently not known before and that it has, arguably, not experienced since."[2] What were the ramifications of that ideal and what were some of the political, economic, and cultural assumptions behind this all-pervasive moral authority? Finally, who was Norman Rudolf? Why were his reflections on the ideal of character so significant?

Some historians recently have linked the concept of Victorian character to the formation of what Andrew Holman terms "a sort of middle-class-led public conscience." The mid-Victorian values implicit in this new meaning of character "combined strict adherence to a work ethic with a code of personal deportment and a sense of responsibility to society as a whole."[3] This idea of character was constructed during an era when the principle of a career open to talent and merit was replacing an earlier Georgian ideal that tied the concept of character to British notions of gentlemanly leadership and the badges of authority of a self-proclaimed gentry.[4]

In the Nova Scotian context the term "gentry" referred to people of good family and social position, such as that held by Norman's father, the Honourable William Rudolf (1791–1859).[5] He was a lieutenant-colonel of the First Battalion, Lunenburg, following in the footsteps of his forebear, Christopher Rudolf, leader of the "Foreign Protestants"[6] who founded Lunenburg in 1751. Unfortunately, like many other businesses affected by the repeal of the British Navigation Acts, the Wm. Rudolf Co., which traded primarily in the West Indies, failed in 1848 leaving the family in straitened circumstances. Rudolf's position as elected member of the House of Assembly in 1827 and then councillor in the Legislative Council from 1837 until his death in 1859, however, gave him power of appointment. He also served as justice of the peace, registrar of deeds and postmaster for Lunenburg County. (Norman Rudolf briefly held the position of postmaster in 1851 before he left for Pictou in 1853; his mother was given the post at her husband's death.) With William Rudolf's power of appointment came a dependence on those in higher authority and a use of power in self-interested ways, an eighteenth-century style of political governance.[7]

In the earlier Georgian ideal of character, classical schooling had been a major vehicle to socialize students and to instill principles of virtue and public spirit, as well as loyalty and good morals. Most of this training was conducted at King's College, founded at Windsor, Nova Scotia, in 1789 and restricted to Anglicans when its 1802 Royal Charter added exclusionist clauses. Education in the colony was conceived as a two-tiered system, an Anglican monopoly on higher education for the character training of sons of the Nova Scotia gentry and elementary schooling for the 80 per cent Dissenter population.[8] As might be expected, there was strong objection to this Anglican monopoly and to Georgian character ideals by a large number of Nova Scotians who had professional aspirations for their sons.

After the 1811 Grammar School Act was passed, most counties established institutions for secondary schooling. Presbyterian leaders, particularly, aspired to a Scottish non-exclusionist form of university education. Led by Thomas McCulloch, a Secessionist Presbyterian minister in Pictou, Nova Scotia, they established Pictou Academy in 1816. It provided a liberal education and opportunity to enter the professions for people of all religious denominations in the province.[9] With similar Scottish aspirations, the Church of Scotland Presbyterians in Halifax, assisted by George Ramsay, lieutenant governor of Nova Scotia (1816–1820) and subsequently ninth Earl of Dalhousie, tried to establish Dalhousie College in 1818. It was planned as a Scottish non-sectarian institution, but lack of funds prevented the implementation of its liberal arts program until 1838, when McCulloch became the first president of Dalhousie College.

By this time a professional notion of ideal character prevailed in the British North American colonies. A number of leaders had had professional training in law, medicine, or theology, and were judged to be in independent circumstances and therefore able to give disinterested advice in political matters. To have a profession was to have a calling, to be committed to the service of others and to the larger social good. As Robert Gidney and Wyn Millar conclude, a key aspect of this professional gentlemanly notion of character was that a "profession was a form of property and, like land itself, freed the gentleman from dependence on the will of others."[10] In Halifax, in Saint John, and in many ports (such as Pictou or Lunenburg) around the periphery of the Maritime provinces, a merchant elite, or "merchantocracy," in the words of David Sutherland,[11] were also deemed "gentlemen" with appropriate character, and thus were eligible to serve in the decision-making processes of government. For instance, William Rudolf, Norman's father, had a powerful control of Lunenburg County politics.[12] Because these merchants shared common values and were the source of prosperity in their communities, they were perceived as carrying important moral authority.[13] They were paternalistic leaders who defined character and respectability for their communities; they expected the people to be deferential and to follow their precepts. In Pictou, Norman Rudolf learned a great deal about ideal evangelical character from three elderly mentors in particular: his employer James Primrose, who was a merchant-banker; Alexander Peter Ross, Pictou's post office commissioner; and J.D.B. Fraser, pharmacist, entrepreneur, and strong temperance leader. Significantly, in contrast to Norman Rudolf's father, all three were long-standing supporters of the Reform or Liberal Party.

After the 1840s, with the collapse of British trade protection, with the establishment of responsible government in Nova Scotia in 1848, and with the disestablishment of the Church of England in the colony in 1851, the Georgian ideal of character began to crumble and the great merchants felt their hegemony in the port cities of Halifax and Saint John threatened. Producers and artisans found that their respectability and status in Saint John as freemen of the city, as well as their trades solidarity, enabled them to establish a strong power base against the great merchants.[14] Artisans, minor merchants, and middle-class prohibitionists belonging to the evangelical churches allied in 1847 to introduce the Sons of Temperance in Saint John and throughout the region; the organization was linked to the political reform movement against the leading merchants. The Anglican Church became embroiled in a split between its evangelical and its high-church wings, the former calling for populist control of clergy, church rituals, and cultural interpretations of dogma while the latter advocated centralization. By this time the evangelical wing of the Church of England was willing to co-operate with Dissenters in inter-denominational projects, such as the British and Foreign Bible Society, Sunday schools, Sabbath observance, temperance, moral reform projects, and the Evangelical Union. As T.W. Acheson observes, the great strength of the evangelical movement was its ability to convince many lay people of the validity of the call to seriousness. Evangelical leaders persuaded them to become leaders in the numerous voluntary associations beginning to spring up in towns and cities across British North America. Their doctrines of vital religion and the sole authority of scripture as the rule of life were to strongly influence a new meaning of ideal character for the rising middle class. The very notion of respectability was redefined by the evangelicals to replace "status, position, or class with attitude and behaviour."[15] This was the cultural and political context of the ideal of character held by many evangelical Nova Scotians, such as Norman Rudolf. How was this ideal cultivated in their early lives? Norman Rudolf's diary provides an important guide to the process.

As the eldest of four surviving children born to William and his second wife,[16] Anna Mathilda Oxner (1811–1886), Norman (b. 27 January 1835) was no doubt exposed to his father's ideal of character and its relation to himself. Norman did not attend King's College, probably because of his father's business failure (he would have been thirteen years old in 1848). Instead, between 1847 and his graduation in 1851, he attended Lunenburg Grammar School (later Lunenburg Academy). Its rigorous academic program, designed by William B. Lawson, principal for thirty-three years, would have been intellectually challenging. Lawson may have influenced the young Rudolf in other ways. He was the co-founder of the Lunenburg Town and County Temperance Society in 1834. During the 1840s, he redesigned the tower and interior of Lunenburg's famous (Anglican) St. John's Church in English Gothic Revival style.[17] Rudolf would become very active in Pictou's Sons of Temperance fraternal organization after signing the pledge when he first arrived at Pictou in 1853.

There was a new emphasis at this time on manly behaviour, which must have weighed heavily on the rather shy sixteen-year-old Norman. At a family dinner party to celebrate his commission as postmaster in 1851, Norman's "health was drunk, and I was called upon to reply to the toast, but my feelings so overcame me that I burst into tears, and had to sit down without being able to utter a word. I was always exceedingly sensitive as a child, and have not quite got over it yet, and the novelty, and nervousness of being brought so prominently forward to notice, coupled with the kind and flattering remarks of my friends, was too much for my sensibilities, and so I made a fool of myself by crying outright" (Journal, vol. 1, 27 January 1863). Nevertheless, Rudolf considered that the responsibilities of this office "developed my self reliance and character—prematurely it may be, but none the less effectually— so that I have always felt that *then*, and *not at 21* I became of age."

By midcentury the notion of character was interpreted in gendered terms[18] and the long process by which the Victorian middle-class family developed had reached its final stage. Increasingly, the private family was separated from the public outside world. While masculine identity was founded on boy-life both within and outside the family, full masculine status was attained by economic or military achievements in the public sphere. As John Tosh writes, "A fine balance is struck between competition and comradeship as young men learn how to become part of the collective (male) voice of the community. But the success or failure of this progress to maturity reflects not only on the young man himself, but on his father. Fatherhood embodies hopes and fears about the future, in the sense that a man's place in posterity depends on leaving sons behind him who can carry forward his name and lineage. Whether that place in posterity is creditable or not depends on the son's masculine attributes—his manly character and his success in stamping himself upon the world."[19] Young Norman Rudolf would have been aware of these family expectations but had not yet acquired the necessary self-control or status to fulfill them. Shortly thereafter, in 1853, he accepted a position with the Nova Scotia Telegraph Co. as a telegraph operator in Pictou, somewhat removed from the influence of his father, who died on 1 January 1859. Meanwhile, in 1854, Norman had joined the merchant-banking firm of Primrose Sons, as a clerk with a modest (one-tenth) share in the firm.

On 15 November 1859, Norman Rudolf attained what would be deemed the fullness of a man's gender identity: he married a suitable young woman, Catherine Dawson, youngest daughter of retired Pictou merchant, Robert Dawson.[20] Cassie had attended Pictou Academy (between 1845 and 1851) and in 1851 was cited in the minutes of the school as a student who exhibited great proficiency in all her studies and who won the French prize as the most advanced scholar. She created quite a stir at the year-end ceremony by refusing to accept any prizes.[21] Her moral uprightness, as well as her dedication to domestic ideals of caregiving and child nurturing made Cassie and Norman enjoy what has been termed a mid-Victorian "companionate relationship;"[22] intellectually and temperamentally they complemented one another.

Rudolf felt he could fully and frequently consult his wife, much as he had his mother. This new "soft-male" style of gender relationship reflected a more "positive view of human nature, a deemphsis on—if not a rejection of—a belief in innate human depravity, and advanced a human-centered [Arminian] theology,"[23] in the words of Donald Yacovone. It was a midcentury evangelical ideal that rejected Calvinist theology and a strongly patriarchal family culture. Rudolf and his wife by and large used persuasion, rather than will-breaking strategies, to inculcate in their children suitable middle-class behaviour and Christian values. They were more optimistic in outlook than their patriarchal forebears. Before major family decisions were made, such as the purchase of a new home, there was full and frank discussion of the issue. In fact, Rudolf's final decision to move to Scotland with his family and mother-in-law in 1870 was made primarily because of "the advantages that would accrue to Cassie & the children, and the happiness it would give to all" (Journal, vol. 2, 19 May 1870).

If mid-Victorian "character" was primarily an ideal of middle-class behaviour and public status, why would Rudolf base this major decision to move on the happiness of his family? Was there something deeper at stake? While many historians agree that evangelical Christianity played an important role in the Victorian concept of character, often they do not elaborate exactly how this influence affected the ideal. Charles Taylor, in a lengthy exploration of the way in which ideals and interdicts affect our modern sense of identity, focusses on three major facets: modern inwardness, the affirmation of ordinary life, and the expressive notion of nature as an inner moral source. His conception of moral and spiritual goes beyond issues of justice and respect for other people's lives and includes universal moral intuitions, such as a sense of meaning and dignity in an individual's perception of his life. The latter criteria are based on a belief that human beings are creatures of God and made in His image, that they have immortal souls, and that they are agents of rational choice—in other words, an ontological approach to morality. Many of these moral beliefs are largely implicit in the average person's linguistic expression; Taylor stresses "the tentative, searching, uncertain nature of many of our moral beliefs."[24] For Christians, however, the affirmation of the ordinary life of production and the family is a fundamental feature of their spirituality. This concept, derived from the Reformation, led Protestant Christian believers to contemplate how closely their everyday lives in marriage, in work, and in voluntary associations conformed to the worship and fear of God; they viewed life as a calling and their task as a quest to make sense of their lives. Their sense of dignity, or character, was derived from their stewardship—as parents, as family leaders, as responsible businessmen, and as social reformers.

We use narrative, Taylor claims, to make sense of our lives; our story is comprised of questions that explore not only who we are but also how we have become and where we are going. We use narrative to "deliberate about our future action, assess our own and others' character, feelings, reactions, comportments, and also attempt to understand and explain these."[25] From these deliberations we arrive at judgments and vocabularies that seem to be the most realistic and insightful for what we deem to be real and morally correct. The Christian goal is sanctification, a sharing of God's love (agape) for the world; this state transforms how we see things and what we long for and consider important. We experience a deeper engagement in our particularity. For many evangelicals this transformation process, sought through frequent prayers, results in God transforming the will through his grace; this was the key to salvation. It involved constant scrutiny of the inner life to bring "thoughts and feelings into line with the grace-given dispositions of praise and gratitude to God. What was remarkable about this discipline is that it wasn't meant only for a small elite of spiritual athletes, but for all Christians."[26]

One of the most important genres for the expression of this inward search was the daily journal or diary. As Robert Fothergill notes,[27] diary writing reached its apogee during the Victorian era. He believes that many people held a conscious respect for the diary as a literary form. Rudolf's diary was begun on 20 February 1862 after reading "Recreations" from George Herbert's *Country Parson*.[28] A seventeenth-century poet and Anglican priest, Herbert emphasized severely practical rules of piety for everyday living (family prayers, daily meditation and Bible readings, reflections, the pursuit of common goodness, and emphases on Sunday School and on church attendance). Even though they came from an earlier era, Rudolf felt that these spiritual practices were appropriate for him. As he wrote, "I do not expect to have the exciting adventures of a traveler in foreign lands to recite, but it may not be an unprofitable expenditure of time to jot down passing occurrences in my quiet life, and if spared in the Providence of God to complete a year's history I trust a retrospective of it, will enable me to correct errors, and to improve any more time allotted to me.—'Time is money'—Yes, and worth far more than silver or gold. Upon our right improvement of it, depends our happiness both for this world, and eternity. May it be my object so to devote my time, that it may be of service to my fellow men, and to the glory of God" (Journal, vol. 1, 20 February 1862).

Patrick Joyce notes that, although the roots of nineteenth-century autobiography lay in the confessional diary and the religious autobiography of the seventeenth century, by the early nineteenth century the relationship between the soul and the world was understood in terms of this world. Everyday life determined an individual's spiritual identity, "an identity which was inseparable from his social identity. The force of the Protestant tradition is obvious; all that stood between a man and his maker was the Bible, which all men were privy to according to their own consciences."[29] At the end of 1863, Rudolf read over his diary and reflected, "I feel that I have come far short of what I might, and ought to have done for the glory of God and the service of my fellow men. Precious moments have been spent idly, and too few given to Gods work. When I reflect on the mercies of God during the past year,— the comforts I have had,—the health enjoyed, and the unnumerable wants supplied, I must exclaim with the Psalmist 'surely goodness & mercy have followed me'—and when I remember how little I have deserved all this, my feelings can only be expressed by the words 'God is gracious even to the unthankful & the unworthy'" (Journal, vol. 1, 31 December 1863).

Like other evangelicals, Rudolf was striking a balance between his worldly shortcomings and his idealistic goals. Character attributes were key. The Victorian ideal of daily Christian duty, which Samuel Smiles took to be the acme of character, could be promoted by strength of will.[30] Smiles used exemplary lives as hortatory devices to promote unselfishness and altruism. Stefan Collini contrasts this evangelical idea of character to the German ideal of *Bildung,* which "in its purest Romantic form, suggests an openness to experience, a cultivation of the subjective response, an elevation of the aesthetic, and an exploratory attitude towards one's own individuality and potential, all of which carry a different, perhaps more self-indulgent, certainly more private, message and political bearing."[31]

Rudolf's diary, with its daily weather observations, its account of family matters, of social and business happenings, and of his own experiences, as well as occasional literary or naturalistic forays, suggests an attempt to follow a disciplined regime of writing, but also has elements of *Bildungsroman,* whose theme was the emergence of a life-shape from these events. As he was later to write, however, "we have two natures, or lives—one our natural one, which is not always allowed to develop or have fair play, and the other the worldly— 'the struggle for life'—the business hard-sided one" (Journal, vol. 3, 17 September 1875). There was obviously a tension between his inner, spiritual search for meaning in his life (evangelical inwardness) and his outward stewardship duties. Rudolf's concept of character, then, involved a type of balance sheet of his evangelical service to his God, his family, his business, and his community. He needed God's help to transform his will and to interpret the world in a constructive, rational manner in order to fulfill his day-to-day responsibilities. This was the underlying intent of his daily journal writing, to keep his commitment to an ethic of benevolence and of the affirmation of the goodness of human beings.

Was the "self" portrayed in Rudolf's diary a real or a fictitious character portrayal? Recent literary criticism suggests that the setting of personal experiences in a narrative format (such as autobiography) reshapes the experiences so narrated, brings them under control and provides outer ordered form to what was formless and less ordered.[32] As Avrom Fleishman observes, "The intention to 'tell the truth about oneself,' like other imaginative projects, is a fictional premise which may issue in highly rewarding constructions of the self."[33] Linda Peterson notes the qualities necessary for self-writing. They include the author's ability to discover or impose a coherent pattern on his or her material, to describe interrelationships or suggest influences of one person on another, to use language with confidence, to interpret and give meaning to history or religious and daily experiences, and finally, to have a concept of the soul that guides one's life.[34] According to all these criteria, Norman Rudolf possessed the appropriate authority to indulge in life-writing.

He possessed one other crucial attribute. Perhaps because of his sensitive nature, perhaps because of his close relationship with his mother, his wife, and some female friends, or perhaps because of his propensity to discuss his experiences openly, Rudolf's diary is an unusually rich source for examining the development of the male concept of character. As Mark Carnes observes, "Victorian men were not given to self-analysis...and they even more rarely committed their introspections to paper."[35] In contrast, Rudolf described his friendship with Fanny Hannington in the following terms: she "was my confidante and correspondent, and although no thought of love save that of a friend or brother was mine, I loved her deeply. Later years of married life and separation from her, have cooled our great intimacy, yet I always enjoy meeting with her as opportunity permits....I pray she may have all the happiness that married life [with Lt. Irvine, RN] affords" (Journal, vol. 1, 26 October 1864). Unfortunately, shortly thereafter Fanny Irvine died of consumption.

Rudolf recorded a perceptive discussion of journal writing with friends in 1865. They were discussing the memoirs of several Maritime missionaries, two of whom had been martyred. A review of Reverend George Patterson's *Memoirs of the Missionaries Johnstone and Matheson* in the local newspaper, the *Bullfrog*, led to their debate on the issue of publishing private diaries. As Rudolf wrote, "The writer of the article finds fault for publishing the private diaries of persons saying that it tends to vanity or fanaticism. John [McKinlay, Pictou lawyer] held something of the same views, and remarked that scarcely any one could or would write anything in their journals which would reflect upon themselves that they were too often written with a purpose in view, and that was, for others to see them—so that they were not to be taken for true indices of men's character" (Journal, vol. 2, 15 February 1865). After listing the type of entries McKinlay considered appropriate for publication—current events or journalistic reporting—McKinlay admitted that he kept a diary of the former type. He recorded his fishing excursions, his hunting tours, and what game he killed, things of interest only to himself; they included occasional comments that he wouldn't want printed. Rudolf replied that

> I too kept a journal *but that if I thought it would be published, I would burn it tomorrow.* It was only kept to remind me in future days of the times past—to shew me how I viewed certain things when they occurred—to tell me what I had been doing day by day, and to compare things past with things present. My remarks in this journal are candid and open—the true exponents of my feelings at the time they are written. I may often modify them greatly, and forget to note it, but yet memory recalls the change, from reading to the first opinions. Many things [in my diary] are of a public nature and might be read by all the world, as records of meetings, and public business. (Journal, vol. 2, 15 February 1865; emphasis in original)

While this is true of the majority of his journal entries, it is significant that Rudolf in this company did not mention his earlier spiritual intent; public discourse among men would not have deemed this revelation appropriate. Since his journal in the beginning was meant for his eyes only, since it did include private as well as public matters on which he could reflect, and because sincerity was a goal of evangelical Christians, one could conclude that Rudolf's narrative attempts in his diary to understand his own ideal of character were genuine and not fictitious.

There are gaps in Rudolf's diary for the modern reader, however, as well as a paucity of discussion on his own spirituality and no account of any conversion experience. Rudolf's diary reflections and daily and weekly rituals—morning prayer, Bible study, Sunday School work at St. James Anglican Church, and mission work in the Pictou area—only imply his deep commitment to his evangelical search for meaning in his everyday life; there is little overt discussion of this commitment. Similarly, while Rudolf describes his companionate relationship with his wife, probably for reasons of propriety he does not discuss his wife's character nor any of his own assumptions about their marriage. While he uses adult mentors, such as Primrose, Fraser, and Ross, significantly Rudolf never mentions the influence of his own father on his early life. Although he may have believed his own public character to have commenced at age sixteen when he began his employment, Rudolf only began his diary reflections when he was twenty-seven. Were there stresses in his life at that time that were also contributing factors in the commencement of his journal?

Between 1859 and 1863, Norman and Cassie Rudolf boarded at her parents' home, in part to save money and in part so that Cassie could help her mother care for her father. In 1861 their first child, Ida, died shortly after childbirth. A second child, Edith, was born in May 1862. From Rudolf's diary entries, we realize that the boarding arrangement proved awkward. The sickly Dawson's querulous behaviour and demands for evening quiet precluded any social activities for the young couple or lengthy visits from Rudolf's mother, Anna, or sister Louisa to help look after their young baby. Rudolf began to participate even more in activities outside the home. As well as serving as warden in St. James Church (1860–1865), he became active in the militia, in June 1862 achieving the rank of senior lieutenant. In 1862 he was nominated (but declined) the office of warden master at the Pictou Masonic Lodge. In that year, under the strong influence of Fraser, he also used his office of worthy patriarch at the meetings of the Oriental Division of the Sons of Temperance to speak out against younger members' attempts to introduce dancing at the Christmas social gathering. In the following year, again guided by his three elderly Liberal mentors, Rudolf participated in the provincial election campaign. His work as clerk for the Bank of Nova Scotia and junior in the firm of Primrose Sons continued to be demanding and to involve family social interactions with the elderly Primroses as well as with their two sons, Clarence and Howard, and their young families. It was during these early married years (1862–1865) that the young Rudolf carried out most of his journal deliberations about the meaning of public character, discussed in chapters 1 and 3–5. His increasing responsibilities with his own and his extended family, discussed in chapter 2, added a private dimension to the concept of character, particularly as he had to discipline his headstrong young daughter and help his mother advise and guide his brother James and his sister, Louisa. These questions of public and private character, intertwined with issues of masculine identity, family status, and liberal ideals of character (chapter 3) are discussed in the midst of a chronological account of Rudolf's life and times.

In the last three chapters, Rudolf's mature public leadership status is outlined. On the retirement of James Primrose in 1864, he became a partner (one-quarter share) in the new firm of Primrose and Rudolf. Norman and Cassie moved first to a rental dwelling in November 1863 and then to their own home in 1866; three sons were born between 1864 and 1868, and Rudolf's status in the Pictou community substantially improved. He achieved the rank of major in the Pictou militia before retiring from military leadership because of the pressures of work and family in 1863. Rudolf became warden master of the Pictou Masonic Lodge in 1868 and throughout these years continued his leadership in the Bible Society and as Sunday School superintendent. In 1868, he was asked to be president of a reorganized Young Men's Christian Association in Pictou, and in September 1869 was nominated as vice-president of the provincial YMCA. His newly acquired public leadership status was acknowledged by his appointment in March 1870 as mark and past-master of the Royal Arch Masonic Chapter New Caledonia No. 11. By this time his ideal of character was qualified substantially by his own life experience.

Chapter 7 outlines the business difficulties faced by the three young merchants in the late 1860s. Rudolf decided that for the sake of his family and for their future financial security he would accept the offer from his brother-in-law, Alex Scott, of employment as commission agent for Scott's firm. Much to the consternation of his mother and many of their Pictou friends, the Rudolfs left for Scotland in September 1870 after effusive tributes were paid to Norman's public character and to his lengthy record of evangelical stewardship in the Pictou community. The last chapter relates how in later life, although far from financially successful because of the continuing worldwide depression, Rudolf achieved the balance he had sought throughout his life between his evangelical character ideals and his understanding of the meaning of his own life and character. Ironically, it was his private character, only implied in his diary and epitomized by his nurturing family relationships, that most closely captured the inner spirit of Rudolf's evangelical ideal.

His diary proved to be the best legacy of Rudolf's developing concept of character. Written in five volumes,[36] the journals provide the reader with a rich source of evidence to explore the dimensions of ideal character held by one very literate mid-Victorian merchant, in the context of the mature evangelical community at Pictou. Despite his initial resolve to write only a one-year private journal for his own reflections, Rudolf seems to have changed his mind and continued the journal for the rest of his life, probably as a memoir of his life and as a repository of evangelical wisdom for his descendants. They did cherish it, finally allowing the public to have access to it when Catherine Weld, Norman's granddaughter, in the late 1970s and early 1980s loaned the journal to the Nova Scotia Archives and Records Management (NSARM) for microfilming. The journal is now in the possession of her son, Robert Weld, who kindly lent it to me. His cousin, Margo Coleman, was able to obtain photographs of Cassie and their son, Robert Dawson Rudolf, and his family. In the Notman Collection at NSARM there is also a good portrait of Norman Rudolf, which was taken in Halifax on 30 January 1878. While few other records of Rudolf's life exist, St. James Church has considerable evidence regarding his service there. As well, there are extensive primary source materials on Pictou Town and on the surrounding region for the researcher to draw on. There is also a rich secondary source literature on the Victorian themes mentioned above. For these reasons I use Rudolf as a case study in the exploration of the Victorian ideal of character, as it was understood by one humane individual trying to make sense of his existence and of his responsibilities in turbulent times.

While the reader may find the mixture of thematic analysis and life chronology somewhat confusing, an effort has been made to introduce the themes early in each chapter and to develop them through the narrative of Rudolf's life. As John Tosh notes, case studies "offer a way into domesticity [and ideal character] as it was experienced at the time....Individual case-histories....anchor...abstractions in lived experience; they also show us, as no other technique can do, how the compartmentalized categories of social analysis were articulated with each other on the ground."[37] As Taylor emphasizes, it was through their life stories and reflections that Victorian evangelicals explored the meaning of their lives, tried to understand the ideal concept of character appropriate for their day-to-day existence, and arrived at judgments and vocabularies most insightful for their daily moral guidance. By the end of Norman Rudolf's life, his earnest search for God's moral guidance of his character proved of great benefit. While we never learn whether or not he had had a conversion experience, as a deeply mature Christian Rudolf was able to accept his terminal illness. His major concern was for the plight of his family, displaying in his altruism another major trait of mature character. Rudolf, guided by his character ideal, had by that time learned to balance effectively his multiple stewardship roles, as well as the conflicting pulls of his outward worldly responsibilities and his inward evangelical search for meaning. His life story, therefore, provides an effective medium through which to analyze the complex Victorian notion of ideal character.

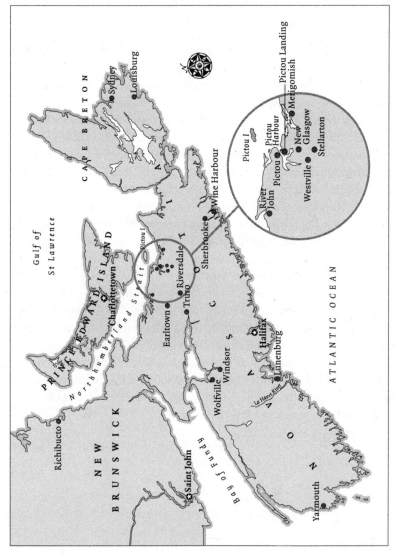

Town of Picton (2) in its Maritime Context, 1860s.

CHAPTER 1

Character Distinctions

A s the young Norman Rudolf approached Pictou Harbour in 1853 on his journey from Lunenburg on the south shore of Nova Scotia to his new job at Pictou, he would have been struck by the attractive view. He had just descended the Cobequid range of hills, which stretched along the southern shore of Pictou Harbour for 160 kilometres. On his right, the East, Middle, and West Rivers met and flowed into the harbour, which emptied into the Northumberland Strait off northeastern Nova Scotia. Here the coal-mining towns of New Glasgow, Stellarton, and Westville were flourishing. At his back were the summits of Mount Thom, Fitzpatrick's Mountain, Green Hill, and Mount William, the sources of Pictou County's timber industry and mineral wealth. In front of him on the far northern shore, Rudolf would have spotted the Town of Pictou, port of entry for the thousands of Scots who had poured into the region since the landing of the *Hector* in 1773.[1] They brought their Highland and Lowland Scottish values into that region of Nova Scotia.

Rudolf may not have been aware of the diversity of settlement patterns that had evolved in the Pictou region, but he would soon learn about them. Approximately five thousand Highland Scottish families had settled in the hilly regions, remote from the shoreline and industrial towns because they wanted to continue their strong clan and religious (Church of Scotland) ties; they were determined to hold onto their Gaelic language and their traditional Highland values and to create homogeneous communities. These Scottish

Nova Scotians had enthusiastically embraced the charismatic evangelical Church of Scotland missionaries sent to them by the Glasgow Colonial Society in the 1820s.[2] By and large they resisted the modernizing trends, including many evangelical campaigns for temperance reform and for orderly commercial development, that affected culture and development closer to the harbour.

Lower down the slopes and around the periphery of Pictou Harbour, numerous moderate-sized farms confirmed the view of J.W. Dawson in 1857 that "Pictou has a larger agricultural population than any of the other counties, and in its older settlements the art of farming is in a more advanced condition than in most other areas of the province."[3] From as early as 1817 at West River and 1822 at East River, gentlemen farmers had spearheaded a (Lowland Scots) agricultural reform movement in Pictou County through the formation of agricultural societies. Professional farming continued to be promoted through the 1830s and 1840s by means of seed and implement distribution and the sale of breeding stock, but as Graeme Wynn notes, between 1837 and 1846 only twenty-three people garnered 80 per cent of the 232 premiums offered by the Pictou Agricultural Society.[4]

On the south shore of the harbour, the industrial towns were being developed by the General Mining Association (GMA), a London-controlled company. Between 1827 and 1837 the GMA had built several railways, two steamships, an iron foundry, and coal-mine shafts going in some places down nearly five hundred feet. It employed over one thousand workers, including highly paid colliers, and it had over 287 horses as well as steam engines doing the work of 459 horses in 1838.[5] J.S. Martell considers that, by the end of 1840, the GMA's coal-mining monopoly had cost it nearly £360,000. Between 1851 and 1861, there was an increase of 121 per cent in the capacity and production of coal. Between 1852 and 1856, 72 per cent of coal exports from British North America were to the eastern seaboard of the United States.[6] In 1858, however, the provincial mineral monopoly held by the GMA was cancelled. This led to healthy competition in the Pictou district, not only in the development of coal mines but also in the growth of small-scale industries. Foundries and sawmills sprang up, followed by gypsum mills, salt works, and iron-smelting furnaces. Secondary consumer goods were manufactured in breweries and flour- and gristmills. By the late 1870s, the industrial towns would begin to manufacture agricultural implements, carriages, and tin and sheet-iron goods. These industries fostered the development of railways and landward expansion of the economy during the 1860s and 1870s. All of these economic trends would affect Rudolf's business ventures and his evolving ideal of public character.

In contrast, the Town of Pictou (population 2,833 in 1861) across the harbour from the coal mines continued to look seaward, serving as a ship-building centre and entrepôt between the agricultural and forested hinter-land and Pictou's extensive trade around the Atlantic "lake." Because of its much earlier development, its centre as a seat of government for the region, and its mercantile-professional leadership, the Town of Pictou differed sig-nificantly in its economy and culture from the industrializing coal towns across the harbour. By midcentury, as well, families had been settled in the town for several generations. The built landscape of the town both reflected and symbolized the Scottish Lowland commercial culture of the town lead-ers. One of the first dwellings Rudolf would have seen as he approached the town was Norway House, a handsome stone structure built in 1813 on McPherson's Point to the west of the town by Pictou's leading merchant at the time, Edward Mortimer.[7] In 1799, he had been elected the first country (living outside Halifax) member of the Nova Scotia House of Assembly, defeating the incumbent treasurer of the Legislative Council, Michael Wal-lace. When the Reverend Thomas McCulloch arrived in 1803, Mortimer sold him land on which he built his house and grammar school. Mortimer served as the first president of the Pictou Academy Board of Trustees from 1816 until his death in 1819. In turn, McCulloch took over Mortimer's leadership of Dissenter interests in the province, combating the Anglican-commercial oli-garchy in Halifax.

The Secessionist Presbyterians[8] were to compete aggressively for the next thirty years with the Kirk, or Church of Scotland, for control of Presbyteri-anism in the province. In the Pictou region both groups were religious activists, promoting Scottish ideals of schooling, evangelical values, and professional leadership. R.D. Anderson describes this as a clerical ideal, evoking "a hier-archical paternalistic society innocent of modern ideas of class [and] bound together...by relationships of a personal, organic kind."[9] This was the cul-tural background of Rudolf's elderly mentors—James Primrose, J.D.B. Fraser, and A.P. Ross. Their strongly principled stance with respect to such social issues as temperance and gender roles, as well as their patriarchal style of man-agement, at first impressed the young Rudolf (perhaps reminding him of his father). His diary assessed their characters at length in an effort to delineate his own ideal concept of character; but he later disagreed with them over such matters as military service, authoritarian rule, and political campaign strate-gies. Like other young evangelicals at midcentury, he believed that talented tradespeople should break through the boundaries previously held fast by the gentry or by the merchantocracy in Halifax. A more liberal society should be constructed, Rudolf believed; but all of this he was to realize in the future.

As Rudolf approached the town he would have noticed evidence of the old order in two prominent church spires. First (or Prince Street, Secessionist) Presbyterian Church had called McCulloch to be its minister in 1804; he served until 1824. Its Victorian Gothic church was erected in 1846. Higher up the hill stood St. Andrew's (Kirk) Church; its main church and spire would be built in 1866. Between the two and acting figuratively and literally (in the case of its rector, the Reverend Charles Elliott)[10] as mediator between these competing Presbyterian groups, was St. James Anglican Church, established in 1829. Another symbol of institutional order was the bell tower of Pictou Academy, erected in 1819. Its graduates would create a professional elite of professors, lawyers, politicians, and journalists who spread the middle-class, modernizing, and mercantile values of Lowland Scotland not only throughout the Pictou region but in towns around the Maritime provinces.[11] Many of Rudolf's colleagues, as well as his wife Cassie, were graduates of this famous academy.

At the Disruption of 1843 when Thomas Chalmers led a substantial minority of ministers and lay people out of the Established Church of Scotland to form the Free Protesting Church of Scotland (and the Free Church of British North America in 1844), the ideal of a parochial community grouped around the church was shattered. A transfer of authority from church to state and from parochial to state-supported schooling was promoted by Reformers. Evangelical Presbyterian leaders came to lead provincial education; J. William Dawson (Cassie's cousin) and the Reverend Alexander Forrester, a Free Church minister, became the first and second superintendents of education in Nova Scotia in 1850 and 1854 respectively.[12] The evangelical campaigns begun by Mortimer and McCulloch to sway public opinion in favour of state-assisted schooling finally bore fruit with the passage of the Nova Scotia Free School Acts of 1864–1865.

Just as the settlement patterns and economic differences around Pictou Harbour continued to diverge from organic evangelical cultural ideals, so the Town of Pictou reflected boundaries between the old and the new sections of town and among mercantile elite, middle-class families, aspiring lower-middle-class youth, and peripatetic Highland workers. Nearing the town, Rudolf would have noticed further signs of the institutional ordering of the town. A wood-framed, two-storey town hall was erected in 1813; it contained six jail cells and the vault in the basement. A magnificent Pictou County Courthouse would be built in 1856; its two rows of rounded windows surmounting the three-storey frame structure, its elaborate plaster work, its stained glass windows, and the judge's raised bench under an arched ceiling strongly symbolized the Presbyterian respect for law and order. The beautiful mid-

Victorian brick house of the customs inspector, David McCulloch, son of the Reverend Thomas McCulloch, attested to the importance of his government office in this main customs and ship-registry port. Another important official was Judge J. Welsford MacDonald, whose handsome freestone, three-storey home was in the west end of the town on Water Street. Built in 1827 and featuring the five-sided dormers so typical of Scottish town style, it housed the Bank of British North America in 1841 and in 1865 was used as the offices of the American Consulate in Pictou.[13]

There were also plentiful signs of Pictou's thriving entrepreneurial economy by midcentury. Lorraine's Hotel and Tavern, built in classical Scottish stone style around 1825 by John Lorrain, a local stonemason, was known for being the centre of St. Andrew's Day celebrations. Another Scottish freestone and granite structure belonged to John Dawson, who owned a general store here beginning in 1833. J.D.B. Fraser, one of Rudolf's mentors, was the first pharmacist in British North America to make chloroform; he operated a chemist shop in a two-storey frame building with Scottish dormer windows. Harper's Hotel, a frame building on Church Street, was a respected hostelry and stagecoach terminus. On a corner lot stood the Hamilton Biscuit Company, which started in 1840 with the manufacture of ship hardtack. Finally, at the east end of town the Pictou Foundry and Machine Company Ltd. was constructed of local brick in 1854; the foundry manufactured such products as cooking, hall, and parlour stoves, as well as steam engines, pumps, and colliery machinery. The owner, W.H. Davies, moved his large family from New Glasgow, where his foundry had serviced the GMA steam engines and pumps, to Pictou so that his numerous children could benefit from the town's educational, cultural, and social advantages.

Shipbuilding was the major industry of Pictou. In the 1840s, sixty-seven vessels were built for the transfer trade—to be sold primarily in the United Kingdom. William Hind sketched many of the brigantines, schooners, barques, steamships, and rowboats that dotted the harbour, as well as wharf scenes of men working on rigging, scraping off barnacles, and repairing sails.[14] Near the wharves were two gristmills, a fulling or carding mill, and another foundry. There were also three tanneries in and one outside the town. In the 1861 census 36 different occupations were listed, including those of merchant (53), seaman (53), farmer (117), ships' carpenter (24), cooper (10), tailor (12), teacher (7), lawyer (8), preacher (6), engineer (6), watchmaker (6), printer (8), and block-maker (5).[15] The Town of Pictou enjoyed a healthy, diversified economy. Rudolf was fortunate to be arriving during a time of prosperity when business opportunities were opening up.

He was also fortunate to be entering Pictou's sophisticated imaginative landscape. It was shaped by over fifty years of bitter religious and political debates, by rigorous intellectual training of young leaders at Pictou Academy, by the ascendancy of print over oral culture through the mediums of Pictou's subscription library (begun in 1822), by its newspaper, the *Colonial Patriot* (established in 1827 by Jotham Blanchard), and by rational debates fostered by the Pictou Literary and Scientific Society (begun in 1834). William Rudolf probably fostered his son's capacity for independent thinking; he himself, although a conservative allied with the Halifax oligarchy, voted consistently in support of Pictou Academy and did not oppose the adaptation of Reform's political institutions to responsible government in Nova Scotia in 1848.[16] Norman Rudolf's discussions with his elderly mentors at Pictou and his early participation in the town's voluntary associations—the Masonic Lodge, the Sons of Temperance, and the Young Men's Christian Association—as well as his work for the *Oriental Budget*, a monthly temperance newspaper that he co-edited with Jim Patterson, all would have helped him develop intellectual and political independence, a necessary prerequisite for rational deliberation and for the cultivation of public opinion. Rudolf's character analyses, written eleven years after his arrival in Pictou, demonstrated that by twenty-seven he was beginning to enter what Jeffrey McNairn calls the "commonwealth of authors" who were capable of judging arguments in print and could transcend hierarchies of society, church, and state. As McNairn notes, "The idea that authoritative decisions about the common good could and should be generated by critical discussion among private persons outside the control of traditional authorities or the most privileged was revolutionary…it marked the birth of the modern political order." This classical ideal of the Kantian and Scottish Enlightenment "was a collective entity—the outcome of prolonged public deliberation among diverse individuals listening to and participating in the free, open, and reasoned exchange of information and argument. Such deliberation gave rise to conclusions that participants accepted as rational, preferred, and representative."[17]

In the small-town environment of Pictou Town, which offered many opportunities for face-to-face conversations and discussion, young clerks such as Rudolf were also exposed to numerous socializing influences. At this time, in an era of progress throughout the western world, the objective of liberal culture was self-improvement, which was considered the key to social responsibility, self-respect, independence, and a universal dignity of character. Thus, as Patrick Joyce points out, the egalitarian narrative about self-cultivation led not only to social discipline but also to moral and spiritual goods. Religion, morality, and a reverence for nature and science grounded the midcentury concept of a common humanity and a social identity tied to it, first by means of public opinion, and then through an ideal of democracy. There was a widespread belief that education and socialization could cultivate bourgeois character; that character was associated with notions of progress and an openended future, notions very suitable for a colonial society such as Nova Scotia in an era of rapid socio-economic development.[18]

A central topic in Rudolf's diary was his documentation and analysis of different character types in the community in an effort to imagine and to construct his emerging ideal concept of character. There were two criteria that emerged and that underlay his ideal: evangelical witness and rational judgment. Clyde Griffen has examined a number of antebellum (before the US Civil War) diaries in order to classify divergent conceptions and styles of masculinity, not only between social classes but within them. As he notes, little is known about the inner lives of male converts, but these diaries revealed not only a great appetite for religion, "but also the persistence of an older, more submissive attitude toward providential workings, coupled with a strong sense of personal responsibility for doing God's work." Evangelicals believed that "economic life must be governed by moral values, that individual and collective righteousness ought to be sustained by public policy, and that the gentler virtues should be applied wherever possible in human relationships. The wider world should be made more like the home."[19] These criteria mirrored the prevalent western cultural phenomena of the rise of independent selfcultivation and of public opinion.

Two characters, for instance, captured the Scottish scientific and wideranging intellectual spirit cultivated by McCulloch and by his successors at Pictou Academy.[20] Alexander Peter Ross, Esq., was a Pictou merchant and ardent Liberal supporter. He held the Post Office Commission until 1864. Rudolf recorded a discussion and wager he had with Ross on the future prospects of Nova Scotia's gold fields. Capturing Ross's Scottish common sense, Rudolf wrote, "Mr. Ross...predicted that the Gold Fields of Nova Scotia would not realize the lofty expectations which are now entertained of them. He thought that an injury, rather than a benefit, would result from them by causing our people to give up their usual employment, to follow after the more uncertain one, of gold seeking, and that they would spend their little resources in vain strivings after speedy riches" (Journal, vol. 1, 21 March 1862). A year later Rudolf showed Ross a copy of his prediction and admitted that he was correct: "Our gold fields have not turned out so rich as was expected, and many have lost a great deal by them" (Journal, vol. 1, 21 March 1863).

A week later Rudolf wrote at length about a conversation he had with Ross on a South African Bishop, John William Colenso (1814–1883), whose

1862 book *The Pentateuch and Book of Joshua Critically Examined* made him the apostle of the higher criticism and provoked a storm of protest in the Anglican Church. It was condemned in 1864 by both Houses of Convocation as heretical; Colenso had been deposed from his see in December 1863 by Bishop Gray of Cape Town. In 1869 Bishop Gray publicly excommunicated Colenso. Rudolf seemed to admire Ross's strong expression of his views on the subject: "Mr. Ross made one of his characteristic speeches 'that Dr. Colenso was an arrant fool to upset the truth, or the ground work of Christianity, for he viewed the first Books of the Bible as such, and to take away the comfort derived from religion, without giving anything in return....He could pardon him for writing his book, if he had discovered a better system to give in place of the one he was destroying'" (Journal, vol. 1, 30 March 1863). Then Rudolf launched into an assessment of the assets and deficits in Ross's character:

> Mr. Ross is an extraordinary man. He is a clear-thinking man—with a critical, and almost skeptical mind with regard to religious matters, but strangely credulous of all earthly marvels. There is no scheme, or wild theory, but would find in him, at least one person, predisposed to favor it. He is exceedingly speculative—not only in idea, but in practice—this latter only regulated by his purse, which has suffered from the failure of several of his enterprizes of a commercial, and operative nature. With a thorough conviction of the truth of religion,—that is an assent of the mind to it—he is yet I believe, not under the influence of it. His religion is that of the mind—not that of the heart. He speaks of it as an abstract idea—one [in] which he himself can have no interest. But he admires—nay venerates it, in others. He is wont to give his views of the value of it in something like these terms "a man's a d—d fool *not* to be religious—he is running a great risk, and even supposing the whole thing to be a delusion, he is at any rate on the safe side. I believe there is nothing than can give comfort—a peace, and a happiness like religion. I don't mean to your canting hypocritical scoundrels, but to those who are really sincere, and good." (Journal, vol. 1, 30 March 1863)

One would suspect that Ross admired Rudolf's sincere evangelical character; but what curtailed Rudolf's full admiration for Ross was his enthusiastic advocacy of the latest scientific fad. For instance, Ross sent one of his plans to the British Admiralty for a fire ship, filled with benzol (a highly inflammable material obtained from coal tar), which could eject the liquid by shell onto an enemy ship, completely destroying it. As Rudolf observed, "On paper, the scheme looks feasible enough, but I doubt if it would work so well, when carried into practice. The Benzol is a horribly offensive compound, and so fiercely combustible, that even water will not put it out. There would be no chance of escape for vessel or crew, should they once get a shower of this

Benzol, unless the efforts to set fire to it afterwards, should fail." Nevertheless, Rudolf copied out the plans for him, as Ross's handwriting was so bad, and sent them off; he reported "the Admiralty declined having anything to do with the thing."

On a public platform, however, Ross demonstrated his intellectual ability and his considerable experience with public addresses: "A.P. Ross, Esq addressed the meeting in his usual fluent, and easy style—setting forth the nature of the [Liberal candidates'] contest about to be entered on, and expressing a sincere hope that all acrimonious expressions should be avoided, but that we should treat our opponents with courtesy and respect. He dwelt especially on the benefits we would derive from the extension of the Railway to Pictou, and gave a most flattering view of the immense traffic which would be carried by it, and of the benefits which could flow from it to this District" (Journal, vol. 1, 23 April 1863). As a shy young man who had difficulty with public speaking, Rudolf admired Ross's public demeanour. He was beginning to realize the importance of public speaking for the promotion of rational arguments, which would become the foundation of public opinion. He was also probably flattered to be treated as an intellectual equal by the older man. As a Liberal, Rudolf agreed with Ross's plans to unify the Pictou district through railway expansion. Ross demonstrated his Liberal leadership role in the district during the nomination day speeches. He praised his nominee, J.D.B. Fraser, particularly because Fraser was attempting to allay party strife in Pictou, a classical liberal ideal. Ross "deprecated the idea of men quarreling and hating each other because they differed on political opinions" (Journal, vol. 1, 21 May 1863). Rudolf held to these ideals and quit working for the Liberal Party when he encountered continued evidence of corruption and the character denigration of opponents.

Another Pictou personality Rudolf admired, Tom Fraser, was the brother of Pictou's pharmacist J.D.B. Fraser; Tom Fraser proved to be so eccentric that Rudolf wrote as if he felt sorry for him. In June 1863, Fraser and his wife moved from New Glasgow to Fall River. Tom had been working on the Sherbrooke gold diggings, managing the operations of a Halifax company, but had left when nothing was found, believing that he had been made the scapegoat of the company's failure. However, Rudolf lauded Fraser's pursuit of his pseudo-scientific hobby:

> Tom is a queer fellow. He has discovered, as he says, the secret of nature, and that secret is magnetism. This property regulates everything around us in the world. By a knowledge of it, he cures diseases, when our ordinary and best skilled physicians fail to do so, and similarly enough, he has quacked so to speak, quite a number of people from sickness to health at the diggings.

There is something in his views, and I believe he has made some discovery, but it is so mixed up with floating debris of all sorts of matter, that I never could thoroughly understand what it was. I have urged him to put his thoughts on paper, or get them printed. He complains that scientific men will not give him a hearing—that they are so prejudiced, that they will not listen to a new idea unless it comes through some of their recognized "savans."(Journal, vol. 1, 4 June 1863)

Tom Fraser moved to the United States where he encountered some doctors and a professor who were sympathetic to his views, Rudolf reported on 13 June 1863. By October, Fraser wrote to tell Rudolf that he was studying medicine at Beland College, New York, and would be able to employ his magnetism practices without fear of prosecution once he had "M.D." after his name. Rudolf's judgment of him was that he "is a good hearted soul, and I believe knows a great deal of *nature* and can treat in some cases, very skillfully. He calls himself *especially* 'a student of nature,' and has a thorough contempt of 'books,' or the well beaten path of writers following one anothers ideas" (Journal, vol. 1, 9 October 1863). What Rudolf admired was that he "strikes out for himself, and follows, what he thinks is the true course of learning—others think he follows the chimera of an excited brain."

By February 1865, Rudolf reported that Fraser was practising medicine in Halifax and was treating his patients successfully. The next year he visited the Rudolfs while en route to East River, where Fraser would sell a coal right of search to a German company for $4,000. They had a long talk about magnetism, but by this time, like Ross, Fraser was getting caught up in the latest technological fad, steam boilers: "He has just broached a theory respecting the cause of the explosion of steam boilers," Rudolf wrote. "He says it is caused by the formation of an excess of Hydrogen caused by the decomposition of the water by chemical action of the water, and the iron of the boiler & that this Hydrogen will explode without a spark or fire touching it. It is a novel idea, and one contrary to all received opinions" (Journal, vol. 2, 7 April 1866).

Without solid training in science, Rudolf was not able to judge the scientific appropriateness of the theories of Fraser or Ross; but he did appreciate their Scottish cultural interest in science and technology.[21] He was also impressed with the results of Fraser's healing powers:

He is a great *Mesmerist*, and performs many wonderful cures by it. He has just made Mrs Capt Cameron to walk after being laid up for 6 months from an injury to her leg, received from being thrown out of her waggon. She was not able to put her foot to the ground, nor to move about without crutches. But to her great surprize and delight she can now walk freely, without crutches, and without pain. This was all done by simply passing his hand over her leg a few times. It was with difficulty she would consent to try to place her foot on the floor, believing herself from repeated failures, unable to do so, but at last trying to do so, she found herself cured. Her husband slipped 2 sovereigns in Dr Toms hand as a fee. The other Drs call this *quackery*, but no matter what it is, [i]f he can cure lame people in this easy manner, God speed to him, say I. (Journal, vol. 2, 7 April 1866)

As Patrick Joyce comments, Victorians had a romantic reverence for science. They believed that the great cities of the East had been made by commerce, which in turn had been driven by the inventions of science and the phenomenal development of industry. Science and knowledge were the keys to the transformation of the world of matter and man's "prison house of instinct. The stream of commerce gave man 'science,' and science promised in turn to complete the work of commerce and liberate man." By investigating the laws of the natural world, including the social, moral, economic, and political spheres, one could then understand how things worked and be released from "the domination of the purely utilitarian, material world of the senses."[22]

Phrenology provided a case in point for this grandiose vision of science. Phrenologists claimed that by investigating the exterior of the human person, especially the cranium, one could reveal the interior workings of the mind.[23] Allied to this was the belief that all knowledge was one, and therefore knowledge/science became the means and proof of mankind's improvement. The laws of nature formed a unity with the material world; the laws of political economy were allied to the laws of the human mind and the natural world. Phrenology, as Joyce relates, held that "there was a material basis, rooted in nature, for moral behaviour and social relations. It promised a 'science of morality,' a science of the social. True knowledge of the organization and function of the brain permitted actual scientific laws of human nature to be derived. Nature was the court of appeal, the element in which 'laws' were felt to be inherent. Phrenology, like science in general, both revealed progress in action in the world, and, in its actual practice, exemplified this progress in action."[24]

Like many Victorians, Rudolf consulted the "science" of phrenology in order to discover the "natural" character of his children. In 1864 Rudolf took Edie, his eldest child, to Professor O'Leary, a visiting phrenologist. He agreed with the analysis of her character: "Said she was a busy, stirring restless active body—always on the move——inquisitive——full of curiosity—wanting to know everything——full of affection and kindness—was proud, ambitious and anxious to please—Had little reverence, very firm, and determined, impatient, and excitable—her head large and the brain more than usually developed—recommended her to sleep a great deal, had great powers of imitation, full of fun, and passionately fond of music" (Journal, vol. 1, 15 November 1864). When his two boys were in secondary school in England fifteen years later, Rudolf again consulted phrenologists, this time to advise him regarding future careers for Rob and Will. The phrenologists picked up Rudolf's professional expectations for them; they predicted that the boys would distinguish themselves at school and that one would be a doctor and the other a minister.

After his experience with the Reverend McPhee, a new Evangelical Union minister who arrived in Pictou in 1863 to replace the departing Reverend McArthur, Rudolf learnt to be more skeptical about a related character type, charismatic leaders. On hearing McPhee's first sermon, Rudolf judged him to be "an excellent preacher, and I think thoroughly in earnest. His text was 'Jesus Christ, the same yesterday, and today and forever.' He spoke of Jesus as the Saviour—as Christ, our King—our anointed ruler—and as our Judge. His thoughts flow with great ease, for he never seemed at a loss for a word. His language throughout was beautiful and appropriate, and it appeared no trouble for him to speak. On the conclusion of the service I shook hands with Mr. [J.D.B.] Fraser, who sat behind me, and congratulated him on his choice of a minister" (Journal, vol. 1, 1 November 1863). He continued to attend services at the Evangelical Union church and to report on McPhee's excellent sermons even though Rudolf was not a member of the Evangelical Union, but a practising Anglican and a Sunday School teacher at St. James Church. During the ministerial hiatus the Evangelical Union Sunday School students had been looked after by the St. James Sunday School. Rudolf was pleased when one of the students, Kenneth J. McKenzie who had attended his class, decided to remain because of Rudolf's effective tutelage.[25]

Rudolf was impressed when McPhee attended a lecture and subsequently joined the Sons of Temperance; but in January 1864, Rudolf was surprised to be approached by McPhee after a temperance meeting and asked to provide him with a bed that night. Apparently, McArthur had returned from Scotland, had visited the home of George Hamilton (owner of the Hamilton Biscuit Company) where McPhee was boarding and had written a letter "aspersing Mr McPhee's character and trying to prejudice [Mrs. Hamilton] against him. This letter Mr H. shewed to Mr McP. and the consequence was that he refused to sleep under the same roof as Mr McA" (Journal, vol. 1, 11 January 1864). Fortunately, Hamilton supported McPhee and told McArthur that he was not welcome either at their house or at the church. At a meeting of the congregation there was unanimous support for McPhee, and within two days McPhee had moved to the house of Mrs. Captain Cameron. For the next three months, Rudolf reported that McPhee continued to give good sermons, but he had not come to visit. In April McPhee explained why. He was court-ing Kate Fraser, daughter of J.D.B. Fraser and friend of Cassie, and they hoped to be married soon.

To everyone's astonishment, however, in June McPhee abruptly an-nounced that he was leaving town. Poor Kate Fraser "had all her clothes—even bonnet prepared. He is going in the steamer by [Prince Edward] Island tonight," Rudolf reported (Journal, vol. 1, 2 June 1864). In September McPhee suddenly returned, but appears to have left again until the following August. At last Rudolf determined what was the cause of McPhee's behaviour: "Poor Mr McPhee is quite *insane*. Mr. Fraser told me so on Saturday and today he is no better. He talks of taking him on to St John to Dr. [John] Waddells care.[26] Poor fellow. Poor Kate Fraser, what a blow it will be to her. They are engaged, and she suffered greatly when he left the congregation so strangely before, what must her feelings be now?" (Journal, vol. 2, 14 August 1865). A week later, McPhee left for his hometown of Glasgow in the care of Mr. Hut-ton of Halifax and of Captain George McKenzie, master of the *County of Pic-tou*. Rudolf reported that his "friends here thought it best that he should go home to his friends in Scotland. He was very much improved before leaving, and he may be better by the voyage, but the Dr says he will never be thoroughly cured. Poor man. It is very sad. He once had inflamation of the brain, and this is the result of it" (Journal, vol. 2, 23 August 1865).

McPhee's story functioned in many ways like Victorian melodrama: it pro-vided a test of the moral order as a test of human nature. As Joyce remarks, the "basic function of the tales seems to have been as a vehicle in which the moral order of the days was rehearsed."[27] Rudolf's three character studies helped him make rational distinctions in his ideal concept of character. McPhee, obviously, had ruined the public respect he had earned with his effective sermons by leaving his post and pleading insanity. Tom Fraser had also left town, but to gain credentials and earn respect for his unusual heal-ing practices. In Rudolf's eyes, Fraser's utility overcame the professional stigma of "quackery." Ross, like other older mentors he was to encounter in Pictou, came closest to Rudolf's ideal standard for public character. He was an effective speaker, a fair-minded Liberal, and, even though not a practising Christian, respectful of Christian values. The qualities that all of these men shared were that they were respectable, educated, and in a community of an informed reading public; in Rudolf's mind, they were of good character.

In these three character outlines, Rudolf employs a descriptive defini-tion of character, referring to the settled dispositions of these individuals; he implies rather than overtly judges the goodness of their dispositions. By con-trast, in the next category of characters to be discussed, Rudolf's definition suggests what Stefan Collini calls an evaluative sense of the term "character." Here "moral" qualities "are confined to those which meet ethical approval, and there can be no doubt that 'character' was used to refer [by negative implication] to the possession of certain highly valued moral qualities in just this way."[28] They acted as cautionary tales. Those characters Rudolf deemed to be of "bad character," for instance, exhibited violent behaviour and were from working-class backgrounds. In June 1863, Rudolf wrote about a fracas outside their window: "Our streets are very noisy at nights just now. Last night we were all alarmed by a report that a man had cut his throat. On running to the place in great haste, I found a woman sitting crying and making a hideous ado. But she was only alarmed. Her husband (Black Hugh) threatened to destroy himself, and drew a knife across his throat, but took care not to hurt himself. A crowd soon collected, and some of us felt very much inclined to give Mr Hugh a sound thrashing for his pain. He is a drunken vagabond, and was a little while ago confined in the Penitentiary for a year for horse stealing. He habitually ill treats his wife, and would richly deserve a good whipping" (Journal, vol. 1, 28 June 1863).

The next year Rudolf wrote about a "most brutal murder…committed near the Mines this evening. A man named John McPhail beat his wife with a stick, to death. They are bad characters both of them I hear but it is a shocking thing for a man to do to his wife. McPhail has been arrested and is confined in the New Glasgow Lockup House. The Coroners Jury returned a verdict of wilful murder against him" (Journal, vol. 1, 19 May 1864). Next day Rudolf reported, "Another terrible crime has been perpetrated at the Mines. A party of men went into a house—tied the husbands hands and feet, and then outraged his wife before him. It is really dreadful that such things should be done in a civilized and Christian land. One of the scoundrels has only been arrested" (Journal, vol. 1, 20 May 1864). The next day Rudolf continued the account:

> But it turned out that this latter gossip was not entirely accurate: It seems that the woman upon whom the outrage was committed at the Mines, and whose name is Turnbull is a bad character, and does not care about the matter at all. She was drunk, and so were the others. She would not appear before the magistrate, saying "they did not hurt her, and she would not do anything to hurt such respectable young men as they were." "That she was used to it." A pure state of morals truly! We need missionaries at home.[29] And this is not an exceptional case, for it is reported that a son of Bill Porters violated a young girl by the name of Tanner going home to the Middle River last evening. The Railway Surveyors heard her screams, and rescued her. Bill himself has been in town, beastly drunk, for two days. He brought down a raft of logs for us,

but they broke loose [and] are now scattered along the shore between here & McPhersons Point. We have had to send men to look after them. (Journal, vol. 1, 21 May 1864)

Rudolf noted the retribution for violent misbehaviour and crimes, which was by this time enacted by means of a well-established legal system:

The criminal business of the Court is very heavy this term. McPhail was tried, and found guilty yesterday of the murder of his wife. Today John Miller of the Albion Mines was convicted of shooting Connelly in the leg, amounting to a felony, for which he will be sent to the Penitentiary, an event he did not anticipate. Connelly nearly lost his life, but it was saved at the expense of his leg, which had to be amputated. Langille who exchanged his own wife and married the mans sister,...was tried for bigamy, and found guilty. The other man cleared out of the country, and escaped justice. Robbie Sutherland was arraigned for stealing clothes from the Lazaretto [hospital on the outskirts of Pictou, which was used for quarantine purposes] belonging to the small pox crew of the Catherine Jane, and found guilty. There are some bad cases yet to be tried, and will likely be brought on tomorrow. (Journal, vol. 1, 16 June 1864)

While these "bad characters" were dealt with by the courts because they had broken the law, there was another group, largely from respectable families, whom Rudolf condemned because they were harming themselves and their families through their addictions. Henry McKenzie, son of Pictou merchant Roderick McKenzie, attended Pictou Academy between 1848 and 1855. He then went to Scotland to study medicine, but led such a "dissipated life" there that he failed his examinations. With an American friend, he escaped to Nassau in the Bahamas and then tried to run the blockade during the American Civil War, but their vessel was captured. The British consul got him released after six weeks of imprisonment and he "found his way back to his parents roof, sick and miserable. He appears to be [suffering from] consumption. What a sad return is this," wrote Rudolf, "compared with what it might have been, had he led a different life. But dissipation has done its fatal work for him I fear" (Journal, vol. 1, 1 November 1862). Rudolf recalled a farewell party MacKenzie's father held for him before his original departure. He was toasted and it was hoped that he would distinguish himself as much as other Nova Scotians had done "at the Universities at home [Great Britain], to which he replied 'that if he did not, he would not return at all.' He has failed," Rudolf judged, "to accomplish his promise in one respect. And he has returned but a disgraced man."

Rudolf's final account of McKenzie's demise revealed a prevalent Victorian attitude towards the problem of addiction to alcohol: "He seemed possessed with a fatal spell, for although he knew his dangerous state, yet he spreed to the last. Whenever he left home for his health for a few weeks he indulged in dissipation. It was this craving which urged him to leave his comfortable home to go to Charlottetown [Prince Edward Island] and there die among strangers in a hotel. His brother, William, went over last week to see him. His parents are to be pitied. They have but little pleasure in their family. Two of them have died young. They have but one left now, and he is a wandering roving fellow" (Journal, vol. 1, 8 January 1864).

Rudolf equally condemned another prevalent addiction, gambling. George Scott, who was the son of Colonel Scott (deceased 1865), manager of the GMA, had been employed at a salary of $2,000 a year by a Halifax group of investors to search for coal and direct their mining operations. At his request the company paid him a year's salary in advance; in five months he had spent it gambling at New Glasgow. For the next few months Scott was in a continual state of intoxication. He began drawing cheques on the bank in Pictou and had them cashed by various merchants in New Glasgow, "having at the same time no funds to draw against. This was on Thursday," Rudolf reported, "and on Saturday he escaped on board a vessel called the 'Spartan' which sailed for Boston. As soon as it was known the parties whom he had swindled came down to town, and were greatly annoyed to find he had made off. His poor mother has however engaged to pay the amt. of his defalcation about $300" (Journal, vol. 2, 12 December 1865).

These addictions of intemperance and of gambling afflicted many young men in the Pictou district, in Rudolf's judgment. He told the cautionary tale of Jim Ross, son of A.P. Ross, who was seated at a card table with three of his young friends playing whist: "Poor Jim looks very miserable, and is yet leading a dissipated life. He was apparently half intoxicated this evening. He laughed, and talked so boisterously, and with so much nonsense and slang that we [he and Cassie] were both shocked to hear him. He has made his Mother believe he takes nothing more than a little Porter at his dinners as a medicine. Infatuated fellow," snorted Rudolf (Journal, vol. 1, 1864). Two years later, he reported the death of Jim Ross in Newfoundland: "Jim had been very ill, but at last accounts he was much better, and they were expecting him home at Christmas, and the blow is all the greater because of the disappointment. Poor Jim, his was a wasted life. He possessed considerable talents, and he was calculated to shine in the world, but he fell into dissipated habits and evil company. He lived for some time in Halifax, gradually getting lower, and then went away to Newfoundland where his uncle gave him employment...his habits were not such as to warrant his friends in assisting him" (Journal, vol. 2, 27 November 1866).

Even those who tried to reform were prone to backsliding. Rudolf recounted the story of Daniel McKenzie who had just died of delirium tremens,

> another victim to intemperance....His was a sad and strange career. When a clerk with Messrs Yorston he refused to enter into partnership with them *because they sold liquor*, and left their employ. He went to California, and remained there for a few years. Came back, and took charge of Arnisons store, and *there* learned to drink. After a couple of years service, he became too much addicted to drink, and was dismissed. He then opened a rum shop on his own account. He was sold out once by his creditors, and managed to start again. But kept constantly drinking. He had two attacks of Del. tremens previous to this, and also of erysipelas in the head, but in spite of warnings of the Doctor, and the entreaties of his wife, he still drank to excess. His widow is left in poverty with three children. What a curse liquor has been to him and his poor family. (Journal, vol. 2, 13 January 1867; emphasis in original)

Rudolf and his friends believed there was "no ray of hope…of his eternal salvation. All is dark and hopeless." Fortunately, the Odd Fellows and the Masons, to which McKenzie belonged, looked after him while he was dying and took charge of his remains.

One other case touched much closer to home for Rudolf. It involved the family of his employer, James Primrose, and his son Clarence, whose family lived with his parents. Henry Carré, who was the brother of Clarence's wife Rachel, came from Halifax to visit his sister at Pictou. He suddenly developed "three fearful epileptic fits. The next day he was better, but that night was attacked with Delirium Tremens, and has been in that state ever since. He was very violent last night and kept them all awake in the house" (Journal, vol. 2, 25 August 1867). Rudolf went over to the Primrose cottage and stayed with Henry for over an hour: "He talked incessantly all manner of nonsense but was a good deal quieter than during the night. The Doctor injected morphia into his neck to induce sleep, but without succeeding. In the afternoon however he got asleep, and continued sleeping all day. Poor Rachel, she has suffered a great deal." Within a year they learned of Carré's death at his mother's home in Halifax; his final illness was inflammation of the lungs after an attack of pleurisy.

From these samples of Rudolf's character sketches, we see Rudolf in the process of forming his own character ideal. By analyzing character types in his community, he was beginning to imagine the outlines of the concept and to analyze some of the causes of character decline. His conclusions were implicit in the first three sketches: the male person must live his character in a public domain, must not become too carried away by intellectual ideas, must be active in his community, and must have some emotional connection ("heart") with his society. His work must be sustained, not abandoned for illness, real or imagined. Bad habits, such as drinking, violent behaviour, or attacks on members of the opposite sex, as his "bad characters" illustrated, were not to be tolerated: in the working class they were punishable by the law; in middle-class society they deserved to be ostracized by the rational, progressive members of the public. Excessive inwardness, as will be shown, and deviations from appropriate manly roles, were also deemed by Rudolf to overstep the balance he was seeking in his life's journey. His was a typical world view of the emergent merchant classes. It complemented, as John Gillis writes, "the rise of the patriarchal household as a spiritual as well as economic center…images of youth were domesticated. An age group that had previously been imagined as brave knights and bonny lasses, venturing far from home, was reconfigured to fit the needs of household production. Henceforth, the ideal was the industrious apprentice and the dutiful daughter." As Gillis observes, commercial capitalism "demanded greater intergenerational continuity and more long-term family planning. Whether the new understandings were causes or effects of commercial capitalism is a question that cannot be answered here. It should be sufficient to point out that Protestantism's innerworldly asceticism, with its emphasis on deferred gratification, would have been impossible to put into practice without the support of images of a continuously developing life in which each age led to the next in an orderly, if not timed fashion."[30]

The tragedy of the bad or sad characters sketched in Rudolf's analyses, then, was that for a variety of reasons their life's journey was interrupted. Trying to understand why, Rudolf's narrative language tended to polarize good and bad character in black and white terms; a laudable "public character," for instance, contributed in practical ways to the amelioration of party strife, or through effective medical practice or spiritual ministry. In contrast, bad characters had crossed the line, both culturally and legally; they had broken the boundaries of rational, respectable conduct with their violent behaviour and as a result had run afoul of the law or had died. The intemperate young men with dissipated life styles, Rudolf concluded as did other evangelical Christians, had weak wills, had succumbed to their "lower" appetitive and selfish impulses, and could not curb their propensity to backslide. Their habits had overcome the rule of their will. He sadly recorded their demise and regretted society's loss of their talents as well as the fact that they would not complete the fulfillment of their natural character development.

At the same time, however, Rudolf optimistically believed that with prayer, determination, and hard work it was possible for meritorious people to rise above handicaps of class or poverty, to contribute to the community, and to achieve the status of a person of "good character." As yet, he did not fully appreciate the complexities inherent in a concept of ideal character. In his experience with the character development of his brother James (see chapter 2), after the death of their father, he was to discover that in difficult economic circumstances brotherly guidance was not very effective. Significantly, his assessment of his sister-in-law Maggie Scott as a person of noble character encompassed someone not pursuing the normal, middle-class role of mother. Rudolf's rational distinctions and character boundaries were idealistic but not fixed. As with many aspects of Victorian culture at midcentury, the notion of ideal character was transitional and its parameters subject to change, based on one's life experience.

CHAPTER 2

Private Character

Victorian men made a distinction between public and private character. The former was frequently debated in public discourse, the latter often implied in more private journal writings. The Victorian family became the major venue for the development of the individuated self; here, young males, especially the eldest in the family, learned their roles and began to feel their identity as head of household. The home, and especially the mother's nurturing role, was increasingly seen as crucial in the moral character training of young children. This ideal role of women was allied to the emerging concepts of separate spheres for wives and husbands, the former to enact her role in the sanctuary of the private home, the latter to prove his mature character in the public domain. This "cult of domesticity," as it is now called, spelled out real and imagined boundaries between the respectable middle-class family and that of the working class. Anna Rudolf's need to have boarders in her home and to work at the Lunenburg post office, then, would have been a step backwards from this ideal middle-class status. That is why her sons tried to help pay off the mortgage on her home and why Rudolf at times speculated on having her move to Pictou.

Both Anna and her daughter, Louisa, frequently came to help Norman and Cassie look after their young children, and Cassie considered it her duty to care for her parents. Extended kinship support systems continued to be vitally important in communities lacking public provision for health and welfare, particularly within the private domain of the family. Its collectivity was more important than a bourgeois person's supposed individuality. The male head of household was obligated to lend support to his own family when his father had died. As will be related, Norman, as the eldest son, was expected to provide his mother with moral and practical aid in his siblings' upbringing. Both here and with his own children he found that the gap between his ideal concept of private character and the realities of his new roles as father, husband, sibling advisor, and head of the family were more complex than he had envisaged. How did his evangelical principles guide him? Insight can be gleaned by a glimpse of his friend, Mary Fox.

When Norman Rudolf first arrived in Pictou in 1853, he boarded at Mrs. George Smith's. She was the widow of a Scottish timber merchant and shipbuilder who in 1819 was elected member of the General Assembly for Halifax County and held this post for nineteen years. In 1838, Smith was appointed to the Legislative Council. He would have been, therefore, an exact contemporary of Rudolf's father in these two posts.[1] While Rudolf gave few details of his bachelor years, one perceptive character sketch was included in his journal. It marked the passing of one of his fellow boarders at Mrs. Smith's, Mary Fox (later first wife of John S. McLean, YMCA leader, Halifax wholesale grocer, merchant, business associate of the Primrose firm, and subsequently president of the Bank of Nova Scotia, 1874–1889). Like his earlier friendship with Fannie Hannington (see introduction), Rudolf's relationship with Mary Fox was a sustaining friendship; in his journal, he fondly remembered many pleasant hours spent with Mary at Mrs. Smith's. He was attracted to her moral earnestness, a key concept in Rudolf's ideal of character, which was symbolized by their temperance pledge:

> She never indulged in the vain and frivolous affairs which take up so much of the time of young girls now, and despised gossiping thoroughly....She was Mrs. Smiths model of propriety....She was strictly upright in her dealings and never seemed at rest with an obligation discharged. Her only fault was that of procrastination. She was always pressed for time. This arose from her trying to do too much....She was a strict total abstainer, and I first pledged myself at her instance [insistence?] in Pictou. She had been either President, or Secy of the Ladies Temperance Society, and one evening looking over her desk, she came upon the pledge of the Society, which she handed to me with a request to copy, and sign with her. (Journal, vol. 1, 9 October 1862)

Rudolf recalled Mary's character at her death in October 1862; she left behind her husband, John McLean, and three small girls. Rudolf's introduction to John McLean, as well as to Mary's temperance activism, were to be important influences on his subsequent life in Pictou.

After his marriage in 1859, however, Rudolf's immediate concerns were his new roles and responsibilities as husband and father, as son-in-law to the Dawsons, and as a surrogate father to his siblings and support for his mother after William Rudolf's death in the same year. His experiences with death, with boarding at his in-laws, and with guiding his siblings would force Rudolf to consider the tension between his rather cerebral concept of ideal character and the emotions he experienced in his day-to-day life. In contrast to his previously independent status, as the senior male head of his own household Rudolf felt that he had to support his wife in caring for her parents, but at the same time, as a boarder in their house, he had to keep the peace with a querulous senior Dawson. His manly identity was limited in this household. Further, Anna Rudolf frequently appealed to her eldest son to assist her in the upbringing of his three siblings. Because of the distance between them (they lived in Lunenburg), Rudolf's influence here also was limited. As mentioned in the introduction, his lack of home ownership and inability to accommodate his family members when visiting also emphasized to Rudolf his lack of independence and limited manly status. In this position, he was learning the necessary self-discipline of character required to bear his lowly status, and it may have contributed another incentive for starting to write his journal in 1862.

More potent reasons, however, were probably Rudolf's need to control his strong feelings: grief over the death of their first child, fear over the successive illnesses of their second child, and his desire to express in private his love for all their children. As Patrick Joyce writes, evangelicalism offered a new access to feeling and to sentiment. These, in turn, led to new notions of manliness, which were marked by sympathy for the weak and helpless, and for women and children; these notions gave rise not only to "the release of feeling [but] inevitably…the problem of controlling this release. The borders of manliness had to be patrolled in order to prevent the licensing of feeling running away into licentiousness and anarchy."[2] Another central conundrum for Victorian parents undertaking the character development of their children was how to foster the cultivation of their natural personalities while at the same time controlling their willful behaviour. In Rudolf's diary entries relating to Edie's illnesses, he revealed these conflicts. All in all, his journal demonstrates that home and family were the locus of deep emotion and provided the important first phase of character development, that of social relations based on kindness, love, and tenderness.

One of the most poignant examples of this tenderness was revealed when Rudolf recalled the death of their first child, Ida, on 26 March 1861.[3] As he wrote, "Her bright happy face was for 7 months our study, and delight" (Journal, vol. 1, 29 May 1862). On the first anniversary of her death, Rudolf admitted his grief: "Strange that though she left us nearly twice as long as she was with us, she yet retains so strong a hold upon our hearts" (Journal, vol. 1, 28 March 1862). They "regretted very much not having a picture of Ida, and resolved to get one of Edie as soon as possible" (Journal, vol. 1, 9 October 1862). With high mortality rates, evangelical Victorians were always ready for death but found it especially difficult for a child, their favourite symbol of life.[4]

Fortunately for the Rudolfs, Cassie gave birth to a chubby, black-haired baby, whom they named Edith (Edie), in May 1862. To their consternation, however, like many children in small towns of North America Edie contracted a serious intestinal disease in August and weighed only thirteen pounds when she was four months old, emphasizing for her parents the continued fragility of their children's lives. Until the beginning of the twentieth century, one out of every five to seven Canadian babies died in the first year or two of life, especially during the hot summer months. Diphtheria, summer dysentery, and cholera infantum were caused by bacteria in impure water systems and by unpasteurized milk.[5]

The Rudolfs decided to have Edie baptized; as evangelical Christians, they were concerned about the formation of her character. They prayed that they would be "enabled to train our child up in habits of godliness and virtue, and see her at last among the disciples. May she, if spared to attain to years of maturity, take upon herself, the promises we have made this day in her stead, and faithfully fulfil them. May she make Jesus, her friend, and counsellor, and through His Holy Spirits guidance Keep in His commandments, and 'remember them to do them'" (Journal, vol. 1, 19 October 1862). One of Rudolf's happiest moments before he died in 1886 was to hear of Edie's conversion as a full member of the church at Towie (outside Glasgow). This was a major goal of evangelical Victorian families and reflected the long-term ideal of their character-formation project, that is, to have their children dedicate their lives to God. It was also a mark of their mature children's self-discipline. As Joyce relates, Victorian self-culture was perceived as divided between the soul or spirit and baser instincts. Since governance of the soul was seen as a key instrument of governmentality, social responsibility, and the government of society, it was important for evangelicals to overcome this division, as well as to control passion and "bestial emotion." Evangelicals believed that actively exercising the good—praising children's good behaviour, exhibiting kindness to others, and doing one's duty to the family and to the community—would result in more equal cultural opportunities and a widening of self-culture among rich and poor, "the good being realised in a human nature under God, of which all individual selves were indissolubly a part." The ability to make personal moral choices, therefore, was a major goal of both the private and the public character-building process. For adult males, the key term for defining manhood was independence, "by which was meant the full control of one's self, one's property, and one's labour."[6]

The difficulty was how to instill self-discipline, particularly when the child had a strong personality, the summer was hot, and her mother was recovering from undulant fever. Rudolf regretfully described how he met this challenge: "Poor Edie has such a terrible temper. I was obliged to flog her for getting into a fearful passion and upsetting and throwing down everything in her way. She took the fit when we were going to bed, and kept us awake for a couple of hours. I am much grieved at it, and trust as she grows older she will be able to have more command of it" (Journal, vol. 1, 5 August 1864). As later chapters will relate, in his evaluation of the guidance of his two sons by James Primrose and in Rudolf's experience with the militia at this time, he was obviously uncomfortable with harsh disciplinary practices and there was no evidence after this of his ever administering corporal punishment to his children. In fact, he seemed to be searching for a more nurturing, more subtle form of character formation for them and for his guidance of young people.[7]

In 1862 Rudolf reported that he had visited an infant school in Pictou, run by Miss Christie, which pointed to a more experience-centred approach to learning: "It was an interesting sight to see, and hear, the children going through their lessons with so much evident pleasure to themselves. These schools are very different from those I went to when a boy. The system of the Model Schools has often been styled jokingly 'learning made easy,' and really one must feel that there is some truth in the remark—for the instruction is communicated in so easy, and pleasant a manner to the children, that they never seem to weary, or find learning a lesson a task" (Journal, vol. 1, 4 March 1862). Following the publicity the Reverend Alexander Forrester, Nova Scotia's second superintendent of Education, gave to the humane model-school teaching methods of Scotland's David Stow, evangelical Presbyterian school culture began to influence common schooling as well as family culture in Nova Scotia.[8] In the "affectionate authority"[9] relationship cultivated by the infant-school teacher, techniques of persuasion were used rather than harsh disciplinary tactics designed to break the will of the child; the goal was to help him or her internalize authority and develop a conscience as well as a capacity for rational obedience.

There was also a transition in parental roles at this time, as John Tosh explains: "There was less talk of 'authority' and much greater emphasis on 'influence.' Because the child's individuality was now more readily recognized, its upbringing had to be carefully adapted to its particular temperament, requiring observation and flexibility from day to day.…The implications of character training pointed in the same direction. The watchword here was 'self-government.'"[10] This called for different methods. The goal, both for family members and for business and professional people, was to be guided less by external authority and more by their inner drive and moral sensibility. Tosh argues that once parenting was seen "in these processual, developmental terms, fathers were inevitably sidelined, since they were less and less available for the extended periods of contact with children which the new wisdom required." In Rudolf's case, however, the small-town environment, the proximity of his workplace to his home, and the type of companionate marriage he shared with his wife, who was frequently pregnant (she had three children in her first five years of marriage), meant that he undertook a great number of these nurturing responsibilities.

This was particularly true when the children were ill. The worst case occurred at Christmas in 1864. After suffering from diarrhea during the summer and fall, in mid-December Edith contracted a high fever and began to scream with pain. Rudolf described his anguish: "Poor little dear it is very hard to see her suffering, without being able to afford relief. We did all we could—gave her injections and warm bath to soothe her, but they did not avail much. The Doctor appears anxious about her today and has been in three times to see her" (Journal, vol. 2, 16 December 1864). Six days later, the fever had gone, and they hoped she would soon recover. On Christmas morning, however, Edie took a turn for the worse; the doctor pronounced pneumonia. Dr. George Christie, recently arrived in Pictou from medical school, was called in and both doctors ordered her chest to be blistered and her throat painted with nitrate of silver; as well, they directed her to drink wine to stimulate her blood. Two days later, her lungs had improved and she appeared to have been spared from death. Rudolf prayed, "God grant us resignation and patience under the trial. We need support and comfort now. Friends are very kind in offers of help and inquiries about her, but no one can render aid to her, as she will not let anyone nurse her but her mother. She is reduced to skin and bone, all her hair has come out, and her head is nearly bald" (Journal, vol. 2, 27 December 1864). Even by mid-January, although improving rapidly, Edith could not stand on her own.

Two years later, Edie cut her hand very badly on a broken plate. Rudolf was called home by their servant because Cassie was caring for her mother. He called the doctor, who applied a compress, but the wound wouldn't close so four days later she had to have it stitched up. Again, Rudolf felt greatly distressed: "It was a severe thing for the poor little pet. I had to hold her, and it was a difficult task. Her cries were very great, and I could hardly bear to hold her, and see her suffering so. But the Dr. said she stood it very well....Cassie could not remain in the room. Indeed I sent her away" (Journal, vol. 2, 4 June 1866). Again, two years later, they were "dreadfully alarmed by Edie being seized with convulsions. About 4 oclock I heard a strange noise in her room, and going in to see what was wrong found her frothing at the mouth, and in a stupor. I could not rouse her....[We] sent for... Dr. Christie. He soon came, and ordered an emetic, we gave her Spec. Wine but it did not affect her much. Violent convulsions came on again. We got her into a warm bath, but it did not relieve her....The Dr....sent for leeches and put them on her temples and ordered her hair to be cut close. After 9 oclock the twitching ceased, and she fell into a stupor and slept all day, until evening when she woke up brighter and better" (Journal, vol. 2, 6 July 1868). Three days later Edie developed measles, the cause of her symptoms, which was a great relief to her parents.

Just as Rudolf gave his wife substantial assistance in the care of their children, especially during emergencies, Cassie played an important role in the character formation of her husband, as he reflected on their third wedding anniversary: "This year 3 years ago I was married. I can scarcely fancy so long a time has passed by, but short as it seems, it has been full of events to me. The birth and death of little Ida, and the birth too of sweet Edith, appears to divide the time into lengthened periods when taken sep[a]rately into view, but it only seems like yesterday since Cassie & I stood together before our friends and in the sight of our God, and pledged our hearts & fortunes to each— through weal, or woe. And I can truly add, I never regretted the step. In my little wife I have found a helpm[ate] indeed, and one who bears my burdens, and shares my joys alike with me" (Journal, vol. 1, 15 November 1862).

Norman and Cassie were great companions, enjoying together games of chess, walks, attendance at church, the upbringing of their children, and social engagements. When Norman suffered severe facial ague, his wife gave him a poultice of oatmeal, camomile flowers, and laudanum, immediately relieving the pain. In December 1862, the Primrose firm ordered a half-dozen sewing machines from Boston, with a 30 per cent exchange rate reduction. Norman took it upon himself "to understand its working, and in less than half an hour [I] learned to sew rapidly with it. I then taught Cassie" (Journal, vol. 1, 6 January 1863). When the machine jammed, Norman had the shoemaker repair it; then he set to work hemming sheets. As they became more affluent, Cassie considered that Norman should acquire more stylish clothes, so he bought "a straw hat, trimmed with blue ribbon tonight at H. Mathesons, to please Cassie. I think it rather 'fast' for me but she is determined I shall wear it. She laughs at me when I tell her it is too gay, and 'buckish' for an *old* fellow like me. (I am going on 29.) I got home my summer suit of clothes from the tailor. The coat is made without a collar. This is the present fashion. It is neat, and airy for warm weather" (Journal, vol. 1, 19 May 1863). As Leonore Davidoff and Catherine Hall remark, for Victorians marriage "provided security and order in personal relationships, the most perfect *friendship*. Furthermore, it created the setting most suited to the bringing up of children, who needed both 'the mother's bosom' and the 'father's knee.' A good marriage rested on the man and woman bringing to it their complementary characteristics."[11]

Norman and Cassie's happy companionate marriage, however, was under severe strain in the couple's first abode. Because of Rudolf's modest income and because of the obligation Cassie felt to help her mother care for her father, they boarded at the Dawsons for the first four years of their marriage. The aging Robert Dawson did not sleep well at night, and most of the day; Rudolf wrote, his "unhappy complaining disposition makes everyone around him feel miserable. It is like a damper on all our spirits, and prevents all society and sociability with our friends for we cannot invite any one to the house, as he does not like company, and the noise disturbs him. He goes to bed at 7 and all evening, we have to go about as quiet as mice for fear of awakening him" (Journal, vol. 1, 15 June 1863). Rudolf was having to learn forbearance in the face of these difficult domestic tensions, and perhaps his journal-writing helped him maintain an even keel. Fortunately, Edie's happy disposition tended to counteract the household gloom. In an effort to cheer up his father-in-law, Rudolf gave him a pair of Canadian moccasins, which he had ordered the purser of the *Lady Head* to bring down on his regular return steamship run between Pictou and Quebec City. For once, Dawson seemed to be pleased.

In March 1864 Dawson died, aged seventy-four, leaving his wife, three married daughters (Maggie Scott living in Scotland, Jane Crow living outside Liverpool, England, and Cassie) and two sons (John Adam and Smith). Rudolf assessed the character of his father-in-law in a charitable vein: "Mr. Dawson was a good man. When his health permitted he was always active in good works. He was mainly instrumental in establishing Sunday Schools here [in Pictou], and was the Superintend[ent] of Mr. Baynes [Prince Street Church] for a long time. He was naturally of a kind and benevolent disposition, but latterly his finer qualities became overpowered by disease and melancholy took place of all else. This engendered a feeling of selfishness, foreign to his nature, but the effect of disease, making him quer[u]lous to a fault about his eating and everything that tended to the gratification of his own wants. He became wrapped up in self, and it was a source of trouble to himself and to all" (Journal, vol. 1, 1 March 1864).

It was a shock to all of them to hear the will of the retired merchant, whose estate was estimated to be worth £9,000. Each daughter was left £200 apiece; the youngest son, Smith, was given the stone house occupied by his brother and family; and Mrs. Dawson was left only the household furnishings with a maintenance allowance from the business for her lifetime. Her house, all the stock and debts of the business, and its sole control were left to the eldest son, John Adam.[12] Smith's hope of a partnership was dashed; his brother was only interested in keeping him on as a clerk with a salary of £100. No one in the family considered this just; but it took the arrival of Alex Scott, Maggie's husband, to bring the issue into the open. He led the "firm conversation" with John Adam and with his lawyer, John McKinlay. They came to the following terms: "John Adam agrees to pay his mother £250 per annum in lieu of his maintenance under the will. She also to enjoy the use of property she lives in for her life. John A. keeping it insured and paying taxes, and to have the shop and business premises rent free. John A. pays Smith one thousand pounds at once, besides the house left by the will to him....John A. gives his notes payable on *one* year for the girls legacies of £200 each. This will give him 3 years to pay them," Rudolf reported (Journal, vol. 1, 2 June 1864).

There were several repercussions from this settlement. After Scott had left, John A. began to abuse his mother and Cassie, insinuating that the latter had only been attentive to her in order to gain an increased inheritance. At this, Rudolf became more assertive, "I told him his insinuations about Cassie & I were mean, and contemptible, and altogether unjustifyable. He apologized and retracted what he had said....I explained to him how groundless his suppositions were about his Mother treating him with coldness....I begged him not to tell the private matters of the family to every one, but let things rest, and as Smith and he had parted to try and not make things worse, but, let them settle down" (Journal, vol. 2, 8 December 1864). Rudolf also persuaded John A. to apologize to his mother for the way he had spoken to her. Smith consulted Rudolf about an offer of a partnership in a dry-goods business with his friend, Joe Gordon. Rudolf advised him to accept the offer without hesitation. These family crises pushed Rudolf to the fore as a family mediator. He also now introduced the notions of unselfishness and responsible family stewardship into his character ideal.[13]

Before Dawson died, Rudolf had accepted another major responsibility, that of setting up their own home. At the death of Mrs. William Primrose, sister-in-law of James Primrose, her daughter, Helen, was told by her uncle, who owned the house, that she could not live there alone and that he wanted her to come and live at Terrace Cottage with him, his wife, and their son Clarence and his family. While Rudolf sympathized with Helen's desire to stay in her mother's house, he wrote, "I could give her no encouragement about it, for I know Mr P has determined she shall go to the cottage, and will not hear of anything else. He said to me, that he would regard Helens living elsewhere, and working for her support, as a reflection upon himself, and he would not permit it. The community would also feel that he was not doing his duty....He added, that if she would not accept of his hospitality and aid in the manner he wished, he would much prefer her going to another country, and work away by herself, rather than remain here and work for her living in his sight" (Journal, vol. 1, 19 October 1863).[14]

As a married man, Rudolf realized that to achieve his full independent status and mature male identity he should provide his family with their own home—in contrast to Helen's unmarried state and lack of rights to her own home. As John Tosh remarks, "*establishing* a household creates the conditions for private life, but it has also long been a crucial stage in winning social recognition as an adult, fully masculine person."[15] Rudolf and Cassie had discussed the matter for some time, and he justified the move from the Dawsons for a variety of reasons:

> We have lived very happily at Mrs Dawsons, and could continue to do so no doubt, but her house is crowded. We have no spare room in it, and if any friend comes along, there is no place to put him, or her. Again our being there gives her a great deal of work. She has too much to do. Mr Dawson makes work enough for her, apart from the rest of the family, and we feel we ought to leave for her sake. It will be a great trial to us all. I know she will miss us, very much, and Cassie will feel the parting keenly. But the sep[a]ration must come one day or another and a way just now has opened that seems to make the present the time. By the death of Mrs Primrose her house will likely become vacant and it occurred to us, that we could take it, and buy the furniture from Helen. I mentioned this to Mr Primrose today, and he immediately fell in with the plan. I told him I would speak to Cassie, and decide upon it. I told Cassie to speak to her Mother which she did and it is now agreed by us that we take the house. Helen will go to the cottage in all likelihood. (Journal, vol. 1, 15 October 1863)

It would seem that Rudolf, rather than Primrose, had initiated the plan to have Helen move out.

Having made this major decision, the Rudolfs became prone to anxiety attacks, but they drew upon their optimistic evangelical resolve to dispel negative thoughts: "[I] had very hard work to get free of thoughts about our housekeeping. Cassie & I resolved when dressing to keep silence on this point, and to banish all thoughts about it if possible. Our weak natures are so prone to sin, and are easily led away, that it requires great watchfulness and care, with the aid of the Holy Spirit ever to refrain from open violations of God's Law, but much more difficult is it to restrain our thoughts from going astray" (Journal, vol. 1, 25 October 1863). Rudolf's evangelical self-discipline was helping him to balance the scales of his life's course by means of positive Christian ideals. His prudence enabled him to take advantage of the house rental opportunity. Rudolf calculated that since his marriage in 1859, "when I had only about $60 clear of my expenses, I have been able to save about $3,000—so that we can buy our furniture and have a good deal to spare. My income is moderate, and I do not expect to lay by much hereafter, as house-keeping will be more expensive than boarding with Mrs D. But I must be grateful for living so long so cheaply" (Journal, vol. 1, 17 October 1863).

The Rudolfs held many consultations in the next few weeks regarding the purchase of Helen's blankets, linens, piano, and other pieces of furniture, as well as her dog, Blarney. Orders were made for building a sideboard, for a stove for their bedroom, and for plate silver, linens, and blankets from Boston. The newly laid carpet had to be lifted to accommodate the installation of a gas pipe from the floor below. Moving day on 18 November 1863 proved espe-cially taxing, as the roads were dreadfully muddy, and the day rainy, cold, and gloomy. Edith slept at her grandparents' house, "but after tea it cleared up a little, and Miss McQuarry wrapped [her] up and carried her over. We got things in order pretty well, and went to bed about 10, worn out and tired, but glad to feel settled in our new home....I feel more than ever the respon-sibility of a husband and father now, and I pray God to guide and bless me in my new home," Rudolf wrote (Journal, vol. 1, 18 November 1863).

Not only had he won their privacy, but the acquisition of their own home earned Rudolf new respectability and entry into the middle class. Cynthia Comacchio writes that, as with later European immigrants, home ownership was regarded as "a stable, concrete and economic foundation for domestic respectability and prosperity....Comprising a breadwinner father, a stay-at-home mother, and dependent children...the middle-class family model became a benchmark of respectability and national success."[16] To mark their newly earned social status, they invited the Primrose family as their first guests: "We had the cottage folks, and Howard & Mrs. Corbett in to tea this evening. Olly [wife of Howard Primrose] was unable to come as she had a headache. We were very sorry she should be missing from the family group. We had a very pleasant party. Rachel [wife of Clarence Primrose] came late and had to return early as her children were not well" (Journal, vol. 1, 3 December 1863).

With Rudolf's new responsibilities and status came opportunities to share household chores. Prior to helping with the sewing, Rudolf had had nothing to do with household tasks. He reported a week after their move that he had "bought a half of a pig today, and we have been reading up the cookery books to get a recipe for carving the pork and hams. These are some of the cares of housekeeping. I was perfectly indifferent to all such matters a month ago, and now, I am anxiously absorbed in all that relates to domestic economy" (Journal, vol. 1, 23 November 1863). As the weeks went by, other decisions regarding choice of wallpaper, carpets, and blinds for the lower windows required regular consultations. When Cassie's mother became ill in February and when Cassie was confined for the birth of their son, William, on 26 March 1864, Rudolf took over the responsibility for Edith's care. He also looked after the year-old Willie a year later, on 29 June 1865, when Cassie gave birth to another son, Robert Dawson.

During the summer of 1864, the house proved extremely hot, being poorly ventilated. First Cassie, and then Willie succumbed to undulant fever.[17] On her twenty-ninth birthday (24 August 1864), Cassie had Norman cut off her hair because so much was falling out as a result of her fever. The doctor persuaded Rudolf to take the family to the farm of George Campbell (brother-in-law of John Adam) at Beaches, at the neck of Pictou Harbour. With fresh air and outdoor activity during September they recovered their health. Rudolf, meanwhile, learned to cope further on his own with the servant attending to household chores. He apparently had succumbed to what current historians term "masculine domesticity...a behavioural model in which fathers agreed to take on increased responsibility for some of the day-to-day tasks of bringing up children....A domestic man also made his wife, rather than his male associates, his regular companion on his evenings out," according to Margaret Marsh.[18] The latter pattern, however, was not the case with Rudolf; his wife was frequently indisposed because of her pregnancies, and he attended a wide variety of male social gatherings.

Rudolf was also very aware, as were many Victorians, of the danger of too much attachment to the home and to the insidious emasculating influence of women on the development of male character. As Davidoff and Hall write, there was a fear that "too much affection for home would promote feebleness of character and dependence, characteristics that could never be associated with manliness."[19] Rudolf considered this fear in his account of the death and his character assessment of James Purves of Pictou. When Purves became ill from erysipelas at the beginning of April 1863, Rudolf spent time sitting with his wife. After sending for their sons who worked in Sydney, Nova Scotia, they sat through his last moaning hours, Rudolf finding the ordeal "distressing." When Purves died on 10 April, Rudolf assessed his character as that of a "true and sincere Christian," who "prayed frequently and most fervently for his family—and shewed a meek and submissive spirit to whatever might happen." Rudolf elaborated:

> *Mr. Purves died this morning* at 8 oclock....His loss will be deeply mourned by his family. He was most devotedly attached to his children, and they in return loved him most fondly. He has been during his whole life engaged in business in this town, and won for himself the character of an upright and honest man by his integrity in his dealings. No one perhaps had fewer enemies, and more friends in this community. He was exceedingly domestic in his habits, and passed a great portion of his evenings, which were almost all spent at home, in the society of his children. He frequently put them to bed, and shewed all the tenderness of a mother towards them in little acts of this kind. He did not latterly take much interest in public affairs. (Journal, vol. 1, 10 April 1863)

Rudolf, in a kindly way, considered that this was his one character flaw; Purves exhibited "a degree of selfishness, which led him to take but little interest in matters of public welfare, but to busy himself within his own home circle, and take the world easy, letting matters around him go as they pleased, as far as he was concerned. This habit often subjected him to remark [public rebuke], and to be considered as a lazy, indifferent man, to all but that which affected himself. But he was not callous, or hard hearted, but on the contrary was full of kindness, and sympathy for the distressed, and his charity was never solicited in vain for the needy" (Journal, vol. 1, 10 April 1863). This would appear to corroborate what Davidoff and Hall describe as a new code for gentility: "Real gentility, like real manliness[,] was a matter of the inner state, not the outer casing. Without salvation men could not aspire to be truly 'fit and proper persons' for in their inner lives they were lost. With salvation they could combine in themselves the authority of God and man."[20] Rather than engage in social activism, Purves preferred to read and to play music with his children.[21] He was an excellent conversationalist, had "a fund of intelligence gathered from close reading, [and] was a pleasant companion at all times." Many people would weep for him, especially his aged mother and his wife. For Rudolf his demise was also a cautionary tale about death; recounting his last visit with Purves, Rudolf wrote, "I never looked on him again. I little thought it at the time but 'we know not what a day nor an hour may bring forth.' God only knows how soon *my* time may come, and grant Lord that I may be as ready and willing as he was to obey Thy summons hence."

Purves's loving relationship with his children must have struck a chord with Rudolf. He was deeply attached to his mother and grateful for her continuing involvement in their lives, even though she lived several days' journey away, in Lunenburg. He recalled his departure: "I well remember her last embrace—so full of love, and clinging to me as if she could not resolve to let me go. I know I tried to escape bidding her goodbye, but I think she suspected my intention, and prevented it. She has been a good Mother to us all, and it is a great satisfaction to me to think I have been able to repay her somewhat for all her toil and care for me when a youngster" (Journal, vol. 1, 14 November 1862). Rudolf, and later his brothers, helped to repay the mortgage on her home, held by her brother, Ephraim Oxner, after the business failure of William Rudolf. As mentioned earlier, at the death of her husband, Anna not only took over his post office commission but kept a boarding house in her home to make ends meet. Her family background,[22] as well as her very active role in St. John's (Anglican) Church in Lunenburg maintained her respectability in the community, but Rudolf always felt guilty that he could not also support her, especially in the upbringing of his siblings. After the death of her husband, Anna increasingly consulted her eldest son, appealing to his moral obligation now to act as surrogate father.

James Rudolf was ten years younger than Norman and had a completely different personality and stature from his brother. Whereas James was five feet, ten inches in height in 1862 and was to gain considerable weight, Norman was one-half inch shorter but weighed only 140 pounds. James teased Norman when he received his first photograph of him; he claimed he would not have known him, Norman reported. "My moustache and whiskers look so different from the Baptist Minister looking portraits at home of me he did not recognize me. He adds that I am very thin compared to him—that he is built on the model of a man, and I am that of a *bean pole*" (Journal, vol. 1, 23 March 1863). The most significant difference between the two brothers was in their relationship with their mother. By 1862, when James was seventeen years of age, he was beginning to exhibit signs of independence and even of rebelliousness, a more traditional male identity role than Norman's "soft-male" image. When he was let go from his first job with Mr. Bent, one of their lodgers, James languished at home. Norman felt that his mother had "done [what] she could to train him aright, but there are times when the more powerful weight of a fathers authority is required. One matter of regret we all have, he does not seem to care about religion. He is exceedingly thoughtless in this respect. All we can do, is to continue to pray that his heart may be touched, and brought to feel the nature of sin, and to seek, and obtain pardon, and forgiveness from his God" (Journal, vol. 1, 7 November 1862).

James's pattern of intermittent employment was to continue for over a year. At first Norman interceded on behalf of his brother, even to the point of inventing his "good character." He wrote to the agent of the Bank of Nova Scotia (BNS) to see if he would accept a trainee as a bookkeeper—"I wrote James and sent him a copy of this letter, and urged him to take pains to improve his writing, and be careful not to do anything to forfeit the good character we had given him" (Journal, vol. 1, 2 April 1862)—an admission that public character was partially constructed by others. When James obtained a position at Canning, in the Annapolis Valley, Norman and their mother corresponded frequently with him, offering advice and sending him newspapers, photographs, and Christmas presents, thereby keeping up family ties as well as the supervision of his character development. Norman approved of James's playing chess with a young lady, but disapproved of his newly acquired habit of drinking cider: "I wrote to him that it was a violation of his pledge as a Son of Temperance, and left it to himself to use it or not. He says he has not tasted it, since my letter. This is a great thing for him to do, and I am much pleased of it, for it shews there is a feeling of regard for his obligation, and a moral principle, in him" (Journal, vol. 1, 6 January 1863). He also noted approvingly that James sent their mother £2, nearly all his first quarter's salary. In August he chastised James for beginning to smoke a pipe; again his brother respected Norman's remonstrance and stopped. Unfortunately, however, he was soon out of work again, his employer bankrupt.

This time James was doomed to unemployment for several months. As an eighteen-year-old male living at home with a working mother and sister, he became increasingly despondent. Norman received a long letter from his mother appealing to him for help: "Mother is very much grieved at James's unpleasant behaviour. He will not go out to see a friend, or associate in any way with persons. He refuses to go to Church, and his whole manner is so disagreeable as to give all in the house a very hard burthen to bear—to be patient under it. I am very much grieved at this. I have written often, and entreated of him to behave better, but he does not mind anyone. His disposition is a marvel to us all" (Journal, vol. 1, 13 August 1863). Two months later, Anna again wrote to Norman complaining that far from helping her or attending church James "lies in bed til 9 oclock, and spends the remainder of the day in idleness, in some of the shops about town, while she does not get to bed until nearly 12, and is obliged to rise before six. I do not know what is to be done with him. I have entreated of him to amend, but he does not mind. I only wish he had a situation away from home so as not to annoy Mother so much. We must only continue to pray that his heart may be changed, and that he will grow better" (Journal, vol. 1, 14 October 1863).

Anthony Rotundo outlines the "boy culture" and behaviour of young unmarried males as they broke free of their domestic culture and upbringing. What Norman and Anna did not fully appreciate was James's attempt to find a manly, independent identity unfettered by female authority. He kept different hours from his mother and sister, refused to help in household chores, exhibited assertive behaviour even to the point of conflict with Norman and his mother, and socialized in the evening with his peers in the town, staying well past the domestic bedtime. Comparisons in age and size with his brother were part of an informal ranking system common in the young single male's culture. In contrast to the collectivity of the family and religious culture, Rotundo argues that the "boys' realm—like the grown-up world of their fathers—was based on the isolated individual." James was intent on self-assertion, but because of his economic circumstances he could not achieve the independent career path of his elder brother, who probably had been assisted by their father. Because of his age and his unmarried state, neither could James exercise the manly role as head of a domestic household. As a result, he was exposed daily to the tensions between the women's sphere and his young man's culture; he was "living a life divided by a boundary between the two spheres. He adapted to a constant process of leaving home and returning. And he quickly discovered that this process entailed a constant adjustment to the clashing values and demands of two different worlds—back and forth from a domestic world of mutual dependence to a public world of independence; from an atmosphere of cooperation and nurture to one of competition and conflict; from a sphere where intimacy was encouraged to one where human relationships were treated as means to various ends."[23] There seemed to be no escape from these tensions with the result, in Norman's view, that James suffered from an arrested character development.

Eventually, in desperation, Norman advised both James and their mother to let him go to sea, in hopes that he would become a captain; but James was not interested. For a brief time in February 1864, he filled in for his sister, Louisa, at the telegraph office. By April he was offered a promise of a job-hunting trip to Boston with his uncle, Reuben; Norman had his senior partner at the BNS, James Primrose, write another letter of recommendation to their Boston agent. The trip was cancelled, however, and James considered himself "born to be unlucky." At last, at the end of April 1864, James was offered a position by a Lunenburg merchant. Rudolf wrote, "I received a telegram last night from Louisa saying James was offered a situation with Eisenhaur…and wanted my advice about it. I replied today to accept it. I have no belief in his going to Boston, and think it useless for him [to] go" (Journal, vol. 1, 27 April 1864). Five days later he reported that he had received "a letter from James tonight. He has accepted Eisenhaurs offer of £40 a year…doing a large [trading] business, and he appears to like the employ. He says people tell him he is fortunate to get such sober people. They are all sons I believe. It is a great relief to me that he has got employment" (Journal, vol. 1, 2 May 1864).[24]

His new public status, however, did not improve James's behaviour at home. Rudolf recorded his mother's report in December: "James is very disobliging, and unpleasant in his manner to Louisa, and all at home. He does not seem to care for any ones comfort but his own. When Mother corrects him, he abuses her, and she is glad to let him alone. It is really too bad. It gives me a great deal of anxiety and annoyance" (Journal, vol. 2, 8 December 1864). While Rudolf attributed his brother's unacceptable family behaviour to his lack of religious commitment, it would appear that James also lacked Norman's ability to relate so well to females, his "soft-male" personality. This was demonstrated by the family dynamics revealed by Norman in an account of his visit home in 1865. Neither James nor his younger brother, Moyle, participated in the evening conversations: "After getting home Louisa, Mother & I had our usual talk in my bedroom until 1 oclock. We generally go upstairs at about 11, after prayers[25] with the intention of going to bed at once, but somehow we never manage it. During the day there are so many interruptions with visitors— visiting—people about the offices, and the household work (Mother has no servant) that we can get no chance to talk to each other" (Journal, vol. 2, 28 February 1865). Norman did not fully appreciate James's attempt to construct his own male gender identity, separate from the increasingly idealized prestige of motherhood and female authority in the private home that characterized Victorian culture at that time. At the same time, denied access to the normal route toward mature manly status—a successful career, proper marriage, children, and a home for which he was responsible—James fell back on his peer group. In nineteenth-century America, as fathers found their household headship under threat by the mothers' increasing authority in the home, they retreated to masculine clubs and fraternities, which Tosh describes as being "rich in paternal and generational symbolism."[26]

James revealed the independent path he was determined to pursue a year later when he announced to Norman that he had joined the Orange Lodge in Lunenburg and had just been appointed its secretary. To his liberal-minded brother, this was a retrograde step in James's character development: "What has tempted [him] to do this I don't know, except curiosity, which he said had something to do with it. I know nothing about the institution, but that it is avowedly hostile to Catholics as a class, one and all. This is bad, and the cause of frequent strife, and the cultivation of a spirit of animosity against a portion of our fellow subjects, who as a whole are just as loyal, as ourselves, though a few are disaffected Fenians" (Journal, vol. 2, 4 May 1866). That summer, though, as James gained respectability and earned enough money to travel to Pictou, both Cassie and Norman noticed a marked improvement both "in his appearance as well as in manners. Cassie was very much pleased with him" (Journal, vol. 2, 2 August 1866). He had obviously gained a measure of self-esteem. His employer raised his salary to $300 per year in 1867. Norman commented on James's reports: "[his] masters seem to like him very much, and want to keep him with them. Mr. Eisenhaur, the managing Partner is in very poor health with heart disease, and does not give much attention to the business now, so that James has all the affairs to look after. He has another clerk under him" (Journal, vol. 2, 18 May 1867). To their amazement, Louisa wrote ten days later that James had just been confirmed, not at the Anglican church in Lunenburg where his mother was so active, but at another Anglican church in nearby Mahone Bay. There was relief that James's character was maturing at last. To mark his newly acquired gentry status, James ordered himself a silver watch from England; Norman had it brought back by a Pictou colleague and wore it himself for a week to try it out. It cost James £6 10s.

Neither James nor his brother were satisfied, however, with James's dependence on an employer. As Tosh remarks, a Victorian father's concern for his son's attainment of masculinity was a generational one: "sons…hold out the prospect of symbolic immortality, reproducing the name, the attributes and sometimes the occupation of the father…this generational concern was focussed on the ambition to establish a son in an honourable and rewarding occupation. This was the vital prerequisite of his future masculine standing."[27] In 1868, James asked Norman to intercede on his behalf with federal members of Parliament to gain him the vacant position of customs collector at Lunenburg. As his father would have done, Norman wrote to the Honourable E. Kenny in Ottawa "urging him on account of the many years of political and business intercourse with my late father 'to give his favorable consideration to this request.['] I also wrote Hon. Jas. McDonald [Pictou MP] to use what influence he could, and also to Albert [Kaulbach, a cousin who was an Anglican priest at River John], to ask him to write [later Senator] Henry [Kaulbach] to do what he could for James" (Journal, vol. 2, 19 June 1868). Family expectations for James, then, were that he would attain not only public recognition as of "good character" but also a measure of economic independence. On the eve of his own departure for the United Kingdom, Norman sat down with his twenty-five-year-old brother and had "a talk…after dinner about business and his future prospects. I would like to

establish him in a trade of his own, and have suggested that he and his cousin
Dan go together and that I would try and arrange for getting him or them a
stock of goods through [Norman's brother-in-law in Scotland] Alex [Scott]"
(Journal, vol. 2, 27 July 1870).

Ironically, the independent-minded James remained in Lunenburg, and
married at the late age of forty-two, a year after his brother and mother died
in 1886. His wife and distant cousin, Edna, was the daughter of Senator
Kaulbach and his wife, Sophie. Before James and Edna's marriage on 7 September 1887, Senator Kaulbach built them a beautiful home, which today is
run as Boscawen Inn in Lunenburg. The couple had two children, Marjorie
and James. James Rudolf (senior) died in 1907.

Rudolf's relationship with and guidance of his sister, Louisa, a year
younger than James, was much more subtle. It revealed a different type of
concern for her character, that she should be sincere and should only carry on
a relationship with serious suitors. In 1863, while staying with them in their
new home, Norman discovered that Louisa had been corresponding secretly
with Smith Dawson, his younger brother-in-law. Rudolf recognized at first
that with such a determined person as his sister it would be imprudent of
him to interfere. After a year, however, he decided to tell his mother why he
objected to their correspondence:

> for they may be led into difficulty bye & bye. One of them may be—indeed
> must be, disappointed in the end. They are insensibly led on writing to one
> another, thinking that they mean nothing but friendship, until something
> occurs to stop the correspondence, and then wake up to find they have been
> deceiving themselves. I don't want Louisa to be made unhappy in this way.
> If Smith *means anything*, all right enough. I have no objections to it, but let
> him declare it. I don't want Louisa to correspond with any gentleman unless
> as an accepted suitor. Cassie thinks Smith is fond of Louisa—and that she
> is not indifferent to him. If that is the case, the sooner they understand one
> another the better, and not be corresponding as *friends*, while they mean, as
> *lovers* to each other. (Journal, vol. 1, 3 August 1864)

As a brother, Norman would feel he could not directly counsel her, even
despite their open family discussions at Lunenburg; that would have been
the responsibility of their mother. Gender roles were becoming increasingly
differentiated, even though Louisa led quite an independent life working as
a telegraph operator in Lunenburg. At the same time, Norman felt a responsibility as her surrogate father to advise the seventeen-year-old Louisa of her
important future role as wife and mother. His recent (June 1864) experience
with Smith's character in the Dawson family crisis would not have inclined
Rudolf to recommend Smith as an ideal husband for his sister. While he could

fraternize with numerous female friends, his sister, Rudolf believed, should behave more circumspectly with male friends. In the next few years Louisa appears to have matured, and she came closer to Rudolf's notion of her ideal character and appropriate social role.

In 1865 Louisa visited the Rudolfs for over five months, helping Cassie with the children and leading a very social life in Pictou.[28] By then, her relationship with Smith appeared to have cooled. Three years later, Norman met her at a hotel in Halifax while there on business. He remarked, "She is a very fine looking girl. She had her hair beautifully arranged in curls, and she looked really handsome. The boarders stared, and several asked me where I picked up such a good looking girl" (Journal, vol. 2, 15 September 1868). Louisa continued to visit the Rudolfs at Pictou for extended periods of time until they left in 1870. In 1878 she married Dr. Charles Gray, of Mahone Bay, a match that the family considered appropriate. When Rudolf was dying in 1886, he wrote that Louisa had just given birth to a baby girl.

Rudolf assumed that his siblings would mature and undertake the roles and responsibilities of a "normal" middle-class family, as he had. That is, James would become a middle-class merchant of independent means; he would marry, produce children, and serve his community in a number of humanitarian volunteer associations. With the help of religion, Norman believed, James's rebellious will would be transformed, and he would approach the ideal of a mature public character. At the same time, Norman recognized that James's major problem was his lack of a job, so he tried his best to help his brother acquire one by constructing his "public" character image. Louisa, in contrast, should cultivate behaviour and attitudes deemed suitable for developing the qualities of private character in her future offspring. She should remain sincere and morally earnest in cultivating relationships; her life's journey would unfold primarily in the home as a companion and helpmate to her husband and as a moral guide and nurturer of their children's character. Rudolf's advice to his siblings, then, was couched in gender-specific terms and adhered to traditional family expectations of their roles. Once his siblings had achieved these goals of mature character development, Rudolf also expected them to act as stewards of their family, their community, and God's mission for them; they were not to retreat inward and indulge their selfish or private tastes. As he himself was striving to do, he wanted his male siblings and later his children to strike a balance between their private and their public responsibilities and between their Christian ideals and their everyday lives. This was his ideal concept of character.

Rudolf did consider those who, because of handicap or illness, could not complete this normal path towards the fulfillment of an ideal character. He greatly admired his sister-in-law, Maggie Scott, when she visited them in Pictou at the birth of their first child. They asked her to name their child, "only stipulating for a single and short one, so she was saluted as 'Edith' on Maggie seeing [her].... This name has long been a favorite of Cassies and Maggies particularly, so they both are well pleased, and we poor men mortals must agree. But I must confess I do not dislike it. The only remark I made was that i[t] seemed too spiritual a name for such a fat little lump of humanity as ours. She is decidedly of the earth—earthy—not much of the *spirituelle* about her" (Journal, vol. 1, 14 June 1862). Maggie later contracted an acute case of lockjaw after a severe dousing from a Scottish rainstorm. She had to have five teeth extracted, eat her food through a straw, and live in a sickroom, which Rudolf (transcribing her letters) described as "a sacred retreat. She says, she feels shut out from the world, and nearer to her God, and when able to go down stairs again to mix with the family, she felt reluctant to do so" (Journal, vol. 1, 21 January 1863). By March her letters reported that her jaw was still not fully open and that her teeth now overlapped, making chewing awkward. Rudolf admired the fact that she could rise above these adversities by means of her strong will and religious beliefs: "But notwithstanding all these things she is cheerful and happy. Her Saviour seems to make up to her all her pains and troubles, and confiding in Him she seems to forget her bodily ailments. Anyone who has any doubts about the unspeakable and great reality of religion, need only converse with her, to find at least that in her case she has found it no idle dream, and thus have their doubts removed. She seems to live only for those around her. Her servants are her peculiar care. She reads and prays with them every evening, and it was a great grief to her not to be able to carry it on regularly, when confined to her room" (Journal, vol. 1, 7 March 1863).

On her thirtieth birthday, Maggie wrote to Rudolf. "She rejoices in the fact of her being so near *home*—near to Heaven. Her letters," Rudolf observed, "are like refreshing showers to the parched earth, to us" (Journal, vol. 1, 26 November 1863). The following year, Norman reported that Maggie was "under treatment for womb disease in Glasgow" (Journal, vol. 1, 2 May 1864).[29] After another trans-Atlantic trip to visit her Nova Scotian family, poor Maggie arrived back at their Scottish country estate/farm, "Scatterly— very miserable in body, but her spirit rejoicing at the beauty around the farm— for the comforts she enjoys, and for the peace of God which seems to fill her soul. She is obliged to recline on a couch nearly all the time. Her letters are written while on her back, but not a murmur escapes her, but on the contrary, her expressions are those of gratitude and praise" (Journal, vol. 1, 15 September 1864). The next year Maggie was described as a "confirmed invalid." Norman reported, " She is under constant medical treatment, but all seems to be in vain. She is going to spend the summer months in the Highlands. Maggie Esson [a Pictou friend] is with her and will accompany her. They expect the fresh air and change will be of service" (Journal, vol. 2, 9 June 1865).

Fortunately, by 1866 Maggie had recovered sufficiently to be able to travel again with her husband, Alex; they arrived at Pictou in time for Christmas. Maggie and Alex remained childless; she, her husband, and her family, like many other middle-class Victorians, believed that mothering should have been her principal role. To make up for their deficit, Maggie undertook to look after her sister Jane's children while their parents were on a business trip to the United States in 1868. Prior to the Rudolfs' move to Scotland in 1870 with the widowed Mrs. Dawson, Maggie offered to supervise the finishing education at Banff, Scotland, of Minnie Harris, an orphan adopted by Mrs. Dawson. Minnie was treated as Maggie's adopted daughter thereafter.

Why was Rudolf so attracted to Maggie as an invalid? Steven Mintz claims that Victorians were fascinated with invalidism and disease because they provided "a counterpoint to the interest in strength, independence, and self-assertion, and it betrayed a profound uneasiness about individualism. There was a deep-seated sense that individualism, unless contained and socialized, would result in a general process of society unraveling."[30] In Rudolf's character analyses of "bad" characters, his cautionary tales about intemperate or dissipated middle-class men, his criticisms of the selfishness Purves and Dawson, and even his fears about James's rebelliousness, there were elements of this fear, particularly of males who were undisciplined by their family's cultural governance.

Rudolf's account conveys more of an optimistic admiration for Maggie's spirit under adversity, however; he envied her strong religious belief. She embodied what Charles Taylor calls "the ideal of altruism." Taylor suggests that "real dedication to others or to the universal good wins our admiration and even in signal cases our awe. The crucial quality which commands our respect here is a certain direction of the will."[31] Its roots are in Christian spirituality and in the love of God. Despite her afflictions, Maggie rejoiced in her ordinary daily life; she had imbued it with meaning and had accepted her invalid state without complaint. In Rudolf's judgment, she had attained self-knowledge, or wisdom, and had discovered the human balance he was searching for in his own life. Above all, Maggie recognized that life must be led in the light of God's ends—to glorify Him, to work primarily for God's purposes, and to serve other people as His stewards.

While this was the ideal character Rudolf would strive for during his lifetime, offering constant prayers to God and reflecting in his diary about how he measured up to this ideal, the emotional travails of his daily life, as this chapter relates, often made it a difficult ideal to attain. Strong personalities, such as those of Edie and James, made direct guidance difficult. Rudolf learned from the loving example of his mother and from the new evangelical culture of persuasion to use sentiment in his child-rearing practices. As Taylor writes, "the affectionate [middle-class] family [during this period] undergoes an intensification and comes to be seen self-consciously as a close community of loving and caring, in contrast to relations with more distant kin and outsiders."[32] Family relationships become central human preoccupations, and even affect relationships with the dead. The hope of immortality was now depicted as a family reunion in Heaven. As Taylor explains, "Sentiment takes on moral relevance. For some it becomes the key to the human good. Experiencing certain feelings now comes to be an important part of the good life. Among these is married love."[33] In Rudolf's case, his love for his mother, his wife, and his children was the source of his sense of continuity with the past and hope for the future. Even Victorian filial rebellion, Mintz suggests, provided Victorian parents with an opportunity to define social roles and middle-class values, as Rudolf's advice to James demonstrated. The language of social relations was changing from the older style of hierarchy and prescription (used by James Primrose and implied in the life of William Rudolf) to one of "sacrifice," "duty," "obligation," and "debt." As Mintz comments, "Such terms at once revealed a desire to place social relations on a more moral basis than hierarchy and prescription and an awareness of the complex and convoluted relationship between social relations and economic obligations."[34] It was to the latter, as well as to his family, that Rudolf bent his energies, as the next chapters will relate. In the public sphere, he would find his own character to be a central benchmark not only of his ability but of his moral trustworthiness. In this evangelical, small-town context, he would also be judged by the status of his family, by his social relations, and by his voluntary service to the community. His own ideal of character was primarily shaped, as this chapter has argued, by Rudolf's own family; in the words of Catherine Hall, the family for Evangelicals "was at the centre of Victorian middle-class social life and the complex set of social values which comprise middle-class respectability."[35]

CHAPTER 3

Public Character

In 1854, Norman Rudolf was offered the position of clerk in the merchant firm of Primrose Sons. James Primrose (b. in Banffshire on 17 June 1802) was the founder of the Pictou firm. In 1839 he had been appointed the first agent for the Bank of Nova Scotia (BNS), founded in 1832 in Halifax. At this time, the agent was not an employee of the bank. He was paid a fixed sum for his services and for those of his clerks and partners, as well as for the use of his office. The bank also paid commissions on business done on its behalf. Significantly, the agent's personal guarantee was required on bills purchased by him, and bad loans were his personal responsibility.[1] In other words, his public character was of prime importance in establishing a culture of trust and confidence in the community. As David Burley observes for the town of Brantford, Ontario, character was also used as a benchmark in the Mercantile Agency of R.G. Dun and Co. from the late 1840s through the early 1860s. It "expressed an appreciation of the ideal of independence through self-employment as the central tenet of the social role of the businessman. Men whose self-employment bespoke independence often received recommendations for credit by virtue of their character despite their limited wealth or trade prospects." After the financial collapse of 1857 in Brantford and the ensuing difficulties of private and public lenders in recovering their loans, this kind of "intangible security promoted a contraction of credit."[2] The Primrose and Rudolf firm in the late 1860s was to experience a similar transition both in the economy (toward larger units of production and exchange) and in the qualities of personality and values necessary for a sound credit rating and for survival in business. Pecuniary strength, rather than character, became the main criterion for credit rating. The elder Primrose was a leader in the community during the first "ideal of independence" phase. Rudolf and the Primrose sons experienced the more precarious second phase; but they retained their admiration and respect for "the old gent's" personal character and business judgment.

When Primrose died in 1882, Rudolf wrote one of his most lengthy character studies, giving insight into how his own public character was materially shaped by Primrose: "He was a model man in many respects and I owe to him very much for any training I have in method, neatness and business habits. He was particularly orderly in every thing and always insisted on plainness of writing and careful formation of figures. A common remark of his was 'every letter should read by itself.' He was rigidly honest and just in everything. I can truly say, he was the justest man I ever knew" (Journal, vol. 4, 19 April 1882).

In his personal character, Primrose epitomized many of the Scottish Whig ideals brought to Pictou by his predecessors, the Reverend Thomas McCulloch and Edward Mortimer. He and the Scottish Pictou cultural community were constructing a Liberal ideal of character that had attained great prominence in the political thought of the Victorian period. Primrose himself had lived through its evolution in Nova Scotia from its Scottish Enlightenment Whig roots, introduced by McCulloch, to its Reform Party political manifestation under Joseph Howe, culminating in Howe's Reform majority victory of 1847 and the introduction of responsible government in 1848, the first in British North America. Both in Nova Scotia and in Britain (with the Reform Bills of 1832 and 1867) the "Country" party had won representation, the commercial middle class had gained respectability, and character based on merit rather than on birth came into prominence. Evangelical leaders, such as Thomas Chalmers in Scotland, preached that character now determined circumstances and a person's progress in life rather than vice versa.

Stefan Collini distinguishes two senses in which the term "character" was used. In the evaluative sense, it referred to moral qualities that were strongly developed or strikingly displayed.[3] This was certainly the meaning that Rudolf invoked in his evaluation of Primrose's character, and in his admiration of Mary Fox and Maggie Scott. In the descriptive sense, the term denoted an individual's settled dispositions and also suggested their formation. Deeds and inward struggle affected one's character. Methodical habits, restraint of impulses, and a strong will, epitomized by Rudolf's depiction of Primrose's character, indicated the importance of psychological factors on long-term moral character formation. Primrose's disciplined habits of early rising, his methodical work habits, and his punctuality modelled the rational behaviour he expected of his sons and of Rudolf.

Collini stresses the cultural impact of evangelical Christianity on this Liberal ideal of public character. The vision of life was seen as a perpetual struggle to resist temptation and overcome obstacles, as Rudolf constantly reflected in considering his own life's course. Collini particularly notes "the way in which an essentially Evangelical moral psychology penetrated the discussion of economic life." Work, rather than the eighteenth-century Georgian ideal of the moral and cultural primacy of leisure, now became the proving ground of moral worth. As Collini writes, "It is not hard to see, for example, how the virtues of character spoke to the economic experience of those groups who made up the urban middling rank. That experience was above all of individual ventures under conditions of uncertainty with no financial safety-net. Stories of businesses which had 'gone down' and of modest fortunes lost in speculations which were imprudent or worse, furnished the moralist with particularly telling illustrations. It was, at all levels, an economic world in which reputation played a powerful part; to be known as a man of character was to possess the moral collateral which would reassure potential business associates of employees."[4] It was this ascribed quality of character that Primrose was cultivating in his sons and in Rudolf. As will be seen in chapter 7, he and his partners were all very aware of how precarious their business ventures were in this transitional era and of what the effect of failure would be on their reputations.

Two other qualities, Collini believes, marked the political culture of mid-nineteenth-century England and separated Whiggism from the developing Liberal ideal of character: "hostility to unreflective and unjustified privilege and a related hatred of being patronised."[5] This involved encouragement of self-assertion, as Primrose did with both Rudolf and Clarence (but not Howard; see below). It accounted for Secessionist Presbyterian Pictonians' traditional resentment of Halifax privilege and of political connections. There was also in vogue at this time a language of "manliness," of "bodily and moral vigour," qualities that Rudolf perceived in his competitive sporting activities and that he commented on at length in his militia experiences. What these character traits were denouncing was "sentimentalism." As will be shown in chapter 4, Rudolf's bonding with other men in the community would help counteract any overly feminine influences on his own manly character. Primrose's direct and frank interpersonal relationship with him and with his sons had a similar astringent effect.

Like his father, who was a Presbyterian minister, Primrose was a strict Calvinist. At first he supported Prince Street Church, where he served for many years as chairman of the Committee of Management. As an evangelical Christian, Primrose also gave liberally to many needy people, to other churches, and to associations in the community. In fact, his own giving was so liberal that many people had a hard time refusing him when he came to solicit funds. He lived so frugally and gave so liberally that he was not, Rudolf claimed, a wealthy man at his death. He took an active part in the social, political, and economic affairs of the county, as he encouraged Rudolf to do, but in contrast to earlier gentry notions of patronage, Primrose refused any honours or offices, with the exception of that of magistrate: "he thought that holding the purse strings of the Community he ought not to be subjected to the implication of favoring one side more than another" (Journal, vol. 4, 19 April 1882).

Like Adam Smith, Primrose believed that there should be a clear demarcation between different forms of government.[6] As justice of the peace for the county, he displayed in his judgments not only his firm convictions but also his prudence; he refused to sit on courts or sign a summons for the collection of debt. His office required him to assist the custos (principal justice of the peace) at the county court sessions (dealing with minor offences) and also to serve as honorary stipendiary (police magistrate). In his judicial role, Primrose was a "terror to evil doers" (Journal, vol. 4, 19 April 1882), but his ability to weigh evidence carefully and to render impartial judgments earned him great respect. This quality, as well as his personal integrity, won the confidence of Pictou County people: "He was trusted absolutely by many as almost infallible. The County people lodged their money in 'Primroses Bank' with implicit faith that it was safe under his management," reported Rudolf. Like English provincial bankers, Primrose used his extensive local knowledge to vet local loans and to establish connections with insurance companies; these protective strategies added to his reputation for trustworthiness. As Leonore Davidoff and Catherine Hall conclude, "The banker was one of the most wealthy and powerful people in the community."[7] Infusing his public responsibilities with moral integrity, Primrose was modelling his Scottish concept of stewardship, and he was also culturally defining middle-class ideals of respectability and order, foundations of the Victorian liberal commercial perspective.[8] Above all, Primrose epitomized the values of trust and confidence, the basis of the colonial financial system.

This system was in transition, however. As T.W. Acheson writes, during the 1840s the imperial mercantilist structure was based on a chain of debt that linked the great commercial firms of Great Britain to the major colonial wholesalers and shippers, through them to the colonial general merchants and retailers, and down to the colonial farmers, fishermen, and lumbermen in the countryside and to the artisans and labourers in the towns. When this system was dismantled with the repeal of the Navigation Acts in 1849, most of the Nova Scotia trade with the West Indies was decimated (hence William Rudolf's financial failure), and there was a serious decline in intercolonial trade.[9]

Reflecting the region's economic stage, Primrose held "transitional" political opinions characteristic of what historians have called "true whigs"—precursors to political Liberals; not only did he oppose patronage appointments in Parliament, but he also disliked standing armies (and, it will be shown in the next chapter, militia activities), and he distrusted the extension of government agencies with their tendencies towards excessive spending and centralization of power.[10] At the same time, culturally and politically Primrose supported all efforts towards unification, such as the formation of the United Presbyterian denomination and later the Presbyterian Church of Canada, the Confederation of British North America in 1867, and the building of railway links to central Canada. Victorian historian Walter Bagehot described this unifying trend in Britain as a Whig effort to build national character and to reconcile freedom with progress and stability.[11] As Rudolf observed of Primrose, "He was a staunch Liberal—the warm supporter in former years of Howe and his compatriots, and entered into all the fights that occurred in the old times over the Pictou Academy affairs. Though he might have had a seat in the House of Assembly he persistently refused it—principally because of his dislike [of] the active pursuit of politics....He was offered a Senatorship (for life) on the formation of the Senate when the Union of the Provinces was consummated [in 1867] but he declined it at once and only informed us of it after his refusal had been sent off, for fear we should try to persuade him to accept it" (Journal, vol. 4, 19 April 1882).

While Rudolf recognized Primrose's tendency to exercise his will inflexibly, especially when he considered he was in the right, and felt that Primrose held his sons too long in "leading strings," Rudolf admired him greatly for his "great force of character—just and upright in all his actions—a thorough, but humble-minded Christian—holding the Calvinistic doctrines of his Church in their fullest degree. He will be very generally mourned for and many will grieve for him as a personal friend, while to his own family his removal will leave a blank that nothing can fill. Howard especially will miss him. He clung more to his father than Clarence, whose disposition is different. But both will miss him" (Journal, vol. 4, 19 April 1882).

Twenty years earlier, Rudolf gave several insights into both the positive and negative effects of Primrose's character-training regime for his sons and for their young business partner. When the "old gent," as they privately called him, turned sixty, they decided to present him with a pair of gold-rimmed glasses that they had ordered from New York. Rudolf's account revealed the kindly yet paternalistic rapport between the younger men and their mentor, as well as the close interpersonal relationships characteristic of midcentury, small-town family businesses:

> Howard, Clarence & I as Juniors of the Firm presented our Senior Mr. P. [Primrose] with a pair of gold eyeglasses this morning....The old gentleman seemed very much pleased to get this evidence of our esteem for him, but in his odd way observed "Well boys I deserve it." I replied, "We thought so, or perhaps you would not have got them," at which we all had a hearty laugh. He said to Hugh [Douglas, his nephew from New York,] "I have just been like a *clucking hen* looking after these boys—trying to keep them straight— Norman as well as the others, for I consider him as one of my boys"—I whispered to Hugh—"and you will now be one of the brood."—It is very happy for me to be so regarded by Mr. P. and I thank my Heavenly Father for placing my lot in so pleasant a situation. Mr. P. is sometimes irritable, and severe in his remarks, but he does not mean to be so. (Journal, vol. 1, 20 June 1862)

The "old gent" proved to be an important mentor for the young Rudolf, training him in accounting skills, introducing him to business colleagues, and offering him opportunities to invest capital in local enterprises in which Primrose himself was involved. Rudolf observed that Primrose, because of his meticulous business practices and his autocratic control of BNS affairs at Pictou, never lost the bank any money through bad debts. Primrose knew every man with whom he conducted business and only loaned to those he believed to be the most trustworthy. The organization of the Primrose firm epitomized another Scottish business tenet—division of labour leading to increased efficiency. Rudolf, with one-tenth share in the company, continued his BNS duties, counting bank notes and money (at that time in a variety of species— Spanish doubloons, American dollars, British pounds sterling). He was also required to calculate interest on bank accounts and on exchange rates, balancing the firm's books every six months, and occasionally he carried gold and notes to the head office of the BNS in Halifax. He wrote that Primrose "was like a father to me. I entered his office at 19 and remained there as Clerk & Partner for [sixteen years], during which time our relations were of the closest and most intimate character" (Journal, vol. 4, 19 April 1882).

Clarence Primrose was the eldest of Primrose's two sons.[12] In the Primrose firm, formed in 1849 as a shipping and banking company, he acted in the capacities of commission agent and auctioneer. He owned the Clarence Mills in Pictou and acted as an insurance agent for Lloyd's of London. Ironically (considering James Primrose's own views on political activism), his father also was grooming him for provincial political leadership. Rudolf found that he had to coach Clarence on the intricacies of exchange rates before his departure for Montreal in April 1863 to purchase wheat and flour for the Clarence Mills (managed for free by the Primrose firm). Under the guidance of the elder Primrose, the firm profited in their commission work, particularly at the time of the American Civil War. Rudolf and Clarence regularly supervised the unloading of cargoes and conducted their auction, the former acting as clerk, the latter as auctioneer. The sale of wheat, flour, molasses, and tobacco at auction added to the firm's profits and cemented the good relationship between Rudolf and Clarence.

Howard Primrose, however, proved to be a more difficult partner.[13] Because of his deafness, he attended to the correspondence of the firm, kept the minutes of meetings, and wrote the annual report of the Marine Railway Co., in which the Primrose firm held shares. Howard also had duties connected to the Customs House and to his directorship (beginning in 1864) of the Marine Assurance Co. Rudolf resented the fact that he had to shoulder Howard's duties when he was away. For instance, early in 1863 Howard left for England, primarily to consult specialists about his ear problems. In his absence, Rudolf had to take on all his correspondence duties and the minutes and annual report of the Marine Railway Co., and still attend to his own duties. Later in the year, when Howard caught a cold after a hunting expedition on a nearby mountain, Rudolf felt that his extra duties in connection with the fall shipment of tobacco were working him "to death" (Journal, vol. 1, 6 November 1863). No doubt the "old gent" would have agreed with Horatio Alger heroes of the time that training in discipline and striving for self-betterment in "a world that was stern and demanding, where character was made by contest and the health of nations forged by diligent obedience to duty" were worthwhile lessons for "bank clerks and schoolboys, and a reassurance to middle-class parents that, despite the expansion of business enterprise, opportunities for their children had not disappeared," as Daniel Rodgers observes.[14]

Several times Rudolf had to intercede in disputes between Howard and his father. The first one was when the "old gent" tried to persuade the elderly John T. Ives, a Pictou merchant who was a member of the House of Assembly, to take early retirement and to leave the position open for Clarence in the 1863 provincial elections. Ives refused. Howard and Rudolf objected to the extra workload this would mean for them, especially as Clarence had an undue share of the profits. Rudolf felt provoked that he had no opportunity to discuss the matter with the elder Primrose because he was tied to the bank office and could not meet with him in private. There was a very unpleasant scene in November of 1863 between Howard and his father over bank opening duties. Arriving at twenty past two, Primrose found the bank still locked and two men waiting outside. He first blamed Rudolf, but was satisfied that he had gone to lunch at one-thirty, so when Howard returned he attacked him:

> Howard instead of offering any excuse, replied impertinently that he was busy with family affairs, and would stay just as long as he pleased if he chose to do so. This at once roused his father's ire, and he asserted that Howard should be in the office at 2, or he would have some[one] else to do it for him. Howard dared him to make any change with him, and added that he (his Father) had just as much right to open the office as he had. His father then said well "I give you notice that at the end of the year the partnership shall be dissolved, and as you are so independent you may set up for yourself." Howard said he would not go out of the Firm, and that he could not be turned out, if it came to that....Much more passed between them of a very fierce and angry nature, for both had now completely lost all control of their tempers. It was very sad to see Father and Son fighting thus. However they at last became cooler, and the old gent. went home, but the row had entered into his soul. Howard saw his error, and Clarence & I told him plainly that he was greatly in the wrong. (Journal, vol. 1, 27 November 1863)

The next morning, when the elder Primrose raised the matter of dissolving the firm, Rudolf asserted at once that he was "ready and willing to allow him to have entire control of the business, and that I knew Howard was sorry for his conduct, and that the breaking up of the Firm should not be thought of" (Journal, vol. 1, 28 November 1863). Rudolf acknowledged privately that Howard was growing careless about his office duties. Howard apologized to his father, but the "old gent" felt very badly about this affront to his authority.

This contretemps may have led to the severe illness of James Primrose from erysipelas, an acute infectious disease of the skin, a month later; he nearly died. He did recover and continued to exert his power over the three younger men until well beyond his retirement. They respected his business judgment. As will be related in chapter 4, Rudolf admired his mentor but did not emulate his style of leadership. He would strive for a more subtle manly role. While continuing to be respectful, Rudolf would soon learn to stand up for his own interests and for his own point of view. James Primrose rewarded Rudolf's integrity by becoming a generous guide to the young man.

In 1862, as a result of Nova Scotia's brief gold boom, Primrose initiated discussions with his partners and with the BNS Board to open a branch at

Wine Harbour at the gold diggings on Nova Scotia's Eastern Shore. Rudolf was offered the position of manager. After consulting with his wife, he refused the offer, giving Cassie's need to care for her mother as his reason. Privately he wrote that he "was not at all sanguine as to the prospects of doing a large business at the Diggings. The gold fields have not yet been sufficiently tested, to make it certain that they will prove a source of wealth—constant, and steady in its flow—nor is the tide of migration commencing in such a way, as will so much increase the population at the mines, that scope enough will be found for a wholesale business such as ours" (Journal, vol. 1, 8 April 1862). Rudolf's doubts, probably reinforced by his talks with A.P. Ross (see chapter 1), proved well founded. Within two months of setting up office there, Primrose's nephew, Hugh Douglas, had to close it. He bought approximately $200 worth of gold altogether, his profit on this giving him a very small salary for two months of labour. Rudolf was thankful that he had not accepted the offer. Production of gold in Nova Scotia peaked in 1867 when eleven sites were in operation. By 1871 production had fallen by 30 per cent because of the shortage of good quality ore.

When the elder Primrose decided to retire from the business partnership on 1 June 1864, he made sure that Rudolf became an equal (one-quarter) shareholder in the new firm of Primrose and Rudolf, and that neither of the sons was senior in status, although together they received three-quarters of the profits. As Rudolf reported, "Mr. P....said there was to be no *Seniors* amongst us. That the man who worked most, and was the best man the world would recognize as the Senior, and that he would give us our Saviours rule to follow, that if any of us wished to be Lord and Master, let him be servant to all. He added you are on a parity and Mr. Rudolf is as good [a] man as any of you only he don't get so large a share of the profits" (Journal, vol. 1, 1 June 1864). This shift to more equality of opportunity with the promise of a career open to talent, as mentioned earlier, would replace the previous Georgian character ideal. In Rudolf's case, it led to an improvement in his status in the community and in his economic standing. He continued, however, to carry a minority weight in the firm because of the brothers' financial superiority. Rudolf received many congratulations for this promotion, particularly from his brother-in-law, Alex Scott, who was already sending out feelers about Rudolf working as his commission agent out of Scotland. Rudolf was pleased for the sake of his mother: "I feel that this advancement is partly due to Mothers earnest, and oft repeated prayers on my behalf, for I know she has been constant in her intercessions for me, as well as for all her children. And one thought delights me that I shall be able to make her declining years comfortable, by giving her a home, whenever she may accept of it." In February 1865, the new firm signed a $3,000 bond for its cash account at the BNS; John T. Ives and James Primrose were its sureties.

The Primrose firm, while benefitting from its senior partner's sound business acumen and banking power in the region, also succeeded because of a number of external structural factors. In 1854 the American government signed a Reciprocity Treaty with the British North American colonies in which there was agreement to have free exchange of natural products. Trade between Nova Scotia and the United States between 1854 and 1860 increased substantially. A railway link between Halifax and the Province of Canada was started. The line from Halifax to Windsor was completed in 1858, and a branch line to the Pictou district was begun in 1864. Maritime commercial interests and political strategists hoped that this overland connection would increase their ocean-going trade. With the cancellation of the monopoly of the General Mining Association in 1858, hopes were high that the exploitation of natural resources would lead to prosperity. Fourteen new coal mines had opened up, and 3,043 men and boys were employed in coal mining throughout Nova Scotia in 1866. Eighty per cent of production in 1865 was exported to the United States. During the minor gold boom between 1862 and 1871, over 192,772 ounces were mined by a labour force averaging 700 people per year.[15]

The Primrose investments in milling and ship-building were part of a general Nova Scotian industrial development trend towards the production of staple commodities and staple processing. Over 60 per cent of the total value of manufacturing in 1861 was in these two industries. Other successful industries included grist mills, tanneries, and brewing and distilling plants that served local markets. Aside from Halifax, which controlled half the manufacturing output, and the large iron production at Londonderry (which annually manufactured $40,000 worth of products), Pictou and Yarmouth had the most developed economies during the 1860s. Profits from the carrying trade were based on locally built, manned, and operated sailing ships. Merchants invested their profits in their communities to produce necessary institutions and local services, thus creating diverse economies as well as establishing greater control over their local affairs. James Primrose, as head of Primrose Sons, was a leader in these new trends in the Pictou region.

He was not always successful, however. During the American Civil War, the firm's gambling on currency exchange rates was at first disastrous. Because of a sudden drop in exchange rates after the capture of Vicksburg by the Union Army, the firm lost $1,000; but shrewdly the partners hoped to recover this loss through an invoice purchased when gold was at $25 and sold when it rose in October to $50. The partners had also gambled on the good luck of

Captain W.A. Fraser, whose ship the *Magnet* ran the Union navy's blockade of shipping into Mobile Bay, outside Wilmington, North Carolina. Unfortunately, the ship was seized at Fernandino, Port of Florida. Fraser returned and sold the cargo; from the proceeds that he had invested (£30) Rudolf gained only £9. Four months later, Fraser's vessel was again seized running the blockade. By this time the Primrose partners decided to purchase their own vessel and gain increased control of its costs.

In September 1863, the partners signed an agreement between Captain Daniel McDonald (4/16), R. McKenzie (5/16), Dr. Johnston (2/16), and themselves (5/16) for a copper-fastened, class A1 barque registered at Lloyd's of London for four years at $41 per registered ton. Although freight rates to Boston had fallen to $2.60 from $3.65 a month earlier, they anticipated that rates would rise again. Rudolf commented, "so many Americans are coming here, that they pull down the freight. Their depreciated currency does not hurt them, and they can carry coals at a less figure (and make money) than our vessels, who have to lose 30 or 33% on their exchange" (Journal, vol. 1, 21 September 1863). By April 1864, Odiorne, their Boston agent, ordered them to get as many vessels as possible at any price for the anticipated increase in the coal trade. Gold had reached $179, and he expected freights likely to be $5 per ton. Unfortunately the Dalhousie Pit, at GMA's Pictou mines, collapsed (with no loss of life) in late April just before Pictou Harbour became ice free. As Rudolf reported, "It will be a very serious loss to the Company, and also to the consumers of coal. They have only about 50,000 tons on the banks, and have only the small cage pit seam to work now. The deep pit near the foundry crushed in last year, and they have not yet got to work at it. We expected a large coal trade this year, but I expect it must now be limited" (Journal, vol. 1, 29 April 1864). Norman and Clarence had taken Odiorne over the ice to visit this shaft two months earlier. As he wrote, it was lucky it hadn't collapsed then. In June their new barque, named *Lord Chancellor*, was launched. Its first charter was to Quebec with a load of coal at 12 shillings 6 pence per ton. Gold by this time had reached $250 in the United States.

The firm began another enterprise in March 1862. The partners rented the tobacco factory owned by A.J. Patterson, with a guarantee of a monopoly over processing in the region. The anticipated profits would accrue because of high US duties and home protection offering them a "large margin." They shipped their first ten kegs of tobacco to Sherbrooke and Halifax in April. The following year, they decided to purchase a steam-driven cutting machine to process tobacco stems, currently unused. The machine cost £140. They also purchased a stove for drying purposes. In October, the tobacco cutter was "working splendidly" and tobacco prices had increased from 2¢ to 4¢ on leaf. In December, the partners made a large purchase of leaf tobacco: "50 Hhds [hogshead, a large cask] costing about $17,000. Our agent [Hunter and Co. in New York] telegraphed us that tobacco had advanced 3c per lb., in consequence of Congress being about to impose a duty of 20c pr. lb. on it, and allow no drawback in what is exported. Should this be done we will make a good business of this lot. We have remitted £2,000 Stg. Exc[hange] to pay for it. Exc. is now @ 64% Prem. in New York" (Journal, vol. 1, 18 December 1863). In late January, Rudolf and his partners were busy supervising the arrival of teams of horses hauling their tobacco overland, the shipment having docked at Halifax and then been transported by rail to Truro.

Because of the promising prospect of coal profits, the elder Primrose in April 1863 proposed that they purchase a machine to bore for coal on the Pictou side of the harbour. Rudolf was offered a quarter share in the speculation. The machine would be rented out for well-boring or other geological explorations, thereby recovering its cost. A year later, the partners applied for a Right of Search for five square miles around Pictou; they sent $20 to the elder Primrose's brother, Alexander, a Halifax barrister, to cover the government fee. Rudolf continued, "We are also talking of sending Mike ONeil to the oil wells in Canada to see the Borers there, and to procure a borer which will work cheaply and expeditiously. Indications of coal have been seen about the Gas Works in Billy Pattersons field. The crop was traced for a little way...dipping towards the harbor. It is useless to build castles in the air, but one cannot help thinking what an enormous fortune it would be to anyone to find a good working seam of coal on this side [of Pictou Harbour]" (Journal, vol. 1, 15 April 1864). The Cape Breton coal mines, now being developed by American companies, provided incentive for this new speculation. Rudolf reported that Dr. McLeod of Sydney had just returned from New York where he sold half his mine for £25,000 in gold. The American company had paid-up capital of $1,000,000 and intended to build a railway from Bridgeport, the location of the mine, to the ports of either Sydney or Louisbourg. Shortly after this, Rudolf and his partners bought a quarter share in a proposed Cape Breton coal mining venture at River Bourgeoise (Journal, vol. 1, 4 October 1864). Rudolf did not mention in this connection the great difficulty J.D.B. Fraser of Pictou was experiencing in selling his New Glasgow–area coal mine (with a mortgage held by James Primrose) to American investors. In October 1864, Fraser successfully sold it for $50,000. By December 1864, Rudolf reported that their boring machine was at work at the Clarence Mills, boring in the existing 180-foot well for water.

James Primrose began several other enterprises in 1864 designed to capitalize on future development both in Pictou and in British North America.

The firm took over management of a brick factory, hiring an American fore-man from Boston; he was paid $75 a month, board included, to modernize the plant. On 18 June 1864, Rudolf walked the dusty road to the brickyard to pay the men. They had just commenced firing the clay bricks for the season. The "old gent" was also very keen on the potential of a ten-mile extension of the Intercolonial Railway (ICR) line from New Glasgow to Pictou Landing, which lay south across the harbour mouth from Pictou Town and which opened on 30 June 1867 at a cost of $2,321,567. The proposed northern exten-sion line would increase trade and the significance of Pictou Town as a port of exchange and distribution. It would also connect the district more securely to the increasing volume of landward trade with other British North Amer-ican provinces. Although this Pictou Town extension, which would necessi-tate a bridge over the West River, was not completed until 1890, railway fever was in the air. Primrose proposed first that John Cameron be supported by the firm for two-thirds of his costs in his tender to do the roadbed work for the New Glasgow line. They sent him to Truro on 26 May 1863 to undertake the bidding. When this scheme failed, they allied with James Fraser Jr. of New Glasgow and a few more "men of property" in April 1864 to go to Hal-ifax and plead for the Pictou railway extension: "Mr. P. [said] that he would take an equal share with [Fraser] in the matter, and was quite willing to go into the business. We have spoken several times of trying to make a contract for portions of the work as it proceeded, but this would give us an interest in the whole construction. It is a large undertaking, but I have no doubt it would be carried out successful[ly] with such men as Jas. Primrose, Jas. Fraser[,] John Crerar [Pictou merchant] & Donald Fraser MPP as head of the concern. But it may never be attempted for we do not know whether the Govt will agree to give a company the building of the entire line," wrote Rudolf (Journal, vol. 1, 8 April 1864). As it turned out, the project was awarded to Sandford Fleming of Halifax, whose project was scathingly criticized by Rudolf.

The various investments of the Primrose firm illustrated what John Reid deems to have been a crisis in the Maritime region during the 1860s. Three strategies were possible, all of which James Primrose and his partners at-tempted. The first was to integrate new techniques into the existing trading economy without fundamentally altering its structure—investing in steam-driven sawmills and brick factories, or building merchant marine and wooden ships. Another strategy was to promote railway and steamship development leading to increased north-south trading links and the generation of capital from international trade. The third strategy was to promote the building of the ICR and begin increased landward links with British North America. As Reid concludes, "The reality was that the Maritime region in the 1860s faced economic choices that were not only difficult but were so complex and so unpredictable in their consequences that they admitted of no clear-cut answers. Only time and experience would eventually determine what these consequences would be."[16] In this economic environment, James Primrose was guiding the three young men in new directions, fostering rigorous discussion about the risks involved, and encouraging them to branch out both in their investments and in their skills. Despite his authoritarian manner, he was cultivating open-mindedness towards the coming expansion in British North American and in world trade. By the 1860s, local merchants' control over economic output (the system of distribution and exchange) and Pictou Town's control of imported goods and services was at its zenith. This was probably the main reason Rudolf cultivated older mentors to help him form his public character ideal. Their endorsement of his own character would also enable him to gain entry to positions of community leadership. The family-based merchant capitalistic ethos in which Rudolf was being trained was shortly to be transformed. The elder Primrose anticipated the coming economic and social changes and attempted to foster skills and character traits to prepare Rudolf for mobility and risk-taking, major characteristics of the rising entrepreneur in the new middle class. A final quality fostered by bankers and epitomized by Primrose's business practice was his use of trust to control credit, which was granted "to those on whom the creditor considered he could rely most fully, that is, people whose characters he knew and to those personally recommended or guaranteed by those he knew and trusted,"[17] according to Douglas McCalla.

Primrose encouraged the young Rudolf to develop his own ideas. When the ways (tracks) of the Marine Railway Co. were found to be riddled with toledo worms and had to be replaced, Rudolf suggested an alternative to the plan offered by "old Mr. Tucker." Rudolf thought railway iron should be used instead of tubular iron; it was much cheaper and would be simpler to lay down. When Tucker heard of Rudolf's alternative proposal he became abusive:

> He says "Do you think I know nothing of ships ways?" I confess [wrote Rudolf] he knows an infinite deal about *ships*, and the *ways* in which they are built, but I also know he does not understand much about our Marine Railway. Mr. P. is rather in an awk[w]ard fix. He thinks my plan a capital one, and feels inclined to adopt it, but Mr. T. has put him in a corner, by claiming to be paid £200 if *iron tracks in any form is used* asserting that my idea is borrowed from his, at least it is tantamount to it. The fact is, I thought of iron tracks, like an ordinary railway long ago, and was more confirmed in my belief of their utility during my journey to & from Halifax. I saw the sleepers embedded in mud, and gravel, with the rails clear off the ground, which

would just be the thing in our Marine Road. We want the cross ties, or sleepers covered with mud, because it has been proved that the worms will not attack wood buried in it. And all we want is just the iron tracks to let the cradle run on. (Journal, vol. 1, 30 September 1863)

In the opinion of the foundry owner, W.H. Davies, railway iron would deflect unless made stronger, and Tucker's proposal was too expensive. As it turned out, the shareholders of the Marine Railway decided to take the advice of a professional engineer, Mr. Crandall, who proposed the building of two cradles and a new track, and the extension of the ways so that the company could double its capacity for ships' repair. Although the cost was estimated to be $11,000, the company had already paid off its $1,600 debt and had given a 6 per cent dividend to shareholders, so it was in a good financial state. The shareholders resolved to increase the capital of the company from $25,000 to $40,000 and invited subscribers for the new shares, the amount raised being dedicated to laying down the new ways. The Primrose firm bought timbers for the purpose in January 1864.

As a result of all these financial ventures, the firm of Primrose Sons in 1862 recorded a handsome profit. Rudolf, with only one-tenth share and his $400 BNS salary (stopped when he later became a quarter partner in the firm), calculated that his profit amounted to $2,639.51 (Journal, vol. 1, 31 January 1863). His expenditures while boarding at the Dawsons amounted only to $754.64; they included a $117 loss on Captain Fraser's seized ship and the purchase of their sewing machine for $51. Even more significant than the profit, however, was Rudolf's commitment to stewardship, instilled in him by James Primrose and by their shared evangelical Christian values. As he wrote, "This is a larger sum than I ever thought to possess, and I humbly thank my Heavenly Father for so largely lavishing upon [me] so much of this worlds goods. It is not because I deserve it, but because He is so kind and good to me. Not rewarding me according to my deeds, but pardoning my unworthiness. Grant me grace Lord, to raise my thoughts and affections above this earth, and suffer me not to set them upon the wealth Thou has given me, and above all, give me a generous and charitable heart, so that I may freely dispense to the poor and needy, and for the spread of Thy Gospel, the means which Thou has placed in my Keeping" (Journal, vol. 1, 31 January 1863). He added that Cassie and he purchased a new dress for her that day from Mrs. Jane McPhail's dressmaking establishment.

A year later, having moved into their first home, Rudolf's cash balance after another very good year amounted to $200. His investments in furniture and in a share of the Marine Railway Co. he estimated to be worth $4,000, almost double his previous year's profit. As he reflected again, "This is far more money than I thought I would possess a few years ago. But the Lord has blessed me abundantly, and I trust the remembrance of His great mercies towards me, may ever incite me to more love towards Him, and a greater desire to serve Him" (Journal, vol. 1, 8 February 1864).

The bank's business was also steadily growing. In June Rudolf reported taking a bag of gold worth $13,000 to Halifax. The partners decided to improve their office entrance by adding a porch and plate-glass panels to the inner door, so that the porch was lit up at night from the gaslight inside. A year earlier, the BNS head office had instructed them to install an iron safety vault at a cost of $200. By the end of 1864, then, the partners looked forward to a promising future. Rudolf's only reservations were the drudgery of eternally counting money, the extra unpaid work he had to do in connection with the "old gent's" propensity (now that he had retired) for liberally dispensing community advice, and the nagging unease he had regarding Howard's bouts of jealousy. When he prayed for a "generous and charitable heart" and for an obliging demeanour, Rudolf referred not only to the poor and needy of Pictou but also to his own disciplined behaviour in his public workplace. In a small town, public scrutiny was ever-present and it was no easy task to control one's emotions in volatile situations.

This was particularly true when one's daily social life merged imperceptibly with one's public workplace, thus merging private with public ideals of character. In his own experience, Rudolf constantly slipped from one sphere into the other; the "old gent's" influence, as well as that of his son Clarence, extended to sporting activities, private family parties, and social gatherings. Most Pictonians, for instance, attended the New Year's day bazaar, but for Rudolf it was "an infliction for I would tenfold rather have spent the evening at home, but the Ladies wanted someone to take charge of their money, and from my position in the Bank, I am generally made Treasurer for all these sort of things—plenty work, but little pay" (Journal, vol. 1, 1 January 1863).

James Primrose was a founding father of the New Caledonia Curling Club in Pictou, which organized challenge matches not only against local teams but also against teams as far away as Truro and Halifax. Local players filled in for absent team members from the "away" club:

> This afternoon a Curling Match was arranged & played between the victorious rink in the Truro game with the Halifax Curlers, and 5 players selected from there left at home. The Truro players were Tho. Meagher—C. Primrose—D. Munro Jr.—Dr. Johnston & James Ives—Skip. Their opponents were James Foote—W.N. Rudolf—J.A. Davison D. Hockin & J. Primrose—Skip. After a very keenly contested game, & the stipulated time being up, the result was a tie—the numbers being 11 each. This conclusion was felt to be

a defeat by the Truro rink, as they went on the ice, with a confident assurance of beating the others by a large majority. But this game has only confirmed the oft repeated adage that curling is a "slippery game"—that it is always best, and safest to boast of skill on the termination of the play—and not to have an o'er weening estimation of ones own ability. Poor Jas. Ives was deeply mortified at his ill luck, and his feelings found unpleasant expression occasionally. But one unfortunate display will not injure the acknowledged superiority of the skill and merit of his players. (Journal, vol. 1, 22 February 1862)

Disciplined self-control under hot competition was the character trait Primrose hoped to instill in his players. As Anthony Rotundo remarks, middle-class male culture cultivated both in the marketplace and in society promoted "constant competitive tests [that] resulted in continuous judgments by peers that, more than anything else, determined a man's status in his profession."[18] The game also provided healthy enjoyment, especially when the harbour was frozen over and work was slack. Rudolf described one afternoon in January 1863: "Mild and fine. Thawing all day. Was out on the harbor curling in the afternoon for first time this winter. We found a good hard piece of ice out in the channel and had a very good game on it" (Journal, vol. 1, 26 January 1863).

The harbour provided a venue for solo sports, as well. Clarence bought a new pair of skates and gave Rudolf his old ones. His skating practice was interrupted, however, "by a man from New Glasgow wanting a che[que] cashed, and I had to go on shore with him just as I was getting into trim" (Journal, vol. 1, 23 February 1863). Two days later, Rudolf managed to get "out on the ice for 1½ hours this afternoon after 4 oclock. Just as I was buckling on my skates Cassie, and Georgina Matheson came down on the wharf to get on the ice. I helped them on it....Skating has become quite a fashionable amusement among the young girls here. The Davies' and a lot more were out yesterday, and today. We formed a line alternately boys and girls and by timing the stroke we went on linked arm and arm together in fine style. It was grand fun for the girls" (Journal, vol. 1, 25 February 1863).

When snow fell on the ice, they tried snowshoeing. After Clarence and his brother used the snowshoes in the morning, "Smith [Dawson] & I went out after dinner. Clarence lent me his shoes. This was my first attempt, and I succeeded very well. Did not get a single fall—was more fortunate in this respect than the others before me" (Journal, vol. 1, 13 March 1863). The next year weather conditions were more severe: "Very cold. Thermo[meter] 9 [degrees] below zero [Fahrenheit]. Was out on snowshoes this afternoon. Howard, Clarence & I started for a walk at 5 oclock. We had great fun. We all got several tumbles, and it was quite exciting sport to run races on them. I borrowed Smiths fitout [outfit]. I almost got one of my big toes frozen though, and had to soak it in cold water on my return. It ached very severely when the circulation was being restored" (Journal, vol. 1, 19 February 1864).

The effect of these intense work and social contacts was that Clarence and Rudolf were fast becoming good friends. Norman and Cassie were invited to the baptism of Clarence and Rachel's daughter at Prince Street Church: "She had her name 'Emma Archibald' selected long ago. She is called after the late daughter of Hon. T.D. Archibald of Sydney, once Rachels most intimate friend" (Journal, vol. 1, 20 April 1863). On his return from Montreal, Clarence brought Edith and Mrs. Dawson's adopted daughter, Minnie Harris, presents from Cassie's cousin, J. William Dawson (originally from Pictou and at that time principal of McGill College). Clarence and Rudolf exchanged photographs of each other. In contrast, Rudolf appeared to be closer to Howard's wife than to him. While her husband was away, Olly had two young men, Fred Corbett and a young member of the large Archibald clan, staying with her. She decided to give a party for them, to which Norman and Cassie were invited. Because of her frequent confinements due to child-bearing, Cassie had "not been at a party for so long a time that her dresses did not suit, and she had no time to get anything ready....Fortunately Kate Fraser [daughter of J.D.B. Fraser and fiancée of Reverend Mr. McPhee] tendered the use of a black velvet jacket of hers, and Mrs. Dawson having got up a suitable head dress at a short notice, she managed to get equipped. She looked very well, and Olly and several others remarked how well she looked. It added a great deal to my pleasure to have her there. Mrs. Dawson took care of baby [Edie] who was very good. I ran home a couple of times during the evening to see how she was getting along" (Journal, vol. 1, 20 February 1863). Rudolf added that the party was a very pleasant occasion.

Numerous other Primrose family parties were held at Terrace Cottage, where, as mentioned earlier, the elderly couple lived with Clarence, his wife Rachel, and their growing family. These parties were notable for the variety of activities engaged in by this mixed-age group. For instance, an informal afternoon tea at which Olly, two Davies girls, their mother, and a Mrs. Dimock from Windsor and her aunt, Mrs. Davis, also attended, resulted in "a great evenings romping. Clarence brought home from Montreal some large india rubber balls[;] these we pitched at one anothers heads until we got as excited as madmen, and laughed outrageously. We also had [games of] battle-door & shuttlecock and 'Cannonade.' The latter is very amusing, and exciting. I never was in such a steam of heat" (Journal, vol. 1, 11 June 1863). The young twenty-eight-year-old Rudolf, despite his earnest evangelical demeanour, proved himself capable of having fun.

Another tea party was held late in June, when the temperature reached ninety-two degrees in the shade: "We were all down at the cottage to tea. We sat outside for a long time in the cool wind. The grounds, and trees about the place look very lovely just now. We sat the entire evening without gas[light]— with all the blinds open to admit the light of the moon which was shining very clearly, and had singing and music of the piano all the time. The harbor looked like a sheet of gold where the moon light streamed on it, and the rest of it by contrast looked nearly inky black. We had a delightful time, and were sorry when half past 10 came to have to go up into the warm, and dusty town again (Journal, vol. 1, 29 June 1863). Clarence also brought a number of games from another Montreal trip: "The old gent wanted to see 'Lotto'[19] played, so we commenced a game, and played for a half hour. I sent for a box of 'Squails,' [an old English game played with discs] and took them home with me (Clarence bought them) and after tea, Mother [who was visiting them from Lunenburg], Cassie, Minnie & I played for an hour. It is a very amusing and innocent game" (Journal, vol. 1, 23 March 1864).

Clarence and family organized expeditions for younger friends. There were several sailing cruises out into the harbour. Rudolf described one in July 1863: "Had a sailing party in the evening. Cassie, Louisa, Smith, Rachel, Clarence, the Davies's, Clara Ross and a lot more. It was rather windy and rough at first, and the boat threw a few sprays over her, wetting some of us a little but it soon calmed off, and we had a delightful time. The moon shone brightly, and gave us light enough to see each other plainly. We sang, and laughed till our throats got sore and our sides ached, and at 10 oclock came to the wharf, sorry to sep[a]rate" (Journal, vol. 1, 1 July 1863). When Captain Clark arrived in Pictou with his new ship, *Duart Castle,* he and his wife (a sister of John McLean's and school friend of Cassie's) organized a picnic tea on board. This time Rudolf arranged to have a ferry transport them to the barque: "There was quite a large party of us—Olly, Rachel, Clara & her two sisters, all the Davies' girls…Cassie & Minnie…also John McKinlay, Howard, & Clarence, the two Davies' boys & myself. We had a great spread of good things for tea, and enjoyed the evening very much. The Cabins are very large and comfortable. Mrs. Clark & her little boy George are going in the vessel for a year, but Anna their daughter, is to be left behind at Truro to go to school. We took our game of Hoops with us, and it was a great source of amusement to those who played with them. Clarence & John McKinlay especially enjoyed them. We returned at 9 oclock" (Journal, vol. 1, 22 September 1863).

By this time, Rudolf was considered so much a member of the Primrose family that at the burial of Mrs. William Primrose he and Clarence were able to rescue the "old gent" from an embarrassing situation: "Mr. P. forgot to order the hearse until just before the funeral. When Mr. Bayne [minister of Prince Street Church] was praying it occurred to him. He dispatched Clarence & I to look after it. We put his horse in [the traces of the carriage carrying the hearse]....Archy drove it. After the funeral Mr. P., Clarence, Howard & I went back to Helen [Primrose's house], where Mr. Bayne had family worship" (Journal, vol. 1, 16 October 1863). Every Christmas the Primroses invited Rudolf over for tea, treating him as very much one of the family: "About 4 oclock I met Howard & Clarence coming up from the Cottage. We walked out the road as far as Blink Bonnie and then down to the Cottage. Mrs. P. saluted me with a kiss, and a hearty welcome coupled with all the congratulations of the season. The old gentleman is very miserable with cold yet. He appeared quite dull, and dispirited. Olly & Howard were there to dinner, but they [went] home to tea. I came up with them as far as our house" (Journal, vol. 1, 25 December 1863). Several weeks later, as the elderly Primrose was recovering from erysipelas, Cassie and Norman visited him and stayed for several hours after tea. Norman lent him several books from his library, realizing that the "old gent [found] the time very long, not being able to go out. His face is so very tender, it was a little swollen from being out on Saturday" (Journal, vol. 1, 26 January 1864).

In this early stage of his maturing manhood, Rudolf's character was being disciplined both in public at his workplace and in private, social settings.[20] He began to acquire self-control, self-confidence, flexibility, and a more resolute personality, perhaps in imitation of his mentor. In this cultural grooming process, James Primrose was teaching his own sons and Rudolf to adopt an optimistic, Liberal outlook towards the emerging industrial-capitalistic economy. Their shrewd, pragmatic attitude towards their investments—shifting away from gold mining and into freight shipping—enabled them to profit from the boom years of 1861–1864. Primrose enthusiastically embraced the implications of Nova Scotia's rapidly improving communications—in telegraph, railways, and roads. He promoted the expansion of banking services to new regions, and his sons acquired extra responsibilities in the rapidly expanding financial institutions, such as marine and life insurance companies. These institutions and improved communications would bring Pictou Town increasingly under the powerful influence of the business cycle of the Atlantic economy and would undermine the strong control Primrose exerted both socially and psychologically on his sons and on Rudolf. Their financial decisions would be influenced increasingly by worldwide factors, such as freight costs, the price of exports in foreign currency, and American inflation. Professional engineers and financial capitalists in Halifax and then in central Canada would control decisions and economic outcomes of large-scale projects, undermin-

ing the regional control of merchants such as James Primrose. Rather than fearing these transformations Primrose, his sons, and Rudolf treated them as
challenges, diversifying their investments and seeking out new opportunities, as future chapters will relate.

In other ways, the small community of Pictou retained its earlier face-to-
face relationships, which also influenced Rudolf's ideal of character. Within
the extended Rudolf-Primrose family, there were frequent interactions
between men and women and between younger and older people. The middle-class male identity fostered by the elder Primrose was not exclusivist, as
numerous scholars of masculinity maintain. Rudolf's own manly public character, as a result, was tempered by both female social interaction and by friendly
interaction with respected elders in his community.[21]

The emerging Liberal ideal of character, Collini argues, was peculiarly
suited to the colonial experience with its future of unknown circumstances,
anxieties about the extension of the franchise, and fears about the breakdown
of habits and willpower in an adverse environment. Character, then, represented "an expression of a very deeply ingrained perception of the qualities
needed to cope with life, an ethic with strong roots in areas of experience
ostensibly remote from politics."[22] As Collini concludes, it was also "the ideal
of moral health and its priority."[23] This was the ideal quality that Primrose represented to Rudolf. What he himself did not fully appreciate was that Primrose would prove to be a healthy antidote to Rudolf's tendency to explore
his evangelical inwardness, through prayer and family stewardship, to the
exclusion of worldly duty. By keeping his focus on the latter through his
work, Primrose broadened Rudolf's concept of character and taught him the
complexities involved with ethical judgments in modern business decisions.
Rudolf's ideal of character would become more sophisticated as he faced the
stresses of his social responsibilities, the complexities of their firm's financial
decisions, and the uncertainties of his economic future. It would also begin
to reflect continuities with the past and his efforts to heal Pictou's culture of
conflict.

CHAPTER 4

Militia Culture

T here was one major bone of contention between James Primrose and his "boys." This was the time they spent on their required militia duties. Norman Rudolf resented this criticism and demonstrated by his rapid advancement in the militia that he had the necessary qualifications and character to succeed in this military culture.

Since the 1753 Proclamation, Nova Scotian males between the ages of sixteen and sixty had to serve in the militia. Compulsory drill, however, was abandoned in 1844. By the 1850s, the imperial government began a gradual reduction of its North American garrisons in an effort to save money and to divert resources to the Crimean War effort. The war spurred a new movement to form volunteer corps. In June 1859, the Earl of Mulgrave, lieutenant-governor of Nova Scotia, sent a circular letter to the commanding officer of each militia regiment asking them to form a volunteer company. By 1860, thirty volunteer companies had been formed, including one at Albion Mines, near New Glasgow, and the Pictou Greys at Pictou Town. The young men of the province enthusiastically supported these companies in the early 1860s. When the American Civil War broke out in 1861, and especially after the US Navy's capture of a British mail packet, the *Trent,* there was a general alarm in British North America and increased interest in defence.[1] Nova Scotia reactivated its militia. Legislation had been passed in 1860 requiring members of all corps to be divided into effective (active), non-effective (sedentary), and honorary members. Each corps was required to pass bylaws and to levy fines—in effect acquiring the trappings of a private social club, especially the volunteer corps, whose members were exempt from statute labour. By 1861 in Nova Scotia there were 37 companies, 1,516 officers and men, and 645 non-effectives; 2,038 rifles had been issued.[2]

It was clear, however, that the members of the provincial militia, in contrast to those in the volunteer corps, were useless, old, and disinclined to resign. Therefore, in 1862 a new militia act was passed that combined all militia and volunteers, thereby gaining young, energetic, and trained officers; the latter were required to pass examinations to prove their efficiency before promotion. The government expended $19,417.69 on provincial defence and increased the number of hours required for drills and for parades. All effective troops had to participate in five days of duty, and officers had to perform twenty-eight drills of three hours each per year. A provincial rifle competition with monetary prizes began in October 1861; a cup was awarded to the provincial champion. The province promised to cover one-third of the cost of new drill rooms, the remaining two-thirds to be raised by local contributors. Finally, a capable staff of field officers, including Lieutenant Colonel John Wimburn Laurie, captain of the Fourth Regiment, were hired to inspect the local corps. Between 1861 and 1867, a variety of British drill sergeants were employed for instructional programs. These efforts led to a high degree of serviceable efficiency during the years of the Civil War (1861–1865). This was the era in which Norman Rudolf served, primarily in the West End Battalion of Pictou Town. He rapidly advanced from senior lieutenant to major.

Rudolf's success demonstrated several aspects of his character. He was able to adapt easily to military culture, in part because of his family heritage; his father was lieutenant colonel of the First Battalion, Lunenburg. Rudolf obtained his first commission as lieutenant at Lunenburg on 4 August 1854 (after he had moved to Pictou). Despite his shyness, he proved to be an able leader; he was also a good athlete and physically hardy. As was the case at the bank, he was a disciplined worker and paid attention to regulations and to new drill procedures. Above all, he enjoyed this new culture, viewed the emerging meritocratic career path as a challenge, and aspired to the status of senior rank. The afternoon-evening militia duties drew him out of the claustrophobic atmosphere at the Dawsons, and he began to experience a new form of peer-group bonding. Jokes, borrowed uniforms, team drill, and rifle cleaning cemented manly cultural identities and established a sense of community, which tended to overcome latent class prejudices held by middle-class officers or lower-class rankings. It was interesting that while Rudolf condemned the violent behaviour and "bad characters" of some working-class people, he strongly identified with the men in his company. In effect, the

small-town culture of Pictou at this time was pre-class: a sense of community and respect for individual character were stronger than any fixed allegiance to class. Militia culture tended to look to the past (eighteenth-century,
gentry character norms); but Rudolf also wanted to introduce changes, especially the principle of merit, which he would embody by means of a new style
of leadership. He began the transition to this new leadership style by participating with his company in a demanding first review:

> ...the wind had hauled to N.E. and a thick, wetting snow storm had set in.
> However, every one was determined to enjoy it, and many were the jokes
> made and cracked on the occasion. Most of the Militia Officers were
> mounted, and served as Cavalry. The remainder were placed in the Artillery
> Co. for the day. By borrowing Undress Jackets, and getting a red stripe down
> our trousers, we made a very close attempt at the uniform of the Co., and
> so did not look oddly. Each man had provided himself with 20 rounds of
> blank cartridge, and we had plenty of firing. The manoeuvres were skir-
> mishing—forming squares to resist cavalry, and marching past a supposed
> General. After 2 hours exercise, we returned home "at the double" to warm
> our benumbed limbs, for we were completely drenched, by this time. How-
> ever dry clothes, and the oiling, cleaning, and rubbing bestowed on the rifles
> kept up a good circulation, and kept us sound in wind and limb. (Journal,
> vol. 1, 1 March 1862)

When the company was inspected by Colonel Laurie in December, Rudolf
demonstrated another asset of peer group identity; he had learned to discern
the difference between individual character and a team's status: "We made
our usual mistakes and with the aid of our awk[w]ard ones, who will remain
so till the end of the Chapter, succeeded in *distinguishing* ourselves as the
awk[w]ard squadron. It was not a *personal* inspection—as one had no chance
of redeeming ones character, but we all sunk, or swum together" (Journal,
vol. 1, 26 December 1862).

Rudolf considered gentry standards of behaviour the appropriate norm.
When Henry Narraway, a Pictou brass founder who was in the artillery company, found that he could not get the infantry to continue subsidizing their
share of the large rent for the drill room, he became very excited and swore
at several officers. He was required to apologize to them "for his grossly insult-
ing conduct," or he would be reported to the adjutant general. Meanwhile, his
name was to "be struck off the list, as being unworthy to associate with them"
(Journal, vol. 1, 14 March 1862). Three days later, Narraway apologized at
length to Major Fraser and the other officers he had insulted. He also wrote
a letter of apology to Fraser. Although this apparently closed the matter, Rudolf
cast disparaging remarks about the fact that Narraway was unable to pass the

militia officers' examination at Pictou and went to West River to pass it. Rudolf believed that an individual's ability should govern promotion. He wrote in disgust, "I must say I can't see upon what principle Col. Laurie passes & rejects candidates. He refuses to pass Murdoch McPherson, who knows more than Narraway will ever learn. I told John [McKinlay], it was enough to make one give up the thing in disgust, as it made no difference whether one knew ones drill or not. All the ignorant ones pass easily, and seniority governs the promotion, so that they get advanced in their turn, always thus keeping their place over smart men—be they ever so intelligent and well drilled, but who happen to be juniors by date of commission" (Journal, vol. 1, 12 May 1863).

When Colonel Laurie arrived to conduct the annual May inspection of Pictou's militia, he indicated that the senior officers had a lot to learn. Rudolf was ashamed of them. He readily agreed with the official policy of headquarters to base promotion on the efficiency of individual officers in conducting their men through drill exercises, and to require all officers to purchase uniforms, similar to British officers of the line. The latter wore blue cloth trousers with a red stripe down the side for full dress and long loose jacket with regulation buttons and shoulder straps of silver lace. Grey homespun trousers were required for undress (informal wear). When in Truro with Clarence for the Provincial Rifle Cup competition, at which they wore their undress uniform, Rudolf "was well pleased with my visit as it gave me a good opportunity of seeing how these affairs are conducted, and also to see something of the Volunteers generally. I was surprized at the evident expense the officers were at in getting up their uniforms and pleased at their neatness and beauty" (Journal, vol. 1, 15 September 1862). The next year, he and Clarence bought the serge for their dress uniforms, which Rudolf admired as beautiful material, to be made into a uniform by Donald McDonald of New Glasgow. Shortly thereafter the Pictou militia officers "met for drill in uniform this evening at 6½ oclock. We had 16 present and those who were fully equipped looked very well in the dress" (Journal, vol. 1, 24 June 1863). Their uniforms served as symbols of the bonding process implicit in this newly constructed male cultural community. They also served as incentives to promote more efficient performance by Rudolf and his younger colleagues.

Rudolf and his friends easily supported another incentive to improve the militia, competitive marksmanship. A field near Norway Point was turned into a three-hundred yard rifle range. It was behind the large stone house, Norway House, where Murdoch McPherson lived. Rudolf reported that he made very good scores for a beginner "7 points at 150 yards—6 points at 200 yds with 5 shots at each range—4 points at 250 yds, and missed every one at 300 yds. The last range I could not get at all, but I attribute it partly to the fact that I was wearied out standing in the sun so long, and my arms got shaky" (Journal, vol. 1, 16 May 1862). Competition with peers was very much part of the exercise: "Howard was out yesterday and only hit the target once out of 16 shots. This morning he hit 3 times out of 10. Clarence fired 15 rounds, and missed every one, which was a great mortification to him, as last evening he baited Howard unmercifully for missing so often" (Journal, vol. 1, 22 May 1862). In June they held their regulation target practice under Sergeant Denning. Rudolf reported that at the two short ranges he earned 15 points, an improvement from his previous month's score and well above the range average of 8.70. Under the stress of competition for the Moss medal, however, Rudolf averaged a score of only 4 points. This happened again to Clarence and to Rudolf in Truro when they competed against fifty other provincial marksmen. The winner, J.M. Murdoch of the Pictou Greys, scored 20 points and won the £10 prize. The silver cup, presented the next day, was won by Major Pollard of Prince Edward Island. At the cup presentation General Doyle urged the *old* officers of the militia to retire and enable younger officers to advance.

In October, Dr. George Johnston and Clarence, rapidly becoming the best marksmen, decided to construct a new range at Lowden's Beach. It was sheltered and had an eight-hundred yard range. Rudolf drove down to this range in March of 1863 with Johnston, Clarence, his two brothers-in-law, and several others, and reported that he "made capital shooting at 300 yd— 10 points out of 5 shots—and at 400 yds made 5 points with 3 shots" (Journal, vol. 1, 24 March 1863). His practice had definitely paid off; but it also provided him with an excuse "to escape from the office...and accept of a seat in Dr. Johnstons waggon, to go down with him to the target. We met quite a party there, and had a very pleasant afternoons amusement. I made very good shooting, and enjoyed the fresh air very much" (Journal, vol. 1, 17 April 1863). About this time, the elder Primrose began to demand that the three young men quit their commissions and petition for lesser duties or leave the militia and pay the required fine. Rudolf asked for the position of paymaster, which would require less work, but wrote, "I am fond of the work, and would not like to give it up. The Col. replied that he had promised Mr. Lane the Paymastership...[and] preferred keeping me where I am, as being of more use, and too good an officer to lose. Under these circumstances I must just be content where I am, and manage as well as I can to do the duty" (Journal, vol. 1, 21 April 1863); but his ambition overcame this intention.

Rudolf took pride in his rising status and the military's recognition of his efficiency, both as marksman and as drill leader. In May 1862 at the annual inspection, Colonel Laurie called out Rudolf's company first to be put through the new British "Field Exercise" manual and platoon's exercise. In June Rudolf recorded his rank of senior lieutenant of No. 7 Militia Company, West End of Pictou Town extending to the Town Gut. At the battalion drill in February 1863, the volunteer companies were divided into four, and Rudolf was acting first lieutenant of No. 4. A week later he was appointed to command No. 3 company, part of the Grey's Company. Rudolf reported, "We had a first rate drill and I enjoyed it very much. This kind of exercise is just what we Militia officers want to qualify us. I wish the whole of them would attend, but they do not. Only Wilson & I were there this evening" (Journal, vol. 1, 26 February 1863). He added that a number of ladies, including the socially conscious Davies sisters, were present as spectators. At this drill the sergeant saluted him as "Major" and remarked that Rudolf would soon be promoted, at which he retorted that it must be a joke since three others were senior to him. When the skating in the harbour proved excellent two days later, Clarence spent the afternoon there while Rudolf wrote rather sanctimoniously, "I would have liked very much to have been on it myself, but drill prevented this. Duty before pleasure is my motto. I could just as easily as Clarence have neglected Drill, but I did not think it right to do so. The Govt are keeping a Sergt here at considerable expense for the officers benefit, and we ought not to neglect or refuse to attend his instruction" (Journal, vol. 1, 28 February 1863).

This extra effort proved worthwhile. The next week Colonel McKinlay recommended Rudolf's name to be major of the First Battalion. Headquarters, however, once again advanced those senior to Rudolf, to his great disappointment. In April, he and Clarence were promoted to the rank of captain; Howard retained his position as quartermaster. Rudolf decided on two strategies to achieve his goal of majority rank. He told McKinlay about his earlier Lunenburg commission, which if honoured would advance his seniority. He decided to improve his company in drill efficiency so that it would surpass all others. He got his subaltern, Lieutenant McPherson, to warn the men of a proposed schedule for July; they expected Colonel Laurie and staff to be assisting them. At the first drill, despite the extreme heat and long four hours out in the field, "The men were very good natured, and shewed a desire to learn. Nothing unpleasant occurred, and we got home after six feeling pretty tired after the days work. Some of my men complained very much of the fatigue, and I know it is hard work from experience, but I have got used to it now, and can bear it better" (Journal, vol. 1, 3 July 1863). Rudolf demonstrated that he could listen, empathize with his men, and even anticipate their needs; he added oatmeal to their water to make it more refreshing.

Six days later, with the temperature at ninety-two degrees Fahrenheit, Rudolf's humane leadership style won him rewards. He reported that, in contrast to his two rivals, Simon Holmes (railway promoter and subsequently

Conservative premier of Nova Scotia, 1878–1882) and Narraway, whose men were very disorderly, "My company behaved in a most orderly and attentive manner, shewing an anxiety to learn, and making a degree of proficiency quite beyond my expectations. They called themselves the crack co. and 'No. 5' was considered *the* company on the ground. Of course I flattered them up in the idea, and got them readily to work, and to take pride in their drill. I had 25 men on today all being present except *one,* of those who are at home. It was very cool and pleasant today, and we had a very good afternoons drill" (Journal, vol. 1, 9 July 1863). The following day, his company participated in a battalion drill with other companies from the east end of town. Not only was this well executed, but the men of Rudolf's company

> requested me to drill them twice a week until the Battalion day. I readily consented to do so, and asked them to name a time. They appointed Tuesday & Thursday evenings at 7 oclock. I was much pleased at this. Because it shewed they were anxious to learn and also that they reposed confidence… in me, and appreciated my labors in instructing them. Before dismissing them I thanked them for the orderly manner in which they conducted themselves, and also for the great attention they paid to the drill, and for their very apparent efforts to learn it. I told them that they had rendered by their conduct my task a very pleasing one, and that I felt gratified at being their captain. After getting the word to dismiss, they gave me three rattling cheers, one fellow roaring out, "Yes, he deserves them." (Journal, vol. 1, 10 July 1863)

The men continued to support Rudolf and turned out regularly for drill. They even wanted to adopt a uniform on Battalion Day, although the expense would have been a hardship for many of them. When a luncheon was proposed by officers to thank Colonel Laurie for his help, Rudolf and Clarence refused to participate, in part because they realized it would be an expense for a number of poorer officers who could not afford it: "They feel mortified at not being able to keep pace with others in their expenditures, and I consider it a duty," wrote Rudolf, "not to sanction these things, so as not to cause some to feel badly about it" (Journal, vol. 1, 23 July 1863). The luncheon was held, nonetheless, while Clarence and Rudolf gave their men refreshments (beer, ham, biscuits, and cheese) after the drill. At issue, also, was the manly drinking culture, which Rudolf, Clarence, and other young evangelical activists eschewed. Rudolf explained why:

> Towards evening some of the officers, and guests were seen with unsteady steps wending their way home from the lunch. It is a pity, people cannot keep sober when they meet together at any kind of social engagement. It brings disgrace on the whole Batt., when a few of its officers get drunk.

There was a great deal of drinking going on all evening. One of the results of it was the tearing down of the Flag flying over the American Consulate [see description in chapter 1] at midnight. The Major [Norton, the American consul] is furious about it, and has lodged a complaint with the authorities concerning it. (Journal, vol. 1, 25 July 1863)

Even though Rudolf kept his distance from this aspect of militia life, he was now being criticized not only by the "old gent" but also by Cassie and Mrs. Dawson, who, Rudolf reported, gave him "no peace about it. They do not like our soldierly propensities, and scold whenever they get a chance about the folly etc" (Journal, vol. 1, 15 June 1863). They objected to the time spent away from home on drill duty, target practice, or, in Rudolf's case, filling out returns. They also strongly objected to the expense of the uniforms. There were the dress and undress uniforms, which included militia cap, special buttons (which had to be ordered by the gross), sword belt, shoulder belt, pouch (cost $10), and sword (cost $16). Rudolf acknowledged, "This Militia affair is very expensive." Officers were required to accept these expenditures; their uniform was an important symbol of their reputation, their status within the group, just as much as their success on the parade ground or their proficiency at marksmanship. Town socialites were often spectators at many of the exercises in the new Drill Hall (three-fifths of its cost was paid for by proceeds from the local bazaar, which netted $404 on 7 August 1862; the government contributed $440); but it was the peer culture and each individual's loyalty to it that also troubled Cassie, Mrs. Dawson, and James Primrose. The militia began to vie with family and business for the allegiance of these young men, as Rudolf observed when his company made mistakes. That was why the emotional thrill of doing well as a company, or even as a county's representative in marksmanship, carried so much weight. The young men were forging their own form of collectivity, symbolized by their new uniforms and by their communal activities. Soon individual prizes added increased significance to their new cultural thrust—a striving for individual excellence and for masculine and athletic prowess (as against self-absorption and effeminacy).

Pictou County by 1864 began to carry off over a quarter of the prizes for marksmanship. Its reputation was advertised in the newspapers. Rudolf "received a note from Jim McIntosh of the Bank N.S. congratulating me on the success of our riflemen. He takes a great interest in all sorts of outdoor sports. He is celebrated as a cricketer" (Journal, vol. 1, 24 October 1863). A year later, Dr. Johnston returned from the provincial rifle championships at Truro to report that "Col. Kitchin of River John obtained the Bridle offered by Col. Laurie, and Captain Jackson of New Glasgow won the sword given by Col. Sinclair. Pictou County has done well. The Dr. says Col. Laurie is delighted with the firing of our chaps, and has staked £50 on a match between Pictou & Colchester, against the whole Province" (Journal, vol. 1, 15 October 1864). Colonel Laurie presented two medals to the Pictou Battalion for marksmanship in July 1864, a silver one for officers and a bronze one for sergeants. These rewards resulted in greatly improved performance and in group pride.

Rudolf's efforts to lead in these new directions would prove worthwhile. A new militia bill was introduced to the House in April 1864, which enabled officers to retire after twenty years of service. As an incentive, they would be promoted to the next rank above their grade. John McKinlay (a Pictou lawyer) decided to take advantage of this offer and was given the opportunity to name his successor. Major Robert Doull, a Pictou merchant involved in shipbuilding and marine trading, was so named but could not decide immediately, so he and several officers asked Rudolf to take command. He declined, but said that he would not object to the major's commission. He noted his lack of seniority: "I am not the Senior Captain & J[ames] Ives [Pictou merchant] is first on the List, but he is not well qualified for it, and I could only be appointed over him, for proficiency—whether I could pass such an examination remains to be seen, but if I got the promotion I would strive very hard for the necessary qualifications" (Journal, vol. 1, 20 April 1864). He added that McKinlay's resignation would lead to increased competition among the officers and more attention to their duties.

This new potential to draw away his "boys" made James Primrose renew his efforts to force their resignation from the Militia:

> When Clarence came up from dinner he said his father had been scolding as usual about our being connected as officers with the Militia, and [he had decided that] "rather than be badgered continually about the thing he would resign." Of course this made me resolve to come to a decision about the matter, and on speaking to Mr. P. about it, when he came in, he expressed himself so strongly and arbitrarily upon it that I decided to stop all further proceedings on the part of McKinlay & Doull for obtaining the Majority for me over Ives. The old gent said if we were determined to go soldiering and tom fooling about we might, but that he would not have us as partners. As usual he would listen to no arguments or reasons, and insisted upon his view of the matter, irrespective of anything we could allege to the contrary. Under such terms, and with such a man to deal with, there is nothing left us but to tender our resignations. I feel very sore about it. I like the drill, and it was mild exercise for me, and I never neglected anything for it. And as to the training in summer, this is an imperative duty imposed upon all, and we cannot escape it. We must pay our fines, and this I feel another hardship. (Journal, vol. 1, 25 April 1864)

Clarence and Rudolf wrote out their resignations, but did not anticipate that they would be accepted; they hoped this would stop the elder Primrose from annoying them with fault-finding. Meanwhile, Rudolf decided to have a long conversation with James Ives about the officers' recommendation that he should be bypassed for the major's appointment. Rudolf reported him to be reconciled now and "that McKinlays manner was so unpleasant, and he insisted upon hurrying the business through so peremptorily, that it annoyed him. He said [James] Fogo [Pictou lawyer] he thought would resign soon, and then he would get a majority...and that he did not expect my resignation would be received; he would propose himself that I should get the vacant majority" (Journal, vol. 1, 26 April 1864). Rudolf's negotiating skills were becoming much more sophisticated; he had anticipated the problem with Ives and had won him around to his side. When the resignations of Rudolf and Clarence Primrose were denied by Colonel Doull, appointed to replace McKinlay, Doull commented that he needed all the officers he could get. James Ives was promoted to major in May 1864, James McDonald resigned because of his move to Halifax (he was re-elected in 1863 and appointed to the Executive Council in Premier J.W. Johnston's Conservative government), and Rudolf became senior captain. Major Fogo resigned in July, and Rudolf was promoted as acting major. He and Ives were examined by Colonel Laurie after his July inspection and passed easily. On 21 August 1864, Rudolf read in the Gazette that he had been promoted to the rank of major. As J.K. Johnson observes, this type of honour was "an almost indispensable mark of local status" in colonial society. Johnson adds, "there is still a sense...in which military service can be said to have taken precedence over civil appointments.... The evidence suggests that a militia commission was the basic status appointment, almost an indispensable requirement for anyone hoping to assume a regional leadership role."[3] Military rank, therefore, provided a benchmark of character and of self-discipline. This would have been part of its appeal for Rudolf.

Having achieved this goal Rudolf was in a quandary: "Col. Laurie said I had better not resign, as in all probability I should be made a Sergeant and have to act as such or pay an additional fine. This would be worse than my present inconvenience about it" (Journal, vol. 1, 21 August 1864). However, he ordered a pair of major's stars for his uniform from Halifax in September. He had practised for the county rifle match, but because Howard was away, Rudolf had to remain in the office. In January 1865, he and Clarence resigned their commissions and this time they were accepted, even though Doull had scarcely any officers left. As Rudolf commented, "The service is growing distasteful to many and a better system will have to be adopted sooner or later.

Business men can't give their time to it" (Journal, vol. 2, 21 January 1865). Rudolf asked a member of his parish, the county custos Daniel Hockin, to get him appointed fire warden. He regretted leaving the militia, especially when the Pictou Battalion was reorganized. John McKinlay was made lieutenant colonel of the Militia Artillery, which organized a new brigade in Pictou, as was the case in seven other communities in Nova Scotia. Five Halifax regiments of foot were also converted into artillery regiments. There was an increased interest in rifle shooting throughout the province, and thirty-eight adjutants received a sixty-day drill course. By December 1865, there were 106 efficient regiments in Nova Scotia with a large number of rifles and over 2,000 uniforms issued. The House of Assembly voted $81,578 for support of the militia.[4] Two external factors spurred this renewed militia activity: fear of Fenian raids and/or invasion by American veterans as they returned home after the northern states' victory in the Civil War.

The old volunteer artillery company was broken up in Pictou and Rudolf predicted that the new "Brigade will be very efficiently officered by them as the Company contained the elite of the town—they are well drilled intelligent and commanding in manner....John [McKinlay] has offered me a Commission in the staff as Major,...but I cannot as yet see my way clear to accept it, although if I had plenty [of] time, nothing would give me more pleasure" (Journal, vol. 2, 23 March 1865). He commented when the militia training program began in July, "It seems strange to me to have nothing to do with it this year. I always used to have so much work with it, and interest in the business. But I am saved a great deal of toil by being free from my commission, and by the fortunate exemption from drill as a Fire Ward" (Journal, vol. 2, 6 July 1865). Rudolf went down to see his old regiment inspected by Colonel Laurie a week later, "almost sighing to be back in the work again" (Journal, vol. 2, 13 July 1865), and was pleased at how well the men were doing. Colonel Laurie dropped by their office later and offered Rudolf his old position back if he applied immediately: "He further urged me strongly to take a commission in the Artillery Brigade....He said the drilling would be done at night, and the 5 days drilling would be devoted to firing shot and shell. I would willingly accept of a commission, but Mr. Primrose is so determinately opposed to our having anything to do with the militia movement, that I suppose I must forego it. Col. Laurie says the Fire Ward exemption from drill clause in the Law, will be expunged from it next year. Then I shall have to drill or be fined" (Journal, vol. 2, 17 July 1865).

As Laurie predicted, Rudolf was obliged in 1866 to pay the fine of $17, which he contributed to the brigade. The next year to avoid the fine he rejoined the militia as a lieutenant in the drill company. He found it rather pleasant exercise and was surprised that he was not nearly as rusty as he expected; in fact he "did better than the officers who have kept on the list" (Journal, vol. 2, 8 March 1867) since his retirement. In April he completed his fifteen drills and only had to pay a fine of two dollars for skipping the summer's training. After Confederation the federal government continued the principle of obligatory militia service, now directed by professionally trained instructors; Rudolf became increasingly involved in his business duties and in his family responsibilities and wrote only briefly of the militia thereafter.

What effect had these three years (1862–1864) of intense involvement with the militia on Rudolf's concept of ideal character and its formation? Because of his family background and training at the bank, Rudolf had quite easily adapted to traditional military culture; he deferred to authority, believed in the importance of (gentry) social decorum, and aspired to rank and status within this military society. As John Keegan effectively summarizes them, the values of this culture were different from those of the larger culture; these included "pride in a distinctive (and distinctively masculine) way of life, concern to enjoy the good opinion of comrades, satisfaction in the largely symbolic tokens of professional success, hope of promotion."[5] The experience of social and emotional bonding with his fellow officers and with men under his command had helped Rudolf gain self-confidence. He learned to distinguish between his own personal character identity and the anxieties and doubts associated with its formation, and allegiance to a military culture based on efficient performance for which all could share blame or praise. The variety of militia duties Rudolf performed and his increasing responsibilities taught him flexibility and skill in management techniques.

At the same time, Rudolf illustrated a new quality of manly character, that was emerging in colonial militias and in northwestern American culture by the mid-nineteenth century.[6] Matching the Liberal culture fostered by the elder Primrose, he valued merit and judgments based on principles rather than on the traditional military custom of basing promotions on seniority or on social favours demanded. In Rudolf's judgment, individual competition in marksmanship and in leadership of parade drill led to increased efficiency; performance and individual effort should be rewarded with increased responsibility and rank. The old values of duty before pleasure were now tempered with a new pleasure in healthy, athletic bodies, in moderate drinking habits, and in humane and teasing social interaction. Rudolf and his colleagues sought to develop a more co-operative leadership style and manly character more appropriate for the amateur militia force than the abusive, harsh discipline demanded of the professional soldier. This leadership style also suited the existing pre-class social relationships of small-town communities and emphasized the evangelical moral economy of Pictou Town.[7] Jock Phillips writes, "Essentially the man of 'character' was one who could repress his desires for a larger moral good. Self-discipline was at its heart...those who campaigned against drinking and gambling looked to 'character' as the ultimate guarantor of the respectable society. It was a civilized gentlemanly ideal, but also a virile one since it depended upon inner steel, the strength to resist cheap pleasures."[8] Rudolf would model this newly acquired character ideal in his successful evangelical campaigns in Pictou and later in England.

What the elder Primrose, and probably Cassie and Mrs. Dawson, also detected in this new manly culture was Rudolf's withdrawal from their restrictive, nurturing control. He and his young male militia colleagues were constructing their own masculine identities and a new style of leadership. Rudolf began to assume credit for his own achievements, ascribing them to his own efforts rather than to God's Providence. He learned to channel his newly emerging aggressiveness and anger at Primrose's attempts to control his "boys" into disciplined forms of response—going through the motions of resignation but not leaving the militia until he had achieved *his* goal of peer-group recognition for his proficiency and the status of a major's rank. Rudolf also constructed a new co-operative style of management, in opposition to Primrose's dictatorial form of authority, which blended sensitivity towards the feelings of colleagues, such as Ives, with masculine hardiness in the field. He learned to balance his newly acquired masculine self-identity with his responsibilities towards the larger social group, learning in the process to listen to others and to adapt to changing circumstances. His pragmatic manly character would prove to be very useful for Rudolf's entry into the world of commerce.

At a deeper level, however, Rudolf's aspiration to achieve rank revealed a tension in his evolving concept of ideal character. Charles Taylor terms this an older style of "honour ethic," which deemed the life of a citizen-soldier as higher than the merely private existence or the ordinary life of commerce.[9] This honour ethic sought fame and glory, or, in public life, recognition. Taylor traces the honour ethic back to Homer and then outlines its transformation by René Descartes into an ideal of rational control powered by a sense of self-esteem, which fuels the individual's continued commitment to virtue. Numerous philosophers drew attention to the effect of this ethic; it engendered feelings of disengagement from the world and the body, as well as a desire for power and glory. In contrast, the bourgeois ideal, promoted by Primrose, Cassie, and her mother, valued the ordinary life, ideals of equality, a sense of universal right, and exaltation of the family and work. They condemned the values implied in the honour ethic as unduly self-indulgent and tending towards aristocratic pretentiousness and fractious conduct. The positive sense of self-worth and accomplishment that Rudolf derived from his militia experience revealed a tension between the construction of his own character and the ideal concepts of character that he and his mentors were promoting. A more firm commitment to his evangelical Christian beliefs, a deeper search for God's purpose for his life, and increased involvement with his family and with benevolent activities in the community would restore the necessary balance and bring Rudolf's ideal of character closer to the altruism implicit in the evangelical, bourgeois ideal.

CHAPTER 5

Stylistic Essays

A s noted in previous chapters, the Pictou region experienced significant cultural change in the first half of the nineteenth century; this necessitated changes in leadership styles. Norman Rudolf experimented in his different positions of responsibility with the old and new styles, at first by analyzing the role models of his mentors. Of course, many of their ways of community management were affected by the cultural history of the district. When Rudolf arrived in Pictou in 1853, the town had already experienced fifty years of evangelical propaganda, primarily issuing from Scotland. This cultural campaign was organized at first by three denominational missionary societies. The General Associate Synod (Secessionist) of Scotland sent the Reverend James MacGregor to the Pictou district in 1786 and the Reverend Thomas McCulloch in 1803. The Glasgow Colonial Society, formed by an evangelical wing of the Church of Scotland in 1824, assisted the Reverend Kenneth John MacKenzie to establish Saint Andrew's (Kirk) Church at Pictou in 1825. The Society for the Propagation of the Gospel in Foreign Parts (SPG) purchased the building lot for the later St. James (Anglican) Church and in 1830 established Charles Elliott, one of its travelling missionaries, as rector for the parish. These evangelical leaders were not only biblical but activist. Their missionary societies assisted local leaders in establishing the first Bible Society in 1813, Pictou Academy in 1816, the first Sabbath School Society[1] and a subscription library in 1822, and the Pictou Literature and Scientific Society in 1834.[2] In 1827, the first temperance society in Nova

Scotia was formed at West River; in 1830 James Dawson and other Presbyterian leaders founded one in Pictou Town; in 1832 the Pictou Temperance
Union was formed. These evangelicals were using educational and institutional
means to accomplish their modernizing and moral ends—to alter the rude
frontier culture of a port town into an orderly, professional, and commercial
centre for the county.[3]

In their struggle to solidify their authority, the two evangelical Presbyterian groups, the Secessionists and the Church of Scotland adherents, waged bitter political battles, dubbed the "petty feuds of Pictou" by McCulloch.[4] His
liberal campaign on behalf of provincial Dissenters (Protestants who belonged
to some church other than the state or established church) and of his elitist
college was heavily embroiled in the feuds; Pictou Academy suffered changes
in policy and in leadership. With the advent of responsible government in
Nova Scotia in 1848, and the arrival of British free trade and the disestablishment of the Church of England, educated professionals began to assert their
newly won political power and to establish their evangelical institutions on a
much broader scale across the province. In 1850 J. William Dawson, son of
James Dawson of Pictou, became the first superintendent of Education for
Nova Scotia and initiated the fifteen-year provincial campaign to establish
free common schools.[5] A Normal School to train teachers was opened at
Truro in 1855, and in 1864–1866 the legislature passed the Free School Acts.

A new spirit of co-operation prevailed; it was epitomized in 1860 by the
Union of the Presbyterian Church of Nova Scotia and the Free Church
(formed when evangelical Church of Scotland ministers broke away from
the established church in Scotland and in British North America in 1843 and
1844). In Pictou the Church of Scotland remained aloof, as it did in 1875
when the Presbyterian Church in Canada was formed; a number of older
Pictou Presbyterians clung to their principles and to their leadership status.
As Rudolf noticed, however, a moderate, more optimistic younger group of
leaders (many having been exposed to Pictou's feuds and to the near demise
of Pictou Academy) began to swell the ranks of the town's philanthropic associations, participate in church management, and campaign in politics for progressive reform. Evangelical culture in the town was becoming more domi-
nant. One of the strongest advocates of this evangelical culture was J.D.B.
Fraser, brother of Rudolf's friend, Tom Fraser. Rudolf was strongly attracted
to J.D.B. Fraser's evangelical causes and his powerful personality. His journal entries revealed that Rudolf was closely analyzing Fraser's leadership style
and character as possible models for himself. During these early years when
Rudolf undertook lower-level leadership roles in the community, he began to
try different leadership styles in an effort to find the most effective strategies

for his type of personality. At first he looked at Fraser, whom he greatly admired.

Fraser established the first pharmacy in Pictou (and the only one in northern Nova Scotia) in 1828.[6] It was an immediate success. The next year he became involved in the Eastern Stage Coach Company, which for thirteen years ran coaches between Pictou and Halifax, one hundred miles away, supported in large part by government subsidies and by a monopoly on the mail contracts. Other business ventures he explored were a diving-salvage operation, a stone quarry at West River, and a coal mine near the Stellar seam (later Albion Mining Company). From an early age, Fraser displayed his benevolent and principled character. He was one of the founders of the Pictou Literature and Scientific Society and frequently contributed scientific lectures on such topics as a model electric light powered by burning charcoal and "exhilarating gas."[7] He constantly ministered to the poor, the sick, and the dying. He also looked after interments.

In 1831 Fraser married Christianna MacKay; they had five sons and four daughters (one of whom was Kate Fraser, friend of Cassie, who was engaged briefly to Reverend McPhee). In 1848 Fraser made history by administering chloroform as an anaesthetic to his thirty-nine-year-old wife at the birth of their seventh child; Dr. James Simpson of Edinburgh had pioneered its use the year before. Shortly after this, Fraser left Prince Street Church and became a leader of the Evangelical Union Church in Pictou; he was primarily responsible for the hiring of McPhee.

Rudolf and Fraser participated in two campaigns: the 1863 Nova Scotia election and the liquor licensing campaigns on behalf of the Sons of Temperance. The young Rudolf was obviously attracted to Fraser's upright character, the same moral Scottish characteristic he admired in James Primrose; but, as he had with the "old gent," he began to question the appropriateness of Fraser's patriarchal leadership style with younger constituents. In some of his own first attempts at evangelical moral leadership, Rudolf imitated their direct style but was disappointed with the results.

In December 1862, Rudolf was nominated for the position of warden master at the Pictou Masonic Lodge meeting. He declined the office, but perhaps in imitation of Fraser and because of this honour and his experience with Pictou's temperance campaign, Rudolf was bold enough to express strong opposition to a motion to have lodge members walk in procession[8] at the St. John's Day Divine Service, arguing

> that the conduct of some of our members was so directly the opposite of what
> it ought to be, that for them to go to Church would be but a solemn mock-
> ery, and that therefore we ought not while such was the case, to go in a Body

to Church. Some of the members were rather surprized at this plain speaking, but I trust it may turn attention to those to whom my remarks may apply, and that an improvement in their habits may be made. I had resolved some time ago to leave the Lodge on account of the irregular living of some of the members, but on reflection I determined to remain and use my influence to improve the state of matters. May God grant me wisdom, and strength for this, as well as for every other duty. I need direction and guidance at all times, for I can do no good thing of my own strength. (Journal, vol. 1, 9 December 1862)

For a time, then, Rudolf ceased active participation in the lodge and focussed his benevolent activities on another fraternal organization, the Order of the Sons of Temperance. As mentioned earlier, Rudolf had been exposed to the temperance cause in Lunenburg; his teacher, William B. Lawson, had been a co-founder of the Lunenburg Town and County Temperance Society in 1834. While boarding at Mrs. George Smith's house in Pictou, Rudolf had signed the pledge of total abstinence under the urging of Mary Fox, who was on the executive board of the Pictou Ladies' Temperance Society. It must have been shortly after this that Rudolf joined the Sons of Temperance. Fraser had been a co-founder when the Oriental Division was established at Pictou in 1848. This was only six years after the order was founded in New York. By 1855, there were more than 134,000 members organized into 3,500 subordinate divisions throughout the world. The order differed from previous temperance organizations, because it offered not only the fellowship and mystery of a fraternal organization, but also economic security, such as sick and death benefits, as well as aid for those in straitened circumstances.

The major task of the Sons of Temperance was to evangelize the province. This is what Rudolf meant when in his discussion of bad characters (chapter 1) he wrote that "We need missionaries at home" (Journal, vol. 1, 21 May 1864). Because of its aggressiveness, zeal, and self-righteousness, qualities Rudolf observed in Fraser, the organization in Pictou, like that in Saint John, New Brunswick,[9] quickly eclipsed the previous leadership of British evangelicals and adopted a more American prohibitionist stance on the liquor question. The order appealed, also, to the respectable aspirations of the middle class; its secret symbols, regalia, and weekly meetings offered a full social life for young men in the community. The major thrust of the order's reforming zeal in Pictou, as in other Maritime communities, was to restrict the sale of alcohol. As will be related, there was considerable lobbying among the county magistrates to try to curtail the granting of liquor licenses by retailers.

At Fraser's death in May 1869, Rudolf remarked that he was distinguished by being a "stern uncompromising opponent of the Liquor Traffic and a great

part of his life was devoted to the promotion of the temperance cause. He
was so much in earnest in this reform that oft times he offended his friends
by strictures on those who could not regard the matter in his light. His nature
was so fierce and vehement that everything he undertook was pressed on
with an energy that set cooler men by the ears. His determination and moral
strength sustained the [temperance] cause in this town many times, where but
for him it would have died out" (Journal, vol. 2, 4 May 1869). Local option
to grant liquor licenses was given to municipalities during the militant temperance campaigns of the 1850s and 1860s. In an effort to convince the Courts
of Sessions (local government entrusted to appointed magistrates) *not* to grant
liquor licenses to local taverns, the Oriental Division celebrated its fourteenth
anniversary by holding a public meeting in Pictou's Assembly Hall. Grand
Worthy Patriarch Fraser was the main speaker, and three Presbyterian ministers also gave addresses. Rudolf assessed the gathering in a realistic vein:

> It was the most crowded temperance meeting I ever saw in Pictou. Indeed
> I have seen few larger on any occasion. The speakers all bore testimony to
> the increase of drunkenness in our town during the last 3 months, or since
> the granting of Licenses by the sessions to a number of Taverns, and called
> upon those present, particularly the young men to unite with the Division,
> as a shield from temptation to themselves, and to benefit others. I sincerely
> hope this meeting may tend to swell the members of our Division, for we
> are at a very low ebb at present. Twenty members can barely be brought
> together on any occasion, and these mostly composed of young lads under
> age—some under 18. What can be expected of these? And yet, the Division
> is the only working temperance Society in this town. It is the forlorn hope
> of the cause here. And should it give up its charter—feeble though its efforts
> are—yet its moral influence is great,....Its bare existence is a standing rebuke
> to our opponents. (Journal, vol. 1, 5 May 1862)

At a meeting in November 1862, Fraser gave statistics on the success of
the provincial temperance campaign: in 1831, six gallons of liquor had been
consumed in the province per inhabitant; by 1861, the average amount had
diminished to three pints. In the Pictou Division Rudolf frequently noted,
however, the low attendance and the lack of persons of standing at the meetings. He was concerned about the division's social status and its power of
suasion.[10] In an effort to raise its respectable image, Rudolf spoke out strongly
against a motion of the majority of young members to introduce dancing at
the Christmas social gathering. As worthy patriarch, or chairman of the meeting, Rudolf felt it his duty to refuse to "put the motion, ruling it out of order,
giving my reasons therefore—that it was inconsistent with the purposes for
which we assembled—that it brought discredit...upon the Division—the

public not being likely to discriminate between the meetings of the Division, and the dances immediately after them, and would very likely class them together, and that we would be regarded as boisterous, and pleasure seeking, rather than temperate and earnest reformers" (Journal, vol. 1, 1 December 1862). Rudolf's evangelical righteousness not only enabled him to overcome his reticence but also justified his early forays into public leadership roles.

The issue developed into a clash of interests. At a meeting the following March, there was a stormy discussion again over dancing, this time in connection with a return invitation to the Sons of Temperance at Albion Mines (later Stellarton). The younger members argued that lots of dancing occurred at their party; they wanted a dance included after the Pictou and Albion Mines proposed joint meeting. The older members strongly opposed this, but the younger members outvoted the motion. In Rudolf's judgment

> This dancing tendency of the majority of the Division will seriously injure our usefulness, and drive some members from it. We have had a great influx lately of members, and they are just a rabble, who care nothing for temperance, but only seek amusement. They never speak in the Division, or suggest anything to benefit the order, but are ready to stamp and make a noise if anything is said which suits their views. The more orderly, and useful part of the Division could keep them in check until lately, but they have grown so numerous by recent accessions that they cannot be restrained. Our only hope is that they will not remain long in connection with the Division. This class seldom do. And when once we get rid of them, we must guard against an indiscriminate admission of members in future. There are a few of us, who carry on the Division, and who are really the mainstay of it, and it is provoking that we should be at the mercy of a parcel of thoughtless youngsters, to thwart us, and injure the cause by their foolishness. (Journal, vol. 1, 9 March 1863)

As with his early leadership in the Masons, on the surface Rudolf appeared to be using older members to advance his own chances of gaining leadership status. His espousal of established authority would also have put him on the side of the elite class. Was he exploring different means to put his evangelizing principles into effect, using the experience of these older leaders as guidelines? As he had done in the past, Rudolf was intent on establishing boundaries—between respectable older men of high status and their orderly control of temperance meetings, and the amusement-seeking younger men of lower station; between an exclusively male temperance association and one open to women for evenings of entertainment. As Cecilia Morgan remarks, "manliness and womanliness were signifiers in these discourses....Their use had meanings that were linked to notions of boundaries and margins, exclusiveness and inclusiveness."[11] Rudolf was learning that in the process of cultural boundary formation he had to adopt different strategies from those of his paternalistic, aging mentors. While he did not reflect overtly on the issues of boundaries or discourse, Rudolf implied that he understood the implications of social status and respectable modes of behaviour in the political and cultural campaign now being waged by the order. He also realized that his major weakness in this campaign was his hesitant public speaking ability, which he attributed to "confusion of mind" and lack of preparation. He decided to study the matter in an effort to improve his delivery.

On less formal occasions, Rudolf was able to speak strongly; for instance, he argued in support of amended bylaws for the division. He noted, however, that none "of the prominent, and really good members were present, except McKimmie, to support me"(Journal, vol. 1, 20 April 1863). Was he relying, as did his forebears in the past, on these older members for support to advance his status? It would appear that they were also to be studied as models. During public meetings, Rudolf began to analyze the speaking style of the major speakers. He remarked that, in a review of the formation and history of the National Division, Fraser attempted to read his speech but could not do so successfully: "His ideas flow rapidly, and he can't control his feelings enough to read anything well. He seemed tied down, and without energy. If he had spoken ex tempore, it would have been far better" (Journal, vol. 1, 29 September 1863). When Rudolf included this criticism in his review of the meeting for the temperance weekly, the *Abstainer,* he was persuaded to delete it: "Mr. F. might not have liked it, & I would not for anything write a word to hurt his feelings" (Journal, vol. 1, 3 October 1863). On another occasion, he complimented the elegant language and variety of words used by the Reverend McDonald, past patriarch, "but his manner nearly spoiled all. It was so deficient of action, and also his delivery was rather monotonous—wanting in pith and force. His elocution was very bad—raising his voice when he should have lowered it, but despite this, he rivetted the attention of his hearers throughout the whole lecture, and was warmly applauded when he sat down" (Journal, vol. 1, 21 January 1864). Rudolf was learning that style mattered but moral charisma won overall.

Rudolf's forte was more in the line of writing. He claimed that a proposed newspaper, the *Oriental Budget,* intended for colonial circulation, was one that he and Jim Patterson had edited as a monthly for the division for over a year. It circulated in Halifax and Wolfville, was reviewed favourably in the *Abstainer* (Wolfville) and the *Eastern Chronicle* (Pictou), but was given up by the two editors as it required too much labour. Rudolf's poetry and several other pieces were republished in the *Abstainer,* and its editor, Patrick Monaghan, grand worthy scribe of the order, asked him to write occasional articles for his weekly. Rudolf was asked to canvass for the *Abstainer* and managed to get thirty subscribers in November 1864. The next February, he was awarded the first prize by the weekly for the highest list of subscribers; he received a copy of a steel engraving of "Shakespere [*sic*] and his friends" (Journal, vol. 2, 2 February 1865).

Deeper evangelical principles, Rudolf realized by this time, would provide him with a more secure foundation for his leadership role. Through his temperance activities, he was developing another strategy. He began to use his moral earnestness to hold people to account for their temperance pledge. His fellow warden at St. James Church, Richard Tanner, a Pictou shoemaker, held a party for a number of Tories, including several magistrates, at which liquor was served. The occasion was a celebration of Tanner's appointment as justice of the peace for the Pictou district. The inclusion of liquor at the party was a violation of his temperance pledge. Rudolf learned about it at the meeting of the division in December, but, he wrote, "declared my unbelief of the story, thinking he would be about the last one to do so [break his pledge]. I determined to call upon him, tell him what I had heard, and ask him if it was true or not…to my sorrow, he acknowledged it was true—that he had liquors on his table, but that he had not tasted any of it himself. He admitted that he had done wrong, and that he was to blame for it. I asked him what he intended doing with regard to the Division. He said, 'he could not bear to go back to it, as he had been so long a member, and was unable to make a public avowal of his offence'" (Journal, vol. 1, 15 December 1863). A few days later Tanner informed Rudolf that he intended going to the division and making a confession of his violation. Rudolf told him he was very glad to hear this; at the meeting he pleaded on behalf of Tanner and helped win his pardon.

Six months later, Rudolf intervened again, in this case for the cabinet-maker, Charlie Wilson, whom he encountered in a very tipsy state at his shop. Wilson later apologized to Rudolf and asked him to draw up a pledge for him to sign, with Rudolf as co-signer. After doing so, Rudolf recorded, he

> talked a long time with him, and told him how wretched he was making his home and himself, and plead with him not to yield again to temptation, and taste liquor. He said he despised himself, and felt ashamed to be seen after a spree, and knew how bad it was for him to get drunk. I urged him to try to live a religious life. He opened the way for this, by speaking of Mr. Pryors Sermon last evening [at St. James Church], with which he expressed himself much pleased, and added he wished that he could be religious. I told him there was no reason why he should not be so—that God was willing and ready to give His grace to help him, and pardon him—and that with-

out His aid, he could not hope to resist temptation. He seemed impressed with what I said, and I left him, telling him I should talk to him at any time I saw him the worse of liquor again very seriously. He begged me not to omit to do so. He said he had so little *"fortitude."* He lost his property—being sold under mortgage—and felt so desponding, that he must take liquor to cheer him up, but he would do so no more. (Journal, vol. 1, 12 September 1864)

Rudolf found that his Christian witness, based on an optimistic belief of evangelicals that control of environmental factors (liquor consumption and distribution) would lead to behavioral change and inclination, was gaining success.[12] His own earnest demeanor, rather than any smooth-talking style, increasingly persuaded young men of all classes to reform their behaviour and become active in evangelical causes.

What Rudolf may not have fully appreciated was the degree to which all the strategies of the order were contributing to a new social and character ideal. By means of rituals, regalias, social protocols, a vibrant journal, individual witness, and vigorous political campaigning, the order was effectively constructing "a general mythology of political reform," in the words of T.W. Acheson,[13] as well as a new set of moral values, which would become more important for evangelical Christians than wealth or occupation. This was a radical cultural movement.

Another symbol of the militant nature of the order can be seen in the *Abstainer's* change in format. Monaghan, the paper's editor, altered the paper from a magazine letter-sized edition to a broadside. Now advertising and additional editorial features, including lengthy lists of people appearing very drunk on the streets of Halifax, were included. These changes, as John MacLeod recounts, brought the paper into court eleven times between 1860 and 1863; only one case of libel, however, appears to have succeeded.[14] Unfortunately, in 1863 the postal regulations were changed and Monoghan had to make the *Abstainer* a weekly to retain its free use of the mails. Competition from other temperance papers led to its demise in 1874. Monaghan believed that, particularly in its first seven years (1856–1863), it kept alive interest in the order and was instrumental in spreading its propaganda throughout the province.

A strategy used to good effect by the order was the use of petitions on behalf of their cause. In February 1864, the Grand Jury of the Court of Sessions rendered its decision on the liquor question. A committee was appointed to go over the names drawn up by temperance petitioners in their bid to defeat the liquor interests. Out of 319 people eligible to vote, 167 voted to have no licenses granted in Pictou Town; but the committee threw off 10 names because they were not ratepayers. This lowered the vote to 157, too few by 3 to carry the motion. In Rudolf's pragmatic opinion, "It is perhaps better that we should not succeed by a bare majority even if we had it, because a vote of this kind should have the weight of a large majority. I advised Mr. Fraser, now that our petition has failed, to abandon all further opposition and allow the Court to grant as many Licenses as it pleased" (Journal, vol. 1, 6 February 1864). The Sessions granted four shop and eleven tavern licenses two days later. Rudolf privately admonished, "let those who refused to sign [the petition], and those of the Bench of Justices, who voted to give them, answer for the consequences" (Journal, vol. 1, 8 February 1864). A year later at the Sessions, when the genuineness of some of New Glasgow temperance signatures was questioned, a committee was struck and found that they were all legitimate. As Rudolf remarked, "The temperance cause is an uphill one. Its supporters have a hard fight. In the sessions a disposition seemed to exist to shew all the favor to the *rum* side of the question" (Journal, vol. 2, 11 February 1865). Pictou Town licence seekers continued to be rewarded. Rudolf's notion of ideal character was being balanced by his experiences with the temperance cause.

Rudolf and Fraser also lost on another front—the provincial Liberal campaign of 1863. Fraser had been the Liberal candidate in 1845 when the possibility of violence at these open polls was so real that the sheriff erected a ten-foot high fence down the middle of Pictou's main street to separate the opposing camps. Fraser won by two votes, but because a riot did break out and the polls had to be closed, the House of Assembly ordered a by-election to be held in which neither Fraser nor his Tory opponent, Martin Wilkins, ran again. Eighteen years later, after a failed attempt at compromise with the local Tory party in nominating candidates, the Liberals chose Fraser as their candidate. Rudolf praised the atmosphere of the "utmost cordiality of feeling" that both parties exhibited towards each other. Remarks were designed "to allay party strife in our midst." Fraser emphasized the promise of progressive improvements: "He dwelt on the value of our Mines and Minerals, and the benefits which would flow from having them worked, by giving employment to our population, and prosperity to the country" (Journal, vol. 1, 21 May 1863). With the Liberal promise of the extension of the railway to Pictou, Rudolf and his Liberal committee colleagues predicted that they would win a majority of one hundred votes in the Pictou district.

While working on the campaign, however, Rudolf began to experience a number of disagreeable setbacks to his liberal idealism. William Davies, owner of the Pictou Foundry and Machine Co. and societal patriarch, refused to give any contributions to the young Rudolf when he came to solicit his subscription. Rudolf commented, "He is very cool about the election, and refuses to use his influence with his men, who are about divided in politics. He gets his living principally from our party, and is interested above all others here, in securing the extension of the Railway to Pictou, and yet he refuses to give aid in returning men who will bring the Railroad to his very door. His Foundry would get infinitely more work to do—his property would be greatly increased in value, and his whole prospects considerably improved by it" (Journal, vol. 1, 8 May 1863). Yet Davies proposed the nomination of Fraser two weeks later, much to Rudolf's surprise. Perhaps Rudolf's junior social status was the reason for Davies's rebuff. The incident made Rudolf reconsider his early reliance on older mentors and their established practices as leadership role models.

On 25 May, Rudolf was again collecting funds and now began to notice corrupt practices, which he attributed primarily to venal habits of country people: "It is dreadful to see the corruption that is going on. Men from the county come regularly in to sell their votes to the highest bidder. Then there are debts to be paid—mortgages redeemed, and money lent on notes, which hold out but little prospect of ever being paid. Universal suffrage is a great evil, undoubtedly. There are many good men, of no property, it is true, who do not use their…privileges in any other way than with the purest motives, but these do not compensate for the great number who abuse it, and degrade it" (Journal, vol. 1, 25 May 1863). Once again, Rudolf was creating boundaries in his mind between righteous urban individuals and country men. As an accountant, he had little sympathy for those whose spending habits and credit worthiness were out of control. He was inclined to agree with the Liberal Party's position that only property holders should be allowed to vote; voting should be restricted to those with the proper character qualifications.[15] What Rudolf deplored was the continuation of the gentry ideals of patronage—political parties conditioned by personal connections and by local ties.

Both parties "hunted up" voters as election day neared. Rudolf noticed that the Tories had "a large, influential, and active working committee in Town, and they brought every one of their men up. Not one was left behind, and all we counted as doubtful went against us. But worse than that, about 20 upon whom we counted changed sides and voted against us" (Journal, vol. 1, 28 May 1863). A number of Liberal supporters stayed home, so they lost over sixty voters in Pictou Town and were defeated by 124 votes in the county: "This result completely took us by surprize," Rudolf exclaimed. He then began to analyze why they had lost. The defeat of the Liberal's franchise bill annoyed many young men, who were angry at the proposal to take their vote away from them.[16] "Bribery open and undisguised was carried on," Rudolf noted. "Offers of £5 were repeated for votes. The Tories seemed to have unlimited supplies, and the result testifies to the fact." Liberals were defeated throughout the province; only fourteen were returned, against forty Conservatives. Premier Joseph Howe was defeated in his Lunenburg riding by five hundred votes: "The whole affair seems like a dream—a farce—so unlike anything that ever happened before that it is almost impossible to believe it a sober reality. Our men bear up very well, and as the result has turned out so badly over the whole Province we are glad our two men have not to spend an ignoble 4 years in a helpless state of enforced imprisonment—so to speak—upon the opposition benches....I only hope," continued Rudolf, "that our Railway will not be stopped, but I much fear it."

To Rudolf's surprise, however, the incoming Conservative government led by J.W. Johnston kept its promise to build the Pictou railway extension; but the Conservatives also continued traditional patronage practices. All Liberal Pictou office holders were replaced by Conservatives, including Rudolf's fellow church warden, Tanner, who as mentioned earlier was appointed justice of the peace. Rudolf rather cynically remarked of Tanner, "He has lately been very indignant at the Govt for not building our Railroad, and has declared several times to me that he would not support them [the Conservatives] any longer, if after the meeting of next session, they did not at once commence the work. We will see how he will act now. This appointment looks very like a sop, to quiet him" (Journal, vol. 1, 22 October 1863). He added more charitably, "With respect to his qualifications, he is far better fitted for it than one half of those already in the commission. Though he murders the Queens English, and gives it a good smack of brogue besides, he is not wanting in sense, or principle." When A.P. Ross was ousted from the post office in 1864 by Simon Holmes, Rudolf condemned the "wretched, pernicious system" that swept out office holders, and he put the primary blame for introducing it on the Conservative party (Journal, vol. 1, 12 May 1864). At the appointment of one of his contemporaries, James McDonald, as financial secretary, Rudolf sarcastically remarked, "Our 'clever young man' Jim is getting on in the world. He is now a Cabinet Minister, and one of the rulers of the land" (Journal, vol. 2, 13 December 1864). McDonald in 1863 had been chief railway commissioner of the province and in that capacity had facilitated the construction of the Pictou railway extension.[17]

At the beginning of the election campaign, Rudolf had entertained ideas of running for a seat in the future: "One or two asked me to try it....I laughed at it, as simply absurd and impossible. But with my present feelings, and if I were 10 years older, and with a business which would leave me more independent of it, than my present one, I do not know, but that I might be induced to offer myself for a member. But this is only a passing thought, and I do not entertain the idea, or wish for the honor" (Journal, vol. 1, 15 April 1863). During the campaign, Rudolf's evangelical spirit was revolted by the self-interest of the electorate: "Men at elections seem to lay aside all consideration for an opponents feelings, and all seem bent on accomplishing their own ends, even at the expense of an adversarys reputation. This begets retaliation, and hard epithets, and often blows are passed, and so the war rages" (Journal, vol. 1, 5 May 1863). He blamed the moral state on the low qualifications of electors: "The rabble have the control,—the deciding of the poll. They must be coaxed, cajoled, and even bought, to give their votes, as they may be influenced…[by] unscrupulous leaders." In these early days, several months before his militia experience with working-class rankings in the militia, Rudolf's judgment rested not only on his experience but on the biases of his own (and Primrose's) gentry background.

As for his own conduct, Rudolf tried to abstain from public criticism of opponents, so as not to give them opportunity for advantage, even though there were "a few men in this Town whose overbearing manner, and presumption are hard to be borne, and it is difficult to come in contact with them, without getting embroiled in a squabble. Bob Doull [Rudolf's militia colonel in 1864] especially is almost insufferable, but I don't want to speak evil of anyone, and I refrain from writing what I may think of him, and the others I have in my mind" (Journal, vol. 1, 28 May 1863). Two days later, "pestered out of" his wits in settling accounts with voters at the office, Mr. Primrose remarked that Rudolf kept his temper much better than he would have. Rudolf replied, "there was no use in getting angry. But I never will undertake the duty again" (Journal, vol. 1, 30 May 1863); and he never did enter the electoral lists. Rudolf's liberal idealism and previous unrealistic expectations for future electoral responsibilities had been considerably chastened by his experience in the field. He began to realize that the long hours and drudgery associated with his duties as Liberal "bag man" were very draining on his health and brought few personal character rewards. Once again he was learning to balance his initial naive idealism with his experiences in the field. In contrast to the political role of his father, Norman Rudolf now sought other venues to conduct his own style of leadership.

Not surprisingly, Rudolf's long-standing involvement with the management of St. James Church proved much more rewarding for his leadership aspirations. As early as 1857, he was recorded as being a member of vestry (representatives of the ratepayers of a parish assembled for conducting parochial business). In that year he delivered a committee report in support of the Pictou branch (established in 1845) of the Diocesan Church Society. This society had been set up by Bishop John Inglis in 1837 to prepare Nova Scotian

Anglicans for the withdrawal of state and SPG support for such endeavours as King's College at Windsor, Sunday School materials, and clerical allowances. This became an urgent need after 1851 when the Church of England in Nova Scotia was disestablished (and thus state support was withdrawn); an endowment fund was set up not only to replace previous external subsidies of Anglican projects, but also to ensure that no parish would be without services or the involvement of a clergyman in the future. Rudolf estimated that a five-fold increase would be needed in the 1857 subscription fund;[18] in 1860, his first year as warden, Rudolf put the motion that his parish support the general endowment fund, set up by Bishop Hibbert Binning. By the end of Rudolf's fifth term as warden, not only were the accounts balanced but the endowment fund for the parish had reached $601.18. There was also a large credit of $1240.30 from the bazaar fund to be used to build a parsonage and a schoolhouse (later abandoned for the building of a transept for the existing church). All glebe lands (previously part of the clergyman's benefice under the established Church of England) had been sold, and the funds attached to the Diocesan Church Society. Rudolf, Davies, and Daniel Hockin (Pictou merchant) had purchased a plot of land for a new cemetery at Dickson's Mill Dam for $83; current church funds and sale of plots were to be used to reimburse them. Finally, Rudolf was appointed to a committee to draw up plans for a parsonage. He and Tanner were warmly applauded on their retirement "for the faithful and efficient manner that their duties have been discharged for the five years that they have acted" as wardens.[19] Rudolf had contributed effectively in his parish to the efforts of Bishop Binning to make all Anglican parishes in his diocese much more independent and self-reliant.

These public records do not reveal two critical issues that were beginning to split the congregation of St. James: harsh criticism of perceived "Tractarianism," emanating from Bishop Binning's office, Windsor College, and the Oxford Movement in England; and Elliott's increasing inability to perform his clerical duties. As a result of these problems, Rudolf found it difficult to collect the required church funds and meet current expenses. At Christmas 1862, Rudolf remarked on the beautiful decoration of the church: wreaths of spruce along the walls and over the chancel, biblical inscriptions over the chancel and organ, and the pulpit surmounted with the initials "I.H.S.,"[20] and a blue cross. He further observed, "These looked very well, and had a good effect. The pulpit, gallery and gasoliers were all entwined with spruce. The Ladies who made the letters, and wreaths deserve great praise for their labors" (Journal, vol. 1, 25 December 1862). However, a number of people in the congregation and his fellow warden, Tanner, strongly objected to symbols of

High Church ritualism, especially the display of crosses; on 30 December the two wardens removed the crosses over the pulpit and reading desk.

In 1863 Elliott was fifty-nine years old and had served the parish of St. James for thirty-three years. He was a skillful manager and had his two wardens firmly on side; Norman recorded that

> Mr. Elliott was in the office this morning, and asked me to go up to the Rectory after tea, as he wished to talk over Church matters with Mr. Tanner…and me. Accordingly after tea we went up, and sat for 2 hours with him. We had a very pleasing and (partially so) confidential interview. Mr. Elliott, after we had arranged a new list of subscribers for Church Record for 1863, spoke about the future of the Church here. He said he had it in contemplation to retire to England in about 5 years time—that George [his son] would be settled in his [law] profession by that time, and for family reasons he would feel then desirous of going home. (Journal, vol. 1, 26 January 1863)

To protect his pension, Elliott intended to remain rector of the parish and draw his current salary even though living in England. He proposed a payment of £50 sterling towards the minister acting in his place. This would be supplemented by subscriptions from the congregation. His chief justification for retaining the post of rector was that if he drew on his pension it would jeopardize the £50 he proposed to donate to St. James Church from his salary. At his death, he and his sister-in-law, Miss Butcher, had each willed £100 to the parish, the interest of which, added to the interest from other investments of the Pictou Diocesan Church Society and to aid from the endowment fund when he died, would make up the salary (estimated at $600 per annum) of future ministers of St. James. Presented to a young warden experiencing difficulty in collecting subscriptions, the argument appeared compelling: "The conversation we had tended very much to increase my respect, indeed I may say, affection for Mr. Elliott, and I only wished," wrote Rudolf, "that more of the congregation could have been present."

Over the next three years, however, this respect rapidly diminished, despite the fact that Elliott successfully begged him to continue as warden. Rudolf noted over sixteen occasions when Elliott was either ill, suffering from a bilious attack, away on visits, or just not in attendance at church. The cause was Elliott's intemperance. At first, Rudolf used gentle methods of reproach. He subscribed to the *Church of England Temperance Magazine,* which he passed on to Elliott urging him to promote the cause and privately wishing that "Mr. Elliott would become a teetotaler" (Journal, vol. 1, 27 February 1863). When the bishop came to Pictou to conduct the confirmation service in July of 1863, he came to Rudolf's office to talk over the future of the parish. While Rudolf mentioned Elliott's ongoing illness and the need for a replacement

when he retired, there was no mention of Elliott's planned English retirement proposal nor of his alcoholism. In fact, all Rudolf suggested was that a
young active man be appointed and that "we all liked Mr. Elliott, and would
be very sorry to part with him" (Journal, vol. 1, 6 July 1863). Rudolf's deference to those in authority and his desire to be seen as a responsible church
steward were reflected in his closing remarks that he was "very much pleased
with his Lordships manner, and the interest he manifested in all that concerns the welfare of the Parish. I shewed him an account of our church monies,
and investments and told him, I had but little doubt, but that we would manage to pay a minister if Mr. E. should leave us."

The reward for Rudolf's respectful demeanour and oblique reference to
Elliott appeared in the *Church Record* several weeks later. It contained "a letter from Mr. Elliott giving an account of the Bishop's doings here…he makes
a flattering allusion to Mr. Tanner & [to me] as Church Wardens, says that the
Bishop was highly delighted with the efficient manner with which we had
managed the affairs of the Parish. Mother saw the notice of it, and spoke of
it to me in her letter. It is a satisfaction to feel that one has [done] his duty,
and a greater one, to find that ones labors are appreciated, although it was not
with a view to obtain praise, that Mr. Tanner & I have so exerted ourselves,
but for the welfare of the Church" (Journal, vol. 1, 29 July 1863). Elliott's
problematic behaviour did not improve, however, and the congregation forced
Rudolf to acknowledge it. While Elliott was in the United States in September, a number of young clerics conducted the services. Rudolf reported,

> It is very trying to hear so many complaints about Mr. Elliott. It would seem
> that the stirring sermons we heard yesterday, have aroused our people, and
> made them compare the rather cold and lifeless ones Mr. E. preaches with
> those of Mr. Richey. Mr. Hockin does not try to hide his ill feeling, and I am
> afraid an open rupture will take place in our congregation. I do wish
> Mr. Elliott would see fit to retire, and make [way] for a younger man….
> Mr. E. has one great besetting sin, which in my estimation lies at the bottom
> of all his nervousness, apathy and eccentricity. And that is—intemperance.
> He is too fond of drink. Everyone sees this, and deplores it. Yet the older men
> will not counsel him against it. Indeed they all use liquor—not to the same
> extent perhaps, but enough to prevent them from reproving others for a
> vice, with which they themselves are tainted.
>
> I have resolved to do something myself to try and make him reform, and
> the first opportunity I get, I will address him on the subject….(Journal,
> vol. 1, 28 September 1863)

Rudolf delayed doing so for another five months, however. His temperance
activism was stymied by his evangelical respect for ministerial authority, as well

as by his desire to win respect for doing his duty. As well, his hesitancy can probably be attributed to his fear of arousing the ire of older members of the congregation, who might retain their loyalty to Elliott.

Meanwhile, Elliott himself approached Rudolf, no doubt because of the growing alienation of several leading parishioners, and told him that he had decided to get a young curate to help him and that he would be willing to pay £60 towards his salary. He regretted not being able to hold regular prayer meetings and a Bible class because of his ill health. Rudolf wrote that he was "really delighted to see Mr. Elliott waking up to more zeal and activity. I know he does not lack the *desire* to do good but he wants the energy and self reliance necessary for the active discharge of his parish duties. He is so nervous and frightened lest he should *fail,* that he is afraid to try anything. He thinks if he had a Curate—young and active—he should feel his hands strengthened sufficiently for anything" (Journal, vol. 1, 1 January 1864). This proposal was welcomed by the leading churchmen, and in due course, after hearing the sermons of several young candidates, Elliott suggested newly ordained Ferdinand Pryor for the post. He had won the Cogswell Scholarship and had shown a pious and evangelical spirit while at King's College, Windsor.

Rudolf had not forgotten his vow. He wrote a letter to Elliott on the subject of temperance and enclosed the January issue of the *Church of England Temperance Magazine* "with a request to read it carefully, and plainly telling him, that it was a great sorrow to me to observe the silence he maintained on the sin of intemperance, and that he continued to stand afar off from the temperance reform" (Journal, vol. 1, 15 February 1864). Elliott's reply, Rudolf wrote,

> was more than I almost hoped to get. He thanked me for the kind way in which I presented the matter to him—acknowledged the good temperance societies were doing—excused his not taking part with them from the habits formed early in life and the training which he then obtained—he shrinks from a committal of himself, lest he should suffer from the giving up of a daily portion of liquors—but promises not to partake of it in other peoples houses—to aid the Curate in doing all I should like him to do, and finally to preach temperance more than he has done. I answered this, and told him it was all I could expect from him at present, but expected to see him yet a "cold water man," and able to indulge in a smile at his present fears about the abandonment of the use of liquors. (Journal, vol. 1, 16 February 1864)

With the prospect of a young assistant, Rudolf noted that Elliott "seems like a different man now....So humble, so full of desire to do for the best, and breathing in all his letters to me, a spirit full of the deepest piety. His character lately has certainly presented quite a new, and pleasing aspect to me and I pray God...that our Curate...may serve the Lord in true holiness, and do much good among us" (Journal, vol. 1, 20 February 1864). Rudolf wrote this, however, just prior to the annual parish meeting and Elliott's request that Rudolf and Tanner serve as wardens for a fifth term.

Pryor fulfilled all the expectations of St. James's evangelical congregation. On the first Sunday after his arrival, he preached two sermons, which Rudolf described as beautiful:

> His text in the morning was "now then as Ambassadors of God, we beseech you in Christ's stead, be ye reconciled to God." He first spoke of the mission of Gods ministers—their high office—then of their message. He said that Providence had called him to come among us, and that he would, in view of the responsibility resting upon him, preach plainly unto us. He might perhaps be blamed for speaking too plainly, but he was determined to do his duty in this respect. He exhorted us "not to mix up the man with his preaching, but to consider his message,"or otherwise we should find many things to find fault with. He concluded with a most touching appeal to us to pray for him, that he might be guided aright—to support him with our aid in all good works, and to consider the solemn words addressed to us in the text. It was a splendid sermon, and it caused many to shed tears. I could not refrain mine, nor Cassie either. (Journal, vol. 1, 26 June 1864)

As with his admiration for the Reverend McPhee's charismatic preaching style earlier in the year, Rudolf's evangelical spirit was moved by Pryor's direct, emotional appeal to the hearts of his congregation and for their personal response to Christ. Pryor followed this up by one-on-one encounters, encouragement of church groups, and mission outreach. By the ninth of July, Pryor had visited forty families. He supported the Sunday School picnic in September, which was pronounced a great success; eighty-one scholars and fifty teachers and friends attended. Pryor, Elliott, and Rudolf (as Sunday School superintendent) were rewarded with three rousing cheers. Pryor instituted a mid-week evening service, organized the appointment of a missionary minister, Albert Kaulbach (a relative of Rudolf's), at River John, and strongly supported the Evangelical Union prayer meetings organized in January 1865. Pryor was displaying the characteristics expected of evangelical ministers: he was engendering a more vital parish life, he regarded his work as a vocation, and he earnestly considered his duties to encompass the spiritual, pastoral, and managerial activities from Sunday services to associated clubs, educational societies, and ecumenical outreach programs.[21] Rudolf and other "home missionaries" believed that these idealistic principles, combining "works" with Christian love, would regenerate society. They were the basis of an initiative in 1846 by Anglican evangelicals and Free Church Scots, the Evangelical Alliance, to mount an international conference on Protestant unity. The alliance was formed in England primarily to defeat ritualism and the alarming number of defections of Tractarians (High Church Anglicans) to the Roman Catholic Church. In 1865, Richard West called for the publication of a "Christian Union" journal whose profits would help to promote a Protestant Mission Fund. This missionary movement was already under way in the Pictou region; it was epitomized by the Reverend John Geddie's 1846 Presbyterian mission to Aneityum, New Hebrides (see next chapter). As John Webster Grant observes, "the Alliance inspired a genuine desire for Christian unity and was one of the significant precursors of the twentieth-century ecumenical movement."[22]

The success of his new curate had a deleterious effect on Elliott. At the December meeting of the Diocesan Church Society, Rudolf reported that the poor man "was so drunk, he knew scarcely anything, and behaved in a very unseemly manner. He rambled on in a silly manner for about half an hour and then adjourned the meeting without doing anything. Not a word was said in behalf, or about, the D.C. Society and nothing was collected for it. Mr. E. has been drinking very hard lately, and things have come to a crisis with us now. It cannot be permitted to go on unnoticed any longer, but how it is to be noticed I know not. The congregation are dreadfully enraged about his conduct, and are determined to take action on the matter" (Journal, vol. 2, 29 December 1864). At a meeting between the two wardens and Hockin over the matter, Rudolf took the responsibility of drafting a note to Elliott, which he showed to Primrose, asking Elliott to resign his duties in favour of Pryor, because of the "social habit" of which they all complained. Although the note was signed by the two wardens and five other members of vestry, Dr. Johnston (brother-in-law of Elliott), successfully prevented it from being sent, arguing that it would lead to Elliott's breakdown. Subsequently, Elliott had a terrible row with Pryor and ordered him out of the house because of a notice in the *Eastern Chronicle* that referred to Pryor as rector and praised him for the way he conducted the prayer meetings. The church wardens were pressed by the congregation to intercede on Pryor's behalf. Pryor threatened to resign and strongly objected to a letter Elliott had written unfairly misrepresenting his participation at the Union Prayer Meetings. Finally, Rudolf was surprised and pleased to receive a curt note from Elliott saying that he intended to prepare for his departure for England.

However, the problem got worse. Rudolf wrote a letter to Elliott asking him to cease controlling parish matters and allow the curate to take over until Elliott's departure. At this, Johnston accused Rudolf of driving Elliott to extremes. Rudolf asked him if he had seen the letter, at which Johnston admitted he had not. With newly acquired assertiveness Rudolf responded that he had better do so and that Johnston would "see that you have received quite a misrepresentation of it. He said Mr. Pryor had behaved in a shameful manner to Mr. E. which I disputed" (Journal, vol. 2, 21 January 1865). By this time the bishop had become involved in the affair. The congregation split into two factions, those supporting Pryor (the majority) and those supporting Elliott, twenty-three of whom signed an address on his behalf. Rudolf characterized several of the latter as "poor miserable drunkards. Mr. Elliott may be ashamed of such a testimonial to his services and worth." Rudolf decided at last to write the bishop giving him "a correct statement of our Parish matters. [The Bishop had written to] Mr. Pryor that he was altogether ignorant of Mr. Es intemperance—that he had never heard a whisper of it. It is evident he knows very little about our affairs, and I have now undeceived him. I have told him fully and plainly of everything. He may, or may not attach any weight to my letter. But that is his duty—I have done mine" (Journal, vol. 2, 26 January 1865). The upshot was that Pryor decided to leave the parish and to accept a call to a parish in Dartmouth, which offered a higher salary. Rudolf begged in vain to get him to stay, particularly when they both learned that Elliott was indeed going to England and would relinquish all control of parish matters by the end of June 1865. At the April parish meeting, Rudolf and Tanner resigned as wardens, nominating John Hockin (who was to replace Rudolf as a merchant commissioner in Scotland in 1871) and Cornelius Dwyer (auctioneer) in their stead.

At the Easter Communion service, accompanied by Cassie and by his visiting sister, Louisa, Rudolf enjoyed Pryor's lovely sermon and "the worship very much, and seemed to realize that Christ died for *me* with more assurance today than almost ever before. One grows so cold, and dead by contact with earths cares and concerns. What a privilege it is to be allowed occasionally to kneel at the Lords Table and have our souls aroused to greater activity and strengthened for the fight against 'the world, the flesh and the Devil.' It was very pleasing to me to have Louisa with us at this communion" (Journal, vol. 2, 16 April 1865). For the first time since Rudolf's note to the bishop, Elliott called him to his house in a disturbed state; the bishop had threatened to stop his pension because he had not kept his pledge to give up drinking. Rudolf promised not to support any plan which would give him more pain. Elliott "said I was very kind to him and thanked me. He seemed quite relieved and happy. Before leaving he gave me a book not of any interest or value, but inscribed 'from an old friend' with a quotation from Scripture *unfinished*—so characteristic of him, which makes it valuable to me only" (Journal, vol. 2, 11 June 1865).

Rudolf's final encounter with Elliott was in September, the day of his departure from Pictou: "He was completely broken down, and unnerved. I never saw anyone so miserable. He has been no doubt keeping himself braced up by stimulants, and they have made him shaky, and wretched. Poor man! I am glad he is gone, but sorry, deeply sorry that it had to be so. What a miserable termination of nearly 40 years ministry—leaving the scene of his labors a disgraced, pitied, and wretched old man. And this all through the demon of intemperance. Another example of the evil consequences of moderate drinking. He could scarcely bid me goodbye. He just shook hands and gasped out 'goodbye,' and turned aside" (Journal, vol. 2, 28 September 1865). The entire experience had been a chastening one for Rudolf and for his ideal concept of character. His public leadership roles in various voluntary organizations exposed him to people of different strata. He learned that the paternalistic style of leadership developed by his older mentors, Primrose and Fraser, was now not as effective in establishing codes of behaviour in the community. Boundaries between the respectable class and the "rabble" were becoming permeable. Women were now introduced into the previously exclusive male temperance organization through the dances initiated by younger members. Moral ideals were being jeopardized by calls for entertainment. On a face-to-face level, however, Rudolf's moral earnestness and personal integrity of character continued to make gains in terms of individual pledges of temperance and in helping to convince Elliott to retire. He was also becoming more realistic regarding the political process and more canny in judging Elliott's chameleon character. While still maintaining his moralistic, evangelical ideals, he had gained a depth of compassion for those with frail or weak characters, and he had managed tactfully to lead the feuding congregational factions into concerted support for Pryor. At the same time, in these first four years of reflection on the nature of ideal character and on his ordinary life experiences, Rudolf was learning to be flexible and pragmatic in the face of change or political decisions, putting his trust in God and/or the electorate for their consequences. He was learning to rise above a feeling of personal failure if events turned out differently from his intended goals. Rudolf also realized that his father's militia and political positions of leadership were not appropriate for him. His style of leadership was one-on-one; his preference was for evangelical mission and for educational work.

Rudolf's writing also reveals that in his diary he was refining his previously naive conception of ideal character by means of diary reflections on his own experiences. He was beginning to balance his evangelical idealism with realistic assessments of what he could accomplish as a leader. He also realized that it was all very well to have ideals, which provided him with emotional stability, but that his responsibility as a leader to bring about positive reform measures required him to comprehend the complexity of issues and to find an effective style of leadership that suited his personality. For their successful implementation he needed to be more judicious in his choice of causes. Above all, he needed to achieve full manhood status before he would be accepted as a major community leader.

CHAPTER 6

Evangelical Leadership

Norman Rudolf's chastening experience with the Reverend Charles Elliott and the growing success of his firm, Primrose and Rudolf, marked a turning point in his own character formation. He began to take on more responsibilities both in voluntary organizations and with his own family. After several years of declining the office, in 1866 Rudolf agreed to be nominated as warden master of the Pictou Masonic Lodge. He did not win unanimous approval so withdrew until 1868. In 1866 he also purchased his first home. This was a significant benchmark of manly identity and status. Over the next two years, his leadership was requested in the Bible Society and, especially as president in 1868–1869, in the reorganization of the Young Men's Christian Association (YMCA) in Pictou. With the birth of a fifth child in 1868 and Edie's continuing illnesses, Rudolf strove to achieve a balance between his family responsibilities and his community obligations. With respect to the latter, he was now deemed to be an evangelical leader, trained for "'practical service work' [which] was considered as an indication of Christian commitment, and implied confronting large numbers of people with a challenge to turn to 'Christian ways,'"[1] in the words of Murray Ross. While in these leadership roles, Rudolf's ideal concept of character appeared to become more sophisticated, approaching the complexity of the human condition with less condemnation and his ability to affect human character with more realistic goals.

Rudolf had been active with the YMCA in the early 1860s. He enjoyed the small group meetings because of their interesting Bible discussions. He also used the Pictou YMCA library when he had more time in his early married life. Unfortunately, the library was sold in 1865, the $60 proceeds going to charity. The YMCA evangelical work appeared to be doomed. As Rudolf commented,

> So ends this good work. It was begun with an earnest desire to make it a benefit to those connected with it. It struggled against opposition, and was for a time prosperous. But it has fallen and I fear it will be a long time before another is formed. There seem[s] to be a fatality attending all societies in Pictou. They last for a little while, but sooner or later they are all dissolved...it is solely due to the apathy and indifference of professing Christians that this one has declined. I regret it very much. I did my part faithfully in office and in attendance at its meetings, and so did Howard [Primrose] and 4 or 5 others, but we could not keep it up alone. (Journal, vol. 2, 13 October 1865)

As noted in chapter 5, in 1813 the British and Foreign Bible Society was established in Pictou. Throughout the next five decades it continued to flourish, in part because of support from the Presbyterian communities in Pictou and in Halifax. The society's emphasis on evangelical co-operation appealed to Rudolf's liberal idealism. After the collapse of Pictou's YMCA in 1865, Rudolf joined the Bible Society and attended weekly Bible study meetings where he continued to enjoy the fellowship of other Pictou evangelicals. He also participated in the Week of Prayer, organized by the Evangelical Union and supported by Reverend Ferdinand Pryor in January 1865 (which led to his row with Reverend Charles Elliott; see chapter 5). The society placed a characteristic evangelical emphasis on the power of love to cultivate humble submission to the events of life and triumph over the world's misfortunes. Steven Mintz suggests that "it was through an experience of Christ's saving love that the soul was instantaneously transformed, that men achieved release from their guilt and sins, and that men's souls found consolation and ultimately redemption."[2] The fellowship of believers had an important role to play in creating this remade person. Evangelicals insisted on a personal response to Christ and championed a doctrine of vital religion, a religion of the heart, which either suddenly or gradually would change the supplicant into a new being. Weekly Bible study, which re-emphasized the Reformation doctrine of the sole authority of scripture as the rule of life, would, evangelicals believed, aid the process of personal conversion, of developing an inner conscience, and of acquiring character and a moral nature. What probably attracted Rudolf and many Pictonians who had endured years of inter-denominational strife in their community was the antisectarian position of the evangelicals. As T.W. Acheson explains, "Believing that there was an essential core to the faith, evangelicals were generally prepared to accept the validity of many denominational paths provided that they contained the essentials. In sharp contrast to the high churchmen within their tradition, Church of England evangelicals regarded their communion as simply one of many valid Christian bodies. The evangelical tendencies toward personal conversion and perfection were reflected at a corporate level in efforts to convert and make better the society in which they found themselves."[3]

Michael Gauvreau defines evangelicalism between 1800 and 1870 as "a transatlantic movement of religious revival, which transformed not only personal piety but also values, institutional life and the relationship of the Christian churches to state and society. Of equal importance...is the fact that 'evangelicalism' was one of the key cultural forces which promoted the emergence of the complex of ideas and attitudes we designate as 'modern.'"[4] In an earlier work, Gauvreau elaborates:"concepts of order, respectability, and patterns of personal and social behaviour which were to prove most influential in forging the values and institutions of the maturing English Canadian society were provided by evangelicalism."[5] Marguerite Van Die observes of Brantford, Ontario, that, like the late 1850s in the urban centres of the United States, the period was characterized by a "particular communal dimension of evangelical religion." These revivals were both individualistic and social, she notes: "the initial catalyst to revival in Brantford seems to have been the shared optimism of church and community building. This interaction between religious and social change, with economic upheavals followed by returning prosperity, would continue to shape the pattern of evangelical life in Brantford during the next three decades." Increasingly, families and institutions reflected the pervasive evangelical culture and youth, "were surrounded by moral influences far more encompassing than those experienced by their parents."[6] Pictou experienced a similar pattern.

The evangelical culture of the Bible Society and of the YMCA suited Rudolf's now more mature ideal of character far better than did Masonic culture. The latter depended on ritualistic examination, competition, and a hierarchical social structure to cultivate manly character. In contrast, the YMCA used psychological strategies, emphasizing co-operation, brotherhood, and nurturing forms of education to develop an inner Christian conscience and middle-class norms of behaviour and spiritual ideals. In the small-town setting of Pictou, multiple daily face-to-face encounters provided the opportunity for evangelical leaders, through discourse, to spell out their moral prescriptions and to embed their religious values in town institutions, such as the

numerous volunteer organizations, schools, and churches, as well as in business relationships.[7] A man's character was judged not just on his success in
his professional career, but now on the degree of self-discipline, sensitivity, and
sense of responsibility—stewardship—that he exhibited in the everyday needs
of his family and community. Rudolf's personal growth in character and the
upbringing of his siblings and his children illustrated this new evangelical
culture beginning to influence homes and communities. He embodied a new
conception of family authority, where fathers took on increased responsibility for the care of their children, domestic co-operation in household planning and improvement was more in vogue, and the process of self-mastery was
considered a "manly" achievement.

The evangelical culture blossoming in Pictou was not restricted to individual households nor to the local region. As early as 1863, Rudolf wrote
about the extraordinary upwelling of community response to the missionary
efforts of John Geddie[8] in the New Hebrides. In 1845, Geddie was appointed
the first foreign missionary of the Presbyterian Church of Nova Scotia with
the mandate to go forth and evangelize the heathen. He arrived at the Island
of Aneityum, in the southern New Hebrides, the following year. On his first
and only furlough (1863–1866) he returned to Pictou and New Glasgow to
pick up a mission brigantine, the *Dayspring*. Rudolf arranged a party to tour
the vessel in September 1863; he described the accommodation as "very superior" (Journal, vol. 1, 17 September 1863). She was to be commanded by
Captain W.A. Fraser (whose exploits running the American blockade are
described in chapter 3). As Rudolf commented, "A series of trifling accidents
has occurred to her [the ship]. I sincerely trust nothing more serious may
happen to her. Her loss would be a terrible blow to all concerned, and they
are *thousands*. Perhaps never was a vessel built in which so many are interested. Her cost has been paid by little sums collected by the Sunday School
children [in the Pictou district], and they are a very numerous body" (Journal, vol. 1, 18 September 1863). Rudolf described the leave-taking of three
other missionaries in October 1863:

> There was a great farewell Missionary meeting held in Mr. [James] Baynes
> [Prince Street C]hurch tonight. The three missionaries Rev. Mr. [James
> D.] Gordon,[9] Rev. Mr. [Donald] Morrison[10] & Rev. Mr. [William McCul-
> lagh],[11] and the wives of the two last, were present, beside[s] a number of
> clergy, and a great concourse of people. The Church was thronged. Rev. Mr.
> Stewart of New Glasgow presided, and commenced the speaking part of
> the programme by dedicating the Missionaries by prayer. It was a very long
> one, and made up of a series of petitions, any one of which would have been
> excellent, had it not been rendered wearisome, by "oft repetition." Mr. Bayne

next addressed the Missionaries on behalf of the Board, pointing out their duties, their responsibilities, and the hopes centered in them concerning the future. He spoke very well, and I liked his address very much. He was followed by each of the Missionaries in turn, who spoke of missions, their rise and progress, and made such other remarks as were applicable to the occasion and their circumstances. The proceedings were terminated by prayer by Rev. Mr. [David] Roy [of James Church, New Glasgow]. The choir sang either a psalm or hymn between each address, and thus rendered the meeting most interesting. (Journal, vol. 1, 21 October 1863)

Another farewell service was held the next day aboard the *Dayspring,* which set sail for Halifax that afternoon. The following month, Rudolf reported that Charlotte Geddie had tea several times with them; her sister, Lucy, attended Pictou Academy. In May 1864, the two girls heard that their new little brother, Alexander, had died. That August the parents returned to Pictou, and the Rudolfs invited them for tea. The Geddies were still at Pictou in December 1864. Rudolf met Geddie in a friend's bookshop where he was shown "a number of curiosities from the heathen islands, consisting of arrows, war clubs of all kinds, and *two hatchets* which were the ones that killed Rev. Mr. [George] Gordon & his wife, in the hands of the savages of Erromang[o]. They were sad momentoes....Mr Geddie has quite a large collection of articles" (Journal, vol. 2, 22 December 1864). A year later, Rudolf described the farewell soiree held in Pictou for the Geddies, who were returning to their mission in the New Hebrides. His character assessment epitomized why they all admired Geddie so much: "The meeting was held enraptured by Mr Geddies description of the Islands and of his experience and labors as a Missionary. He is the most earnest, unassuming, humble-minded man I ever saw. No one could fancy to hear him speak of the wonderful work which he has done in Aneityum that he had anything particular to do with it. The whole island has renounced heathenism, and professed Christianity. I think there are 3,000 natives on the Island" (Journal, vol. 2, 28 November 1865). The next day, Rudolf described a farewell prayer meeting at which Geddie recounted "many interesting anecdotes and short sketches of individual conversions" (Journal, vol. 2, 29 November 1865). Geddie would continue his mission for another five years after which he retired in Australia. He died there in 1872. This evangelical cultural context no doubt also affected other organizations; Geddie's mission was a reflection of the strong influence of evangelical religious culture in the Pictou district at this time.

Another influence was the activities of the Masons. One of the principal functions of Freemasonry was to establish intergenerational bonds between young males in the community and older, middle-class leaders. Rudolf noted in 1862 that by midcentury a reformed fraternal movement was attempting to purge an earlier intemperate culture and replace it with a more sober and orderly social regime. The American orders used a ritualistic approach to effect this change, replicating in their initiation ceremonies the stages of manhood from entering apprentice to mature master mason. The English fraternal movement, in contrast, stressed a more evangelical approach. While the former apparently adopted a rhetoric of gender, emphasizing the differences between a masculine moral order and the mother-son bonding inculcated during childhood, the latter stressed human reason as a means of attaining Divine Truth.[12] Rudolf's diary rarely referred to his involvement in Pictou's Masonic Order except during the period 1866–1867, just as he was competing for leadership status in the community. It would appear that his major objective to reform the lodge and his desire to achieve the status of "leading man" in the community were his primary reasons for remaining with the Masonic Order.

Because of his close relationship with his two mentors, James Primrose and J.D.B. Fraser, and his experience with the Temperance Division, Rudolf quickly integrated into the ranks and felt that he had won the support of the older Masons by 1866. He accepted the nomination of W.M. Richard Tanner, his co-warden at St. James Church whom he had named when declining the nomination the previous year. Rudolf's only condition was that he be accepted by a near-unanimous vote of the members present. As in the Temperance Division, however, he found himself stymied by younger members of the lodge. He ruefully explained later: "It appears that [Samuel] Rigby [Pictou lawyer and later Supreme Court Justice] was anxious to be elected, and had, with the active aid of Joe Gordon [business partner of Smith Dawson] canvassed a part of the Lodge, whom I have opposed on several occasions, when I deemed it my duty to do so, and they went in a body against me on the vote being taken. The foundry men, and a few of their class who were only admitted within two years past...on the examination of the ballot there were 2 of a majority against me in favor of Rigby, but afterwards two more ballots for me were found in the box, which tied us" (Journal, vol. 2, 11 December 1866). At this Rudolf rose and stated that he would not consider running if half the lodge was against him. Rigby was chosen, and Rudolf admitted that though he was glad not to shoulder the responsibility, "yet one does not like to get beaten." He thought Gordon had "dealt very deceitfully with me," but was encouraged that "all the old and influential members of the Lodge voted for me." In public perception, Rudolf was associated with venerable elders currently holding power; newer, younger members were contesting them for a share of this power. Ironically, Rudolf's use of older mentors as models and supporters of his leadership aspirations and his goal of imposing evangelical principles on the community had backfired. He now learned to work within the organization and with the younger members—his own age group—at the lodge. During that year, Rudolf's business skills were exploited by the lodge. He had proposed the sale of their property on Prince Street so that Prince Street Church could build a Sunday School. With the $600 thus raised, the lodge accepted James Munro's plan that a third storey be built on his proposed new shop, which would be a lodge temple. Rudolf served on a committee of seven, which supervised its construction. Rigby and Rudolf were asked to revise the bylaws and report back to the lodge. When Rudolf was finally elected warden master in 1868, he became responsible for arranging the ritual ceremonies and initiations, supervising the tenders, adding a gallery to their new meeting room, and organizing a fundraising bazaar, which netted over $1,730. The hall (temple) was officially opened in September 1870.[13]

One of the highlights of Rudolf's year of leadership was his attendance at the Grand Lodge meeting in Halifax in May 1868. A unanimous feeling was expressed, no doubt because of Confederation the previous year, that Nova Scotia's twenty-eight lodges, currently under English jurisdiction, should become an independent Grand Lodge with Deputy Grand Master Alexander Keith (Halifax brewery owner) at the head. Rudolf noted the heated debate between the "old Halifax men" (Journal, vol. 2, 6 May 1868), who could not see the necessity of having any country representatives on the union committee, and the "fired up" country representatives, who resented their omission. Rudolf proposed his Pictou colleague and Reverend Charles Elliott's brother-in-law, Dr. George Johnston, as committee man from their lodge. Significantly, Rudolf did not remain for the dinner and toasts because he did not care "to partake of the wine provided." His evangelical principles precluded Rudolf's full socialization into the Masonic Order's bonding culture; but he had fulfilled his Masonic duties effectively and was duly rewarded by his male peers. When a new Royal Arch Masonic Chapter, New Caledonia No. 11, composed of Masons who had already attained a higher ranking, was formed in 1870 at Pictou, Rudolf was awarded the degrees of mark and past master. Thus he achieved an important stage in his ascent to evangelical leadership; he would now be recognized as a man of good character, a worthy community leader.

A second arena in which Victorian men were required to prove their character (albeit what is termed private character) and their social identity was in the home. As John Tosh observes, "To establish a home, to protect it, it, to provide for it, to control it, and to train its young aspirants to manhood, have usually been essential to a man's good standing with his peers."[14] Whereas with his marriage, the birth of their children, and the rental of their first house Rudolf had established a household, in his own mind he had not achieved his final goal, to own his own home. As he remarked, "The possession of a house, or the building of one, has so long been a dream of Cassie & mine" (Journal, vol. 2, 2 May 1866). For Victorians, home ownership was an important aspect of bourgeois respectability. Andrew Holman associates the size and appearance of the home and its garden with the aspirations of the middle-class couple: "The size and appearance of the home was to reflect one's social station. To the middle-class mind, propriety and orderliness were important measures, reflections of homeowners' pragmatic values. Middle-class homes were not to be unadorned but decorated in measured, natural refinement....A moderate number of bushes of various sizes and neatly mown grass were considered appropriate; a well-pruned tree, even better. A well-kept yard and garden were a credit to the homeowner and the neighbourhood."[15] Homes, therefore, engendered feelings of refinement and desire for emulation among neighbours. As Richard Bushman notes, emulation harked back to an earlier culture of gentrification and aristocratic refinement: "Emulation meant acquiring a refinement of spirit, a sensitivity to beauty, a regard for the feelings of others, a wish to please, all long associated with aristocracy at its best."[16]

Not only was the home a badge of social position for mid-Victorians, with its interior design and furnishings designed to impress visitors, but it also embodied a new, evangelical, moral vision. Here, intense family relationships could be cultivated, including sharing of advice and burdens between husband and wife; enjoyment, nurture, and moral guidance of children; invention of family rituals, discourse, and nicknames; and for evangelical Christians, cultivation of order, deference, and harmony through their religious practices. As Tosh notes, "At its most elevated, the idealizing of the home extended to the belief that domestic virtues would triumph over a heartless world."[17] Men's conduct was measured against this ideal. Their duty was to protect the home, to continue to provide for its maintenance, and to act as evangelical leaders speaking out in the public arena for its values. At the same time, Victorian evangelicals valued their homes as private retreats, designed to shut out the world. Their gardens were cultivated to revere nature and to allow their children opportunity to develop their distinctive characters through play. Behind the private fence, children could be shaped by careful nurturing and led away from the evils of the street. Family members, therefore, in their private retreat would grow together in this spiritually infused atmosphere; their humanity would be fully realized, their characters enabled to reach maturity.

Many of these values were implicit in Rudolf's resolve in March 1866 to buy a house and garden lot from George Archibald, Pictou tanner. By this date, Cassie had given birth to four children in six years. During Cassie's confinements and Edie's crises, Anna or her daughter Louisa had frequently stayed with the family to help them. Space was at a premium. After consulting Primrose, who agreed to continue his £500 mortgage on the property, Rudolf bargained and won a lowered purchase price of £600 and a proviso that they would have water privileges from the abandoned tannery immediately adjoining their property. A drawing card was the number of rooms and ample garden space in which the children could play. Cassie was delighted; the kitchen and principal rooms were on the ground floor, allowing space for them to entertain guests more frequently.

They moved on the long weekend of 23 May 1866; after their first night's sleep all felt at home. The children played out in the fresh air all day, and their neighbour, Mrs. John Crerar,[18] came over to visit "in a friendly way." She told them that her husband planned to tear down his father's old house, which would give them a fine view of the harbour and town to the south. Rudolf noted that this would enhance the value of their house. On Edie's fourth birthday, they all watched a pair of robins feeding four little ones. As Rudolf observed, "It is such a pleasure [for] us to have trees about us, and to hear the birds chirping, and to watch [them] hopping from limb to limb" (Journal, vol. 2, 29 May 1866). He himself particularly enjoyed supervising the spading and fencing of the garden, building a poultry yard, and planting fruit trees. The garden also represented for Rudolf, as for other Victorians, a place of seclusion and repose.

Rudolf quickly found that he had to expend more money to protect his privacy. In June 1866, Archibald offered to sell him the adjoining cottage lot for £117. Rudolf decided to borrow money from Mrs. Dawson for the purpose. The purchase gave him a garden frontage of fifty-seven feet on Spring Street and a source of income when he rented it. A new downstairs bathroom, wall and roof repairs, garden drains, and frozen water pipes in their house required further outlays; but the most serious threat to their peace of mind occurred in April 1868 when Archibald decided to sell the tannery and garden. Just prior to the sale, Rudolf noted for the first and only time that he "had an unhappy feeling all day from something Cassie said to me last night. She will never know here how much pain it has caused me" (Journal, vol. 2, 20 April 1868).[19] At issue was probably the cost and prudence of their purchase of the tannery to safeguard their property and water rights. Because of Cassie's strong protests, and against his own better judgment (Primrose was out of town), Rudolf did not bid for it at the sheriff's auction. It was purchased by his *bête noire,* Robert Doull.[20] Next day Rudolf suffered the rebukes of his friends and acquaintances. He explained that although he wanted to buy it

"Cassie would not hear of it saying we had property enough. Doull I hear is going to convert the Old Tannery into a tenement and it will probably be filled with all sorts of people to our annoyance. I went to him today and offered to purchase the whole thing from him, and he has promised to give me a reply on Monday. But I expect I shall have to give him a high figure for it, as he has the whip hand of me" (Journal, vol. 2, 25 April 1868).

"Old" Riley and his many Irish friends came up on Sunday to view the lot next to Rudolf promised them by Doull. Rudolf feared that they would not give up their claim. As it turned out, Doull decided to sell Rudolf the tannery lot for £80, guaranteeing thereby the protection of their water supply. Old Riley built a new house and the tannery was torn down; but the incident illustrated Rudolf's concern for privacy and compatible neighbours, as well as highlighting his financial power in the household. The original mortgage for their property was signed by him and by Cassie, but her father's final $800 legacy (invested in the Building Society) and her mother's house served as collateral, and Rudolf had the final say as to the purchase of further property. While the pattern for separate spheres and manly power was apparently being extended, with Rudolf by this time firmly in charge of the financial domain, in fact there was continuing contestation of these new power relationships and the construction of middle-class boundaries.[21]

Christmas and birthdays provided opportunities for Rudolf to demonstrate the continuities he believed his family culture should perpetuate and to symbolize, with presents, the material benefits of his newly won status. At their birthday, children could choose their own pudding for dinner, as was the custom in Rudolf's Lunenburg home.[22] Willie's fourth birthday was marked by a change of costume into coat and trousers.[23] Rudolf reported that he "looked very comical, and Edith declared she was *ashamed* to walk down the street with him. They however with Rob too went down to their Grandmothers" (Journal, vol. 2, 3 May 1868). The family always doted on the newest baby, so much so that when Prim was born Robbie commented, "'I am not the little pet any longer—the little baby is. I am going to be only a little boy now'" (Journal, vol. 2, 21 November 1868). Of course, when Prim reached his first birthday, they all celebrated his progress, "walking about freely—four teeth through—two above and two below, and very hearty considering the hard *fall* he has [had] with the whooping cough. He is the centre of attraction in the household as babies generally are," noted Rudolf indulgently, "and little Jim [later called Prim], though not perhaps conscious of power is a very tyrant in his demands. He asserts his wishes in such a way that all must yield to them, however it is baby's prerogative, and must be submitted to" (Journal, vol. 2, 21 November 1869).

It was significant that all three boys were named after their grandparents and Rudolf's key mentor. Willie, born on 20 March 1864, was named after William Rudolf, Robert Dawson after Cassie's father, and "Prim," or James Primrose after the "old gent." Begetting of children, especially sons, was an important aspect of masculine status and represented a bequest for the future. In their naming, Rudolf symbolized his concerns about his lineage and the heritage he would be leaving.

Christmas Day proved to be, as in many other middle-class Victorian families, a child's form of heaven. Rudolf described their delights: "*Christmas Day*—A lovely day—the children were awake before it was light, and came down to our room to examine the contents of their stockings with eagerness .and delight. Edie was in extacies [*sic*] over a pair of skates. Robbie & Willie were more than pleased with a *popgun* each, with sweets, figs, raisins etc.—not forgetting a large sugar Dog apiece. Edie had some money given her yesterday by her Mother which she expended in little things for the servants, and her brothers, not forgetting a sugar "Rooster" for me. She also cut out and sewed together a lot of pieces of paper, for *shaving* papers for me. This is [her] first handwork. (Journal, vol. 2, 25 December 1868). Rudolf approved of evidence of Edie's concern for others (servants), her use of money to give gifts, and the handwork demonstrating the beginning of her domestic skills; their nurturing of evangelical values and appropriate gender roles was bearing fruit. Play was also cultivated as an acceptable form of self-expression, however. The children received a Noah's ark, dolls, a drum, and a horse and cart: "The excitement was great, and the uproar nearly deafening for awhile." As was the custom each year, Rudolf stopped in at the cottage and the "old gentleman" gave each of his children a gold dollar. In the afternoon, while the children were playing with the ark, Robbie asked his father, "Papa, *can't I send out a dove?*" Their father apparently had been telling them the story of the Flood, and he remembered enough of it to ask the question. Rudolf was obviously taking a major role in the upbringing of his children and in the inculcation of evangelical Christian precepts.[24] The Rudolf children do not appear to have been spoiled with excessive Christmas presents, as were other more worldly children at this time. Even the fact that their mother, rather than their father, gave them money to buy presents for their father and for the servants suggests that their parents' roles as providers were interchangeable in the children's eyes. Tosh's statement that presents "from father were the prime symbolic evidence of his exclusive duty as provider for his children"[25] is not appropriate in the context of this small-town Canadian evangelical home.

Rudolf continued to exercise his role as family protector and moral guardian both in his own and in his Lunenburg family. On New Year's Eve (traditionally celebrated by Scots), for instance, he declined an invitation to a temperance soiree with the Templars in their new hall, in order to guard Cassie, who was alone: "It was well I was not away, as three drunken fellows called, and came in. However after drinking my health in ginger beer, they departed quietly" (Journal, vol. 2, 1 January 1868). A month later, they declined another invitation to a grand party by the Primrose family at their cottage, "as Sunday next is our communion day, and we did not think it right to go to so large a party so near it—indeed we do not approve of these large dress parties at any time" (Journal, vol. 2, 31 January 1868). However, Rudolf and Cassie led a social life, holding frequent tea shines (parties), musical hymn-sing evenings, and the occasional large party at home, especially when there were visiting family members present. For instance, a week earlier the Rudolfs had held a party for one of their Lunenburg friends, Nepean Owen: "report says he is fond of Louisa, and she of him [he courted her for ten years but never proposed]—have not heard anything about it from home. He is a fine look-ing fellow, but a *fast* living young man, or inclined so. He has been in the society of the wildest young men of the town since he came here" (Journal, vol. 2, 24 January 1868). By this time, the Rudolfs did not seem to be inter-fering overtly in Louisa's choice of suitors (see chapter 2).

Daniel Owen a year earlier had replaced Rudolf's brother Moyle who had worked as clerk with Smith Dawson and Gordon in 1866 while staying with the Rudolfs. In 1867 after meeting their uncle, Ephraim Oxner, Moyle decided to go to sea.[26] Oxner had stayed for several days with the Rudolfs in Novem-ber 1867, and Norman was impressed with his gentle treatment of their chil-dren. Oxner had promised to leave his sister, Anna Rudolf, the remainder of the mortgage on her house (which he held) in his will. Before leaving for sea, however, Moyle brought back quite a different perspective of their uncle, "He lets me understand that Uncle Ephraim is not at all agreeable, and makes very unpleasant remarks about his owning the house Mother lives in [should she default on her mortgage with him]. I wish they [his mother and Louisa] were with me, and let Uncle shift for himself. I don't see why their happy home should be disturbed by a crabbitt old sailor. It was what I expected, and it has unfortunately proved so," wrote Rudolf sadly (Journal, vol. 2, 30 May 1868). He and Moyle had sent their mother twenty dollars, the latter's con-tribution from his first paycheque in 1866. Before leaving in 1870, Norman sent his mother $209.92, to be her final payment for the mortgage on the house held by Oxner. Moyle, meanwhile, signed his articles and lived at sea for a number of years, rising to the rank of captain. Norman arranged to have him serve on their firm's ship *Rothiemay* in 1869. He described his brother by that time as "rough looking as any common sailor could be.…yesterday morning, he came up after breakfast, and stayed with us" (Journal, vol. 2, 7 June 1869). In contrast to the respectable character he was constructing for James at this time (see chapter 2) Norman seemed to have no qualms about the image of his younger brother.

Norman and Cassie wanted their children to continue to have this close relationship with their Lunenburg relatives. During the summer of 1867, Cassie and the children, accompanied by Minnie Harris, visited Anna Rudolf for several months at Lunenburg. Rudolf returned home to work and to help their servant look after baby Rob. In 1869, he proudly clipped out of the paper an announcement of Great-Grandmother Kaulbach's one hundredth birthday on 11 February, and noted that their "children are the only ones of the *fifth* generation and great regrets were expressed by those who were assembled that they, or one of them, was not present. Had it been at a more moderate season of the year, I would have most certainly made a great effort to have taken Edie or Willie on. However she *has* seen this generation for two years ago we had them both on to Lunenburg, and she then fondly [greeted] them and kissed them. She is a wonderfully smart old woman" (Journal, vol. 2, 25 February 1869). By this time a long life was considered no longer a sign of God's grace but an accomplishment attributable to the virtues of the individual; hard work and right habits of consumption were deemed sure signs of moral maturity.[27] Family continuity was beginning to be valued over previous spiritual models of aging and death, the latter epitomized by Rudolf's ideal character studies in his obituaries (see chapter 1).

Rudolf's diary entries demonstrate that he was intimately involved with the day-to-day raising of their children. He delighted in their antics, their playful discoveries and their humorous discourse. His appreciation of their spontaneity reflected a Romantic view that the "child within" the father should be nurtured in the company of children; he was beginning to realize that children had "redemptive power."[28] In contrast to American culture at this time, where there was increasing absence of fathers from the home and increasing involvement in men-only clubs, English culture through art and literature continued to affirm the centrality of children and childhood for a fully realized humanity. This culture, which Rudolf endorsed, gave men a language in which to articulate a new style of evangelical leadership that reflected the emotional satisfactions of fatherhood.[29] Rudolf's nurturing personality, developed through his militia leadership skills and his role as a father, had proven invaluable in his work with the temperance division. The resulting self-esteem would help him play an important leadership role with Pictou's revived Young Men's Christian Association.

Rudolf began to exert a stronger leadership role in this evangelical movement in 1867. He was primarily responsible for the hiring of Mary E. Swan for the Bible Society and later for the YMCA. She had conducted similar work in Halifax, acting as local Bible missionary and distributing tracts to townspeople and to seamen arriving at the port. On 10 June she began her work and a month later handed the Bible Society her first report. Rudolf "was astonished at the number of persons who [were] without religious instruction, or do not attend Church" (Journal, vol. 2, 15 July 1867). A committee was formed, with Rudolf as chairman, which engaged Miss Swan at a salary of $200 a year for six months as an experiment. Subscriptions were to be solicited to pay for her salary "trusting that the Lord will influence the hearts of the people in this town to contribute what will be required." Rudolf tried to get a committee of ladies together to support Miss Swan, but only Cassie attended the initial meeting in September. Two weeks later they got fifteen ladies to attend their committee meeting, to appoint officers (Cassie became secretary-treasurer), and to solicit funds on behalf of Miss Swan. Rudolf noted the support of a number of socially important ladies, such as Mrs. Primrose, Mrs. Davies, and Mrs. Gordon. He concluded, "The meeting was very satisfactory and I trust may result in permanently establishing the 'Missing Link' [female philanthropic work] in Pictou. Miss Swan felt a want of sympathy, and support in her labors, which she felt could be only supplied by those of her own sex to whom she could freely converse and report matters which she could not state to gentlemen. So we have now handed over the active management of the work to the Ladies" (Journal, vol. 2, 20 September 1867). By October, the young women solicitors had collected over $125, more than enough to pay one-half her year's salary. By December, Miss Swan was also running a ragged school for children of poor families, with over twenty-six students in attendance. Rudolf was not only helping to create structures in which respectable women could more directly help the poor, but he was also broadening the moral authority of evangelicals in this social construction process.

Rudolf was also participating in the rising tide of evangelicalism that would lead to the revival of the YMCA in Nova Scotia. John McLean, eldest son of the Reverend John McLean who was one of the first graduates of Pictou Academy's theology class, was a prime leader in the movement. Husband of Mary Fox, Rudolf's boarding-house friend, and now a prominent Halifax businessman, McLean's leadership of the YMCA movement in the province and later at the international level earned him the fond title in Y circles as the "Bishop of Nova Scotia." His home had a room called the "'prophets chamber,'" in the words of Murray Ross, "which he reserved for all Y.M.C.A. leaders visiting Halifax. Throughout his life, he carried with him the devoutness traditionally associated with the Scotch Presbyterian family....Like many of the other Association leaders of the time, [McLean] combined deep devotion with determination to succeed in business life—that combination of Calvinism and Capitalism so typical of outstanding men of that day."[30] In October 1867, McLean and other Halifax leaders urged the Christian churches around the province to send delegates to a large convention in Halifax, designed to revitalize the YMCA movement. Marking the public recognition of his maturity as an evangelical leader in Pictou, Rudolf was nominated along with John Hockin from St. James Church, and Clarence Primrose and Dr. Christie from Prince Street Church. There were seventy-eight delegates from the country, all of whom were put up in Halifax homes. Rudolf stayed with the McLeans, old friend and business partner of their Pictou firm. He reported, "Nothing can give an idea of the interesting meetings held. The prayers were so fervent, and impressive—the addresses so stirring, full of practical suggestions, and breathing a tone of love, and Christian fellowship throughout.... Nothing denominational shewed itself. The result, of this convention must be great good....To the City by strengthening and encouraging the young men to labor more than they have done, and to the country by shewing the Delegates what can be done for church and opening up to them new fields of labor, and giving them directions how to work therein" (Journal, vol. 2, 8 October 1867). Before the end of October, the Pictou committee had met, drawn up rules for their new YMCA, and submitted them to a public meeting, which Rudolf chaired.

The new ecumenical tone of the organization was struck by the address of the Reverend George Grant[31] of Halifax. He stressed practicality, co-operation of all Christian denominations, and a new optimistic spirit, extolling the enjoyment of life: "There was nothing in it to make a young man love his manly sports less. He urged upon the young men to have an aim in life—to work steadily—perseveringly to attain it—to work for their God, and for their fellow men embracing each opportunity as it presented itself—not waiting for some *great* thing to do but taking hold of the little things as they present themselves, count them as the things which they are to do," reported Rudolf (Journal, vol. 2, 29 October 1867).

After Grant's lecture, the new YMCA officers were elected, with Rudolf as president. Thirty-nine young men gave in their names as members. As Rudolf commented, the meeting was successful beyond his expectations. Although hesitant about accepting the office, he did so as an example to others, viewing it as "one of the things God designed me to do...*My aim is to be a successful man in my occupation as a Merchant and to do all the good I can while in the world* taking the *everyday duties* of life as they arise whether of business, or of the Church, or of the state as my work, and not to seek for great opportunities of doing good which may never arise, or putting off until I have a more convenient reason" (Journal, vol. 2, 29 October 1867; emphasis in original). He asked for God's guidance to accomplish this purpose.[32] Rudolf's idealism by this time had definitely become tempered by the realities of his day-by-day existence. It was significant that he did not mention his family responsibilities in this Christian endeavour; the two spheres were perceived as separate in public discourse. This did not mean, however, that they were not culturally connected. Rudolf's style of management at the YMCA very much resembled the one he adopted for his own children and for his siblings.[33] He and other YMCA leaders took Grant's message to heart. They organized for the meetings a group of speakers who were entertaining and interesting, as well as morally enlightening. Most employed narrative strategies to convey their moral message. Their first speaker, Mr. Passow, for instance, recounted a humorous piece about the mistakes of a Frenchman with the English language. The Reverend Hill from Halifax described his visit to Paris and London to a rapt audience. The Reverend Foster Almon of Halifax gave a lecture on the "Modern Developments of Christian Philanthropy," dwelling particularly on the total abstinence movement. He also spoke about prison reform, slavery, pauperism, missionary labour, reformatories, orphan homes, the social evil (prostitution), and sailors' homes. Many people declared it the best lecture of the season. At the closing meeting, Rudolf thanked the public for its appreciation of the lecture series and privately judged them "very successful...and the lectures have been of a high order" (Journal, vol. 2, 19 March 1868).

The YMCA joined with the churches in leading the Week of Prayer in 1868; this gave the organization more exposure. The committee also agreed to share their new reading rooms and library with the local branch of the Mechanics Institute, an educational and social club designed for the working class. As Ken Dewar writes, these associations by midcentury were creative forums, "intermediary between the state and society, in which the rules, practices, and proprieties of public discourse were informally and provisionally agreed upon. They were institutions, that is, of civil society, and just as important in the creation of politics as the laws and conventions of the constitution."[34]

In March 1868, a YMCA committee was formed to organize a literary and debating club. At their first debate on the subject "Should Public Opinion be the Standard of Right," Pictou Academy's principal for that year, Aubrey Lippincott, gave "a very neat and elegant speech," in Rudolf's opinion. He continued, "He will make an excellent speaker and will be an ornament to the pulpit for which he intends to study" (Journal, vol. 2, 23 April 1868). (Lippincott returned to Dalhousie College in the fall of 1868, enrolling in the first year of the newly opened medical faculty).[35] The Reverend A.W. Herdman, minister of St. Andrew's (Kirk) Church, preached a sermon praising the YMCA. By May 1868, Rudolf reported that they had a membership of nearly one hundred, their balance of funds amounted to $100, and everything was looking prosperous. The old officers were re-elected, with the exception of George Hattie. Hattie was replaced by Rudolf's old friend Jim Patterson (with whom Rudolf had edited the *Oriental Budget*), who had returned to Pictou after several years of mission work in Halifax.

Patterson alerted the Pictou YMCA about the distress of people in Cape Breton; the organization decided to solicit subscriptions on their behalf. Rudolf and John Hockin collected over $70 which, added to the $40 collected at the annual meeting, enabled them to buy 175 bushels of potatoes, just arrived at Fraser's wharf from Prince Edward Island, and to put them up in barrels and send them off to Inverness for distribution. Pictou YMCA leaders also helped establish Ys at Three-Mile House, at Durham, at Fisher's Grant, and at River John. With all this experience, Rudolf noticed to his surprise that he could now speak with comparative ease, especially if the topic was something he knew about, such as the nature and objects of the YMCA.[36] He reflected, "It is strange how time passes when one is speaking and interested in the subject. I used to think when I first commenced to speak in public that every minute was ten—and I can recall the horrible sensation experienced after first getting on ones feet, and opening ones speech. Even yet with all the practice I have had, I never have to speak without a tremor, and fluttering at the heart until fairly launched into the middle of my remarks" (Journal, vol. 2, 23 December 1868).

As a delegate at the 1868 Halifax convention, Rudolf was called on by McLean to speak for five minutes on their Pictou work. The next year he was able to report at the annual meeting that there were 119 members, that their reading room was well stocked with papers and magazines, and that prayer meetings were regularly held. Rudolf was nominated again for president, but declined, explaining

> I have had a great deal of work to do in working up the Assocn. to its present condition, and I thought it but fair that I should retire and allow someone else to step into harness. Dr. Christie was chosen in my place. Before the meeting was adjourned a vote of thanks was moved by C. Dwyer and seconded by Dr. Christie in most flattering terms conveying the thanks of the Assocn to me for my past services. In acknowledging this vote, I said that it was a labor of love to work for the Assocn and that to God only must the

credit be given for the success which had attended the Assocn, and that, in
answer to the prayers that had been offered up for a blessing upon our work;
it is satisfactory beyond measure to me to contemplate what has been achieved
in Assocn work here, and I fervently pray that we may be blessed tenfold
more, until all the young men of this town have been brought to Jesus.
(Journal, vol. 2, 13 May 1869)

Although not accepting the nomination for reappointment as president, Rudolf
was voted in as a delegate at a large YMCA convention in Portland, Maine, in
July. At this convention the Portland Basics, a guide for the association which
was used until 1924, was drawn up. It assured control by evangelical church
members and focussed the association's function within the accepted religious and social structures of the day. When Pictou Town became host for
the very successful provincial YMCA convention in September 1869, Rudolf
was chosen first vice-president for Nova Scotia. An evangelical awakening
occurred as a result of this convention. Rudolf spoke and prayed every night
at their YMCA rooms as scores of earnest young men were brought to God.[37]
He mentioned numerous conversions of men and women that he had wit-
nessed. At a prayer meeting on 31 October, Rudolf judged that over five hundred people were present. Later, he reported that it "was observed by many
that the streets were never so quiet on this anniversary and that less
drunken[n]ess and rioting were noted than on any previous New Years Day"
(Journal, vol. 2, 1 January 1870). The goal of evangelicals to effect a transformation of culture in Pictou had been achieved.

There were benefits and costs to bear from this new evangelical culture.
On the one hand, creative philanthropic associations, such as the YMCA, fostered compassionate, less violent behaviour among men. They tried to develop
true Christian charity and friendship. Strong personal bonds were forged,
especially in smaller towns. It was a remarkable evangelical heritage for family life and for many men aspiring to middle-class status. Their moral authority now had a legitimate place in the political and social process. A new concept of psychological/spiritual influence entered social and political discourse;
invisible forms of restraint prevailed much more in social interaction.

On the other hand, tensions were embedded in this new ideal of Victorian evangelical character. Christian nurture in the home, in Sunday Schools,
and in young people's societies such as the YMCA enabled adults to supervise children's training but tended to reduce religion to morality. While
attempting to instill a degree of independence and autonomy in children,
their psychological strategies tended to cultivate intense emotional dependence on parents and on charismatic community leaders. David MacLeod
believes that these character-building endeavours were "an anxiety-driven

struggle" to balance competing contradictions within the evangelical move-ment—strength versus control, manliness yet dependence, virtue without femininity.[38] On the home front, domesticated wives, lacking power over their finances and wholly dependent on their husbands for material security and status, often used feelings or psychological strategies to influence their hus-bands' decisions. Men were urged to cultivate a high degree of self-reliance and self-sufficiency, and yet were enjoined to develop self-restraint and a strong sense of obligation to the needs of others. The concept of companion-ate marriage based on love, common values, and shared interests worked at cross purposes to the rising cult of domesticity, the notion of separate spheres of responsibility, and the increasing influence of mothers on their sons. By the 1870s, bourgeois men were disturbed by the identification of the home with the feminine. Their public character and its values were beginning to conflict with private domestic ideals.

While Rudolf in his diary reflections had only a limited understanding of these contradictions within his ideal of character, he did clearly enunciate in a public forum his deep commitment to evangelicalism. His prayer meetings and nightly talks at the YMCA rooms attested to his personal spiritual search for the inner meaning of his life; his attention to the daily needs of his fam-ily and the start-up work for the YMCA demonstrated his affirmation of ordi-nary life; and his joy in the natural development of his children and the sim-ple pleasure of gardening, as well as his daily journal writing, were testaments to his continuing search for moral understanding. He believed firmly that he and other human beings were creatures of God and were made in His image. As president of the YMCA, Rudolf was able to convey to many young men the vision that they had immortal souls and that they were agents of rational choice. This was the evangelical ideal of character. Rudolf had now acquired the self-esteem and mature self-confidence to be able to enunciate this ideal in public. He was recognized as a deeply committed Christian leader by the time of his departure from Pictou in 1870.

CHAPTER 7

Mature Character

A major test of public character for mid-Victorian self-employed males was whether or not they had succeeded in business and could provide their families with secure incomes and respectable status. In a business culture lacking our modern regulations and financial institutions, and with spheres of business, politics, and government intertwined, the individual's trustworthiness, or character, was assessed through face-to-face business dealings with family members and social colleagues, usually at the local or regional level. Business or bank failures (Bank of New Brunswick in 1868), or bank fraud (Commercial Bank in Saint John in 1868 and Bank of Nova Scotia in 1870) were thus perceived as the effect of managers with weak character. Such failures are now also recognized as symptoms of a changing financial order (see chapter 3) from one controlled at a local level by an elite group of merchants to an economy, after Confederation, increasingly regulated by the state and more and more affected by international trends. New endeavours were promoted that required a redeployment of local capital and a search for international capital. Railway building was supported by modern entrepreneurs in order to develop the hinterland, seek out markets in Central Canada, and connect isolated communities and entrepôts around the periphery of the Maritime provinces to major ports, such as Halifax and Saint John.[1]

Not only were there considerable risks involved in doing business, as the economy began to change from a traditional mercantile one into a form of proto-industrialization, but new roles were required of entrepreneurs.

They had to acquire larger amounts of venture capital, now by means of public share offerings; they had to learn management skills for more complex enterprises; they had to correctly forecast market demands; and they had to sell their product successfully. Above all, they had to rely increasingly on more distant investors for capital and for help in promoting their industrial projects.[2] A mistake in judgment regarding expansion or a faulty project reflected on the public character of the entrepreneurs, as Rudolf and the Primroses would discover.

Rudolf's diary, while giving his perspective on their ventures, also reveals his growing appreciation of the fact that financial acumen, size of capital, and social connections, rather than just personal character, increasingly determined a businessman's success in this transitional economic era. He was becoming far more realistic in his judgments. Rudolf was also aware that national political issues, resulting from the Confederation of all the British North American provinces would lead to a major reconfiguration of trade and to his future prospects of business success. His Pictou neighbours realized that the newer vision of an economy based on the Intercolonial Railway would seriously compromise their older mercantile trading economy; like other Maritime coastal communities, they opposed Confederation. At the abrogation of the Reciprocity Treaty with the United States in 1866 and with the increase of tariffs, Pictou's north-south coal exports received a setback. As outlined in chapter 3, the retired James Primrose continued to advise the three younger partners in their vigorous debates over the most feasible financial ventures to undertake in these uncertain times. While the 1864 launching of Primrose and Rudolf appeared to mark the three young men's coming of age and independence, their public characters and business judgments were still largely guided by the elder Primrose. As in the past, their main investments were in the exploitation of local resources and in shipping; but they were also venturing into new territory. They would learn, however, that their combined lack of expertise and their lack of control over external factors made them vulnerable to financial loss and character assassination. In Rudolf's case, it made him seriously reflect on his future and on the best path to safeguard his wife and children's security. It was in his decision to move that Rudolf displayed the maturity of his character and judgment. There was no guarantee that by leaving Pictou and the Primrose firm he would attain his goal of being a successful merchant or increase his reputation as a public figure. By 1870 the community recognized Rudolf as a mature evangelical leader. His acceptance of the firm's business failures and his realistic appraisal of his minority status in the Primrose firm would be looked on as his humble submission to events. His YMCA leadership would be seen as the result of a deeply developed inner conscience and resolve to improve society. His lengthy years of church work convinced the congregation of St. James Church that Rudolf had indeed gained public status and was their epitome of a responsible evangelical character. The excellent stewardship of his own and his extended family—his private character—as well as his achievements as a respectable bourgeois homeowner, would have reinforced Rudolf's public status. He had successfully balanced competing responsibilities, had reached a deeper sense of the meaning of his life through his diary reflections, and was willing to put his liberal idealism to the test—to entertain new challenges in an ever-shifting economic world.

But this runs ahead of the story. Five years earlier, buoyed by the enthusiastic reports of J.W. Dawson and other geologists, who were conducting extensive explorations in the area,[3] the three young partners and their elderly advisor continued to invest in mining ventures in hopes of future profits. In July 1865, after sending a miner to Polson's Lake, they bought shares at $20 each (Rudolf bought two shares) in the newly formed Mount Pleasant Copper and Iron Mining Co. In August 1865, their miner, Penrose, discovered copper at another place on the Salmon River, Guysboro County; they secured a license to search for the mother lode; J.D.B. Fraser and A.P. Ross of Pictou judged that Penrose's sample contained 60 per cent copper; a new company was formed and the stock issue was immediately subscribed for. By 26 August there was great disappointment. Rudolf reported,

> Mr. Primrose & Mr. Fraser returned from the Copper Mine this morning. The hopes of shareholders with visions of great fortunes are again doomed to disappointment. They report that the "lead" is small, and the rich specimens formed were in a corner of a wedge-like end of it next the brook. There is a small vein of very rich ore, nearly pure, which Mr. Fraser thought worthless, but he has since tested its value. This may lead down to the lode. It would be necessary to sink 50 feet or more down in the rock, before it might be found, if it exists. This would involve a great outlay and the company will have to be called together to decide whether they will go on or not. It is not likely they will do so. (Journal, vol. 2, 26 August 1865)

Rudolf's judgment was wrong. At a September meeting of the Mt. Pleasant Co., it was resolved to amalgamate with the Salmon River investment, pay expenditures of the latter out of company stock, abandon Polson's Lake, call a meeting to increase the capital of the company by $2,000, and develop the vein of copper at Salmon River. The elderly Primrose, however, was so disgusted with the risks involved that he transferred all of his shares to the firm of Rudolf and Primrose, so that each partner now held five shares: "Plenty to bring us a good share if it turns out well, and not a 'killing matter' as Mr. P.

says, should it be a failure. The ore found is exceedingly rich," Rudolf related, "and from an Assay made by the State Assayer, Mr. Hayes of Boston, of some samples sent, it contains 37 per cent of copper worth $180 per ton U.S. c[urrenc]y" (Journal, vol. 2, 25 September 1865). Rudolf sent specimens to Professor How at King's College, Windsor, who corroborated the Boston assayer's analysis. The following March, Rudolf noted that Penrose was continuing to tunnel and asking for direction. By May Penrose reported that prospects were "rather more encouraging, and also says he has heard of indications of coal oil being found in a well, and wants orders whether to do anything about it" (Journal, vol. 2, 8 May 1866). After a meeting of the directors of the company, it was resolved to keep the news of the oil quiet, lest the owner of the property learn about it, and to requisition the government for an extension of their lease for another year. In May 1866, John Hogg returned from the Salmon River exploration, reporting that very little oil existed. The Copper Co. directors decided to secure leases of the properties around the well on condition of payment of 5 per cent of oil raised. There were no further reports on the Mount Pleasant Co. before Rudolf left. According to Ray Guy, Pictou County's copper discoveries were not exploited.[4]

Another mining venture closer to home, however, produced great excitement. Coal exports in 1865 comprised 30 per cent of Nova Scotia's total exports. As noted in chapter 5, Fraser, with New York interests, organized the Acadia Coal Co., which worked the Acadia seam at Westville and built the connecting railway to Stellarton and to the pier at Pictou Landing. John Campbell secured another lease near Westville, which was sold in 1867 to Montreal interests and became the Intercolonial Coal Co., under the presidency of G.A. Drummond. In 1868, their first slope developed 14,000 tons of coal, and the company built a railway line to Middle River. In 1869 the Drummond Colliery, under James Dunn, Esq., began rapid production, reaching 105,545 tons by 1872, second only to the Acadia Coal Co. In 1869, as well, the Nova Scotia Coal Co. was founded at Westville; it built another railway to Middle River in 1871.[5] Pictou Town was challenged by this huge development of coal mines across the harbour. Entrepreneurs such as the Primroses and Fraser realized that coal, iron, and steel, stimulated by external demand, would spearhead the transition from a mercantile to an industrial economy.[6]

Rudolf reported in May 1865 that the firm's boring machine had bored 540 feet at the mill in Pictou. It passed through red sandstone, magnesium limestone, and fire clay, and managed to reach coal when its "shell" stuck. They got it free and followed the seam as far as Prince Street Church. They were searching at the gas works for a seam that cropped out above Patterson's field. Ross found the outcrop of a seam at Carriboo, but it was only six inches thick at the surface. The partners decided to secure two leases adjoining his. There were so many miners engaged in exploration in the Pictou area that they couldn't get anyone to investigate their claim at River Bourgeoise, Cape Breton. Another prospect near Truro, in which they sank $800, proved a delusion. As Rudolf commented, "We are paying for our experience in mining business" (Journal, vol. 2, 24 July 1865); but the young partners were not discouraged. They sent a miner to Pictou Island and to Merigomish, but neither proved worth developing. In April 1866, Rudolf reported, "[they] offered T.S. Lindsay $2000 for his quarter of the McKay coal mine near New Glasgow. It contains a seam of about 4 feet of coal, and a seam of 'oil shale' of 7 feet thickness; some of this yields 60 gallons of crude oil to the ton. We agreed to give $500 down, $500 each in 3, 6 and 9 months. He promised to let us know whether he would accept our offer in a few days. There is a demand for oil coal [coal oil], and we think we could make something out of it. The remaining 3/4ths is owned in New Glasgow" (Journal, vol. 2, 13 April 1866). Rudolf and his partners were learning to be more efficient in their assessments. They were also profiting from coal freights during a period of demand occasioned by the US Civil War. They chartered two Cape Breton coal vessels for Boston at US $3.00, but Rudolf noted in April 1866 that Pictou mines (at $2.50) were priced higher than Cape Breton mines, which were selling at freight rates of $1.50 to $1.87. After the United States' abrogation of the Reciprocity Treaty in 1866, the US duty on coal was $1.25 a ton; therefore it was more profitable for Americans to buy cheaper Cape Breton coal. A combination of new American duties, competition from Pennsylvania coal mines after the Civil War, and eventual closing of American markets for coal led to a recession in the coal industry beginning in 1867.

Two years before he left, Rudolf reported that petroleum, or coal oil, had been discovered near Lake Ainslie in Cape Breton. A company was formed, with the Primroses and Rudolf and six others as shareholders. They made an agreement with the proprietor, John McDonald and his siblings, to buy five acres for $1,200 with the right to bore anywhere on his two-hundred-acre farm for $800 more, and to receive every thirteenth gallon. (The proprietor owned the mining rights.) The Lake Ainslie Oil Co. was formed in November 1868; Rudolf was appointed secretary-treasurer and his neighbour, John Crerar, chairman. They were planning to bore in the spring. Unfortunately, there were no further reports of this venture before Rudolf left. Petroleum had been discovered in southwestern Ontario in 1857, and with landward economic development after Confederation, Nova Scotia's deep underwater resources of oil and gas remained untapped until recently.

One other mining venture was embarked on, that of iron ore at Merigomish: "Dr. Dawson, who has examined specimens of it, says it contains 55 percent of iron, and is valuable especially for the finer kinds of iron. It is only a few miles from coal, and a like distance from a shipping place. Mr. Copland of Merigomish who brought it to our notice has a share in it. There are five of us—P & R—Copland—Dr. Dawson, Jno. Crerar & A.P. Ross. Mr. Ross went down today with Sir Wm. Logan [first director of the Geological Survey of Canada] to examine the place and to see whether it exists in quantity or not" (Journal, vol. 2, 26 October 1868). In 1872, the Hope Iron Works were founded at New Glasgow with capitalization of $4,000. Rudolf and his partners, it would appear, were anticipating the successful transition to a new economy of industrial capitalism. In fact, two of his partners, Clarence Primrose and John Crerar, in 1882 were listed as leading mercantile families in Pictou with an estimated pecuniary strength of $75,000–$125,000 and extensive shares in the Nova Scotia Steel Company, established in 1882 with capitalization of $142,000.[7]

Shipping was a more successful venture for Rudolf during the late 1860s. The *Lord Chancellor* spent ten months carrying freight to Quebec, then on to Ireland, from Troon, Scotland, to Havana with coal, and then to New York with sugar, arriving at Pictou on 24 May 1865 with three hundred barrels of flour and twenty barrels of crushed sugar. Rudolf also noted that it brought back fifteen tons of Scottish coal, which they sold among the owners; it was much superior to Pictou coal, which he said was now largely mixed with stone. On 9 June the *Lord Chancellor* left the loading ground dock (across the entrance channel to Pictou Harbour from Pictou Town) with 828 tons of coal on board, priced at $2.70 (gold standard), bound for Boston. Rudolf judged the prospects for shipping then to be "very dark looking. We do not know what to do with her next. She may find employment at Boston" (Journal, vol. 2, 9 June 1865). Rudolf next reported her at Barrington, NS, in mid-January 1866. Captain Daniel McDonald informed them by telegram that she had twice been blown off course with loss of sails. He was loaded from Cardenas, Cuba, with molasses for Boston. Delay for repairs would be necessary. In mid-February, the barque had arrived at Saint John to load shooks (wooden pieces for making boxes, barrels, or furniture) bound for Cuba. By mid-May she had arrived at New York after only a ten-day passage.

While not revealing any profits made from these ventures, Rudolf and his partners considered investment in shipping to be lucrative enough to expand. In May 1866, they bought one-quarter ownership of a new brigantine called the *W.W. Lord*, built in Prince Edward Island. She weighed 271 tons and was classed A4 (surveyed good for four years) at Lloyds.' They paid $9,200 and considered it cheap. One-quarter was paid in cash out of earnings from the *Lord Chancellor,* and the remainder was to be paid in six months. The brother-in-law, George Walker, of one of the partners (Forbes) was to be captain, and Walker's brother, became mate. Rudolf and his partners decided to invest their earnings from shipping in more vessels.

In September they seized their first opportunity. Captain Forbes purchased a wrecked barque, the *Henquist,* and its cargo for $10,400. The cargo was oak and pine timbers and spars, invoiced at over $9,000. The vessel was copper-fastened and classed for seven years at Lloyds': "We have a great bargain in her," reported Rudolf, "She will want new rigging, and spars, having been dismasted, and will probably cost $8,000 to refit her. After sale of cargo, and paying for repairs, she will cost us about $12,000, or half her cost. Capt. Forbes, Capt. Burchell, Capt. Knowles [who subsequently declined the offer and was replaced by Alex Patterson], and we are each owners of a fourth. Capt. Burchell will likely take command of her" (Journal, vol. 2, 7 September 1866). They hired a steamer, *Napoleon 3,* at $300 per day to tow the *Henquist* from St. Georges Bay, Newfoundland, to Pictou (total cost $1,000). By November she was repaired and ready for sea, displaying a private flag, blue with a white cross. Rudolf considered it "very conspicuous. It was my design, and I had hard work to get it adopted, as the old gentleman don't like *crosses.* He calls it a Roman Catholic affair" (Journal, vol. 2, 10 November 1866). On 21 March 1867, the *Henquist* arrived at Boston after only nineteen days from Cape Clear, Ireland; she had £824 worth of freight on board. On 6 April, Captain Burchell sent a telegram to them reporting that he was going to Navassor, a small island near Jamaica, to load guano for Hamburg, Germany, at 30 shillings 6 pence per ton.

By this time the *Lord Chancellor* was running into difficulties. She arrived in New York in late April 1867 from Buenos Aires, Argentina, and was reported to be leaking. In October, Captain McDonald had to be replaced because he was unwell. Captain Lauder was appointed master and was assisted by Captain Page because Lauder was recovering from fever. In November 1867, Rudolf reported that the numerous storms caused many wrecks, making local insurance companies suffer. But the *Will Lord* got to Shediac, New Brunswick, before the last storm. She was to load deals (softwood rough planks each measuring a minimum of six feet long, seven inches wide, and three to four inches thick) at 80 shillings for Bristol Channel. The *Henquist* was to sail on 24 October from Boston to Melbourne, Australia, and the *Lord Chancellor* was to sail from Boston for Falmouth, England. By 1 January they heard that both vessels had arrived safely, the former at Gloucestor, New South Wales, Australia, and the latter at Antwerp, Belgium.

On the strength of these successful voyages, the partners signed an agreement with James Kitchin of River John to purchase one-quarter ownership of a new barque, "at $36 per ton register—to be classed 1½ for 7 years American Lloyds. Mr. Kitchin is anxious to sell," reported Rudolf, "as he does not want to hold so much shipping and has asked that we keep the price a secret as he would not build another at such a price. His vessels have a reputation, and he says that this one is superior to any that he has built, as he was desirous of giving a standing to his survey having been recently appointed Surveyor to American Lloyds" (Journal, vol. 2, 27 March 1868). Two other people were to purchase a one-quarter share each, and they intended to give Captain MacDonald (now recovered) a one-sixteenth ownership and appoint him master. For the first time, the young entrepreneurs contradicted their mentor: "Mr. Primrose has bitterly opposed this speculation," continued Rudolf, "and predicts all sorts of things from it, but we have looked at it, and think we see our way clear and will come out all right."

Meanwhile, the *Henquist* made it safely to Melbourne and by May 1868 was returning to London "at 1 penny for wool, 3/4 for unwashed and 70/ for tallow, and [Captain Burchell writes] that her freight will amt. to £3000 Sterling which is very great. We are greatly pleased at this result," Rudolf reported, "for we feared she would do badly when she went out. Freights have since declined and now only half the above rates for wool could be had. West India freights are also good [60/ for sugar]....We hope the Lord Chancellor will arrive to catch this rate as well as the W.W. Lord, both of which are now on [their] way to Cuba, and must be there" (Journal, vol. 2, 13 May 1868). Ten days later their new barque, to be named *Rothiemay* after the birthplace of James Primrose,[8] was safely launched. This was the ship on which Rudolf arranged to have his brother Moyle serve. It was towed from River John to Pictou on 2 June 1868. Rudolf described her as "a very nicely painted [ship] and in good order. Said to be a pretty model, and well built" (Journal, vol. 2, 4 June 1868). He was proud of her appearance going up the harbour with their private flag on the foremast. Her first charter was to load deals from Richibucto, New Brunswick, for Liverpool at 85/, considered a good freight. On 5 June, Rudolf spent the day getting her papers made out, including the declaration of ownership and the ship's registration. Kitchin sold out his quarter to A.J. Patterson and to Captain McDonald (his increased ownership was one-eighth).

In October 1868, Rudolf noted the return of Captain McDonald from Quebec by boat. He had sold the *Lord Chancellor* at a good price; she was now called the *Harriet* of Bordeaux. McDonald was appointed surveyor to the Bordeaux Lloyds.' Captain Lauder now was master of the *Rothiemay* and was reported to be in Fernando Po (off the Nigerian coast) in January 1869, hoping to get a redwood freight from a river nearby to take to England. When Rudolf was preparing to leave in July 1870, he listed their fleet: three ships chartered out of Boston at $20 for lumber to Buenos Aires—the *Rainbow,* the *Rothiemay* and *Wenonah* (just launched at Tatamagouche); the *W.W. Lord* loading coal for Portland; the *Amoy* coming to Pictou from Castine, Maine; and the *Henquist* at Chifu, China, seeking freight. When he left Pictou in September, Rudolf kept his interest in the ships and was to add further English vessels to his portfolio when he moved to Birkenhead. Less risky than mining, shipping was proving to be profitable. Rudolf knew his co-owners and ships' masters, and he trusted the Primrose firm to continue to manage their ships prudently. It was estimated that shipbuilding and ship materials from the Pictou Ship Registry gave entrepreneurs a 7.62 per cent return on their investment in 1870.[9] Pictou was to remain the fourth ship-building region in Nova Scotia until 1914. Vessels in Nova Scotia's merchant fleet, as the Rudolf-Primrose ships epitomized, were world class in both size and efficiency. They benefitted from the rapidly expanding world-trade opportunities, especially after the opening of the Suez Canal in 1869. As Eric Sager notes, the shipowner was a trader first and a shipowner second. He considers this the reason why shipowners such as James Primrose were receptive to a landward development strategy: "Confederation afforded new opportunities for commercial activity because of the promised railroads and entrepôt growth. Shipowners have a vested interest in high freight rates; commodity traders have a vested interest in low freight rates."[10] The Primrose sons and Rudolf, however, also recognized the value of continuing the Maritime tradition of seagoing trading.

As a strong supporter of Confederation and future trade with central Canada, the elder Primrose believed that railways would be the major engine of the region's economic transformation towards modernity. He had already introduced steam-powered technology for their tobacco plant in Pictou (in April 1866); anticipating the completion of the eastern extension of the Intercolonial Railway to Pictou Landing (completed 1867), Primrose correctly forecast rapid expansion of new roads, opening of new towns, and development of Nova Scotia's extensive inland timber resources along these new transportation routes to its numerous ports.[11] As related earlier, he had tried to win the government contract for building the railway, but Pictou's local contractors lost out to Halifax's distinguished civil engineer, Sandford Fleming, who in 1857 had been chief engineer of Ontario's Northern Railway and in 1863 was chief engineer of the Intercolonial Railway (ICR). He was awarded the contract for surveying the line of the ICR's Eastern Extension. The railway was to be completed by 1 October 1866. The work was not nearly ready on time, however, probably in part due to the pluralistic work patterns (farming, timber-cutting, fishing, and stevedoring) of Pictou County labourers. To avoid jeopardizing his contract, Fleming staged a mock opening at Fishers Grant on 29 September, which Rudolf described as a "great farce....At 4 oclock the track was not all laid. Men were busily engaged ahead of a trolley with rails, laying the sleepers on the mud, without any ballasting. In some cases the sleepers were *hanging* from the rods, instead of the rails resting on *them*. By six oclock, a track was thus complete, and Mr. Fleming, Mr. Longley, Railway Com[missioner] and a few others rode over the line at a slow rate, came across [by boat from Pictou Landing] to Pictou [Town], and went to Halifax next morning to blazon abroad in the city papers the completion of this part of the road" (Journal, vol. 2, 29 September 1866).

In contrast to his earlier conciliatory stance towards those he disliked, Rudolf now strongly condemned Fleming's business practices, moral character, and political abuse of power: "How any man could have the hardihood to thus insult the common sense of the inhabitants, and those who came from abroad [to see the opening], is surprizing, but when one considers all the circumstances connected with Mr. Flemings obtaining the contract for the road, wonder ceases, for he is equal to any degree of effrontery and deception. The road is not fit for travelling upon—Station houses are not even commenced—there are no wharves—no steamer—nothing in fact, that ought to be completed at this time to put the line in working order" (Journal, vol. 2, 29 September 1866). Rudolf was proved wrong, however, and (as chapter 5 discusses), probably because of lobbying by Pictou's James MacDonald, the Conservative government completed the promised Pictou Extension.[12] These railway developments proved to be a foretaste of the future; contracts, political power, and business decisions would increasingly be made outside the Pictou district. With improvement in transportation, connection to central Canada, and bigger projects, financial capital was needed on a much greater scale. The elder Primrose eagerly sought out the opportunities offered by what would prove to be an era of rapidly growing world trade. He began to invest in enterprises beside the proposed railway line.

In September 1865, Clarence and his father went to the Black River, near the source of the Salmon River, to look over a mill and 1,100 acres of woodland connected with it, which had just been purchased by James Porter and Alex Douglas from Captain McKenzie. Acting on behalf of Helen Primrose, whose 1,000-acre inheritance from her father (William Primrose) had mistakenly been regranted to someone else, they were impressed with the location of the Porter and Douglas land, excellently situated beside the proposed railway line, with crossroads leading to Truro, to the nearby Highland settlement of Earl Town, and to Stewiacke in the centre of the province. The settlement was named Georgetown and a railway station was planned. Porter and Douglas proposed that the firm take one-third interest (outlay of £330) with them in the mill and property, that the firm lease 3,000 additional acres of Crown land as a source of timber, and that when the railway was completed the partners advance more funds to build a lumber mill. They pointed out, as well, that "there are many valuable sites on the property which runs for 5 miles along the [Black R]iver, for manufacturing establishments, and some day may see cloth and cotton factories in operation there. We have agreed to join with them in the speculation, and have sent to Truro for a plan of the county to enable us to select the land required" (Journal, vol. 2, 29 September 1865). At this initial stage, the six entrepreneurs shared an optimistic dream of future capitalistic opportunity; they had little inkling of the risks involved and the complexity of their undertaking. Nor did Rudolf and the Primroses consider their lack of expertise in the lumber industry. Their main consideration was that it would prove to be a profitable investment and that the land could "probably sell for a high price should a town spring up there" (Journal, vol. 2, 30 September 1865).

When Rudolf and Clarence took a sleigh trip to Georgetown at the end of January 1866, they were given a tour of the site by Porter and a millwright, Mr. Leake, from Amherst. Rudolf enthusiastically endorsed the site ("I am very much pleased with its appearance, and think it will be the centre for a great settlement and trade"[Journal, vol. 2, 30 January 1866]) and the plans for a new dam and mill. They asked for specifications to be drawn up for the timber and frame required and also asked for a tender for the work from Porter. These were presented in February. After lengthy business consultations, the partners decided to postpone building the new dam and mill and to repair the old mill (estimated cost $200). They agreed to a contract to have Porter and Douglas saw 200,000–400,000 feet of flooring of specified lengths: "12–14 & 16 ft. and 1½ thick—part of it may be 1 in. thick, to be delivered and piled on the railway trollies for transportation @ $6.50 per M [thousand feet] superficial measure. They are to have the use of the Mill, and also the gift of the trees on the land, and the above price is for getting out, and sawing the stuff" (Journal, vol. 2, 5 February 1866).

The first sign of trouble appeared when discussion began on future plans, estimated to cost $12,000 for a new dam, a new mill, and machinery. Porter and Douglas acknowledged that they could not take on one-third of this cost, and would only be able to assume one-eighth (Porter) and one-tenth (Douglas) of it. The other shareholders authorized the partners to sell the remaining shares, leaving a profit of $250 to Porter and $280 to Douglas. Howard was to act as trustee of the property and the mill henceforth would be referred to as Howard Mills. Porter and Douglas asked for an advance of funds and pay of $100 to enable them to get provisions and to commence work before the expected arrival of the railway in May 1867.

Rudolf was charged with the task of lobbying members of the House of Assembly to ask for a repeal of the act authorizing railroad companies to cut down trees on Crown lands for their railway sleepers (a bill to that effect was introduced in the House), and to secure more Crown land leases. In May, he and Clarence went to Georgetown to meet the arbitrators appointed by the government to award damage done by the railway to tree cutting on their property. A new ten-horsepower engine was delivered to the mill in June; by August, the mill was in operation cutting floor boards. A road to Truro, Rudolf reported, was partially opened and graded. The property was still remote, however, and in November Rudolf and Clarence had to walk five miles inland after being dropped off the Truro stagecoach at Waters. They found railcars travelling daily from Truro carrying stone for the railroad bed; the bridge over the Calvary River was near completion. Passengers and mail were expected to be able to travel from Truro to West River by January 1867. A telegraph was in operation at the new station and accommodation was available at the new Government House. A road was being built to connect Earl Town with Georgetown. The street was laid out at the rear of the station, and they expected soon to be selling lots to settlers. Above all, 150,000 feet of flooring had been sawed, and was ready for the arrival of the railroad. Because of similarity of name with Georgetown, PEI, the railway commissioner was ordered by the House to change the name of the settlement. Primrose chose Riversdale as the new name.

Just before shipment of the lumber, the shareholders inspected the site and found the management of Porter and Douglas wanting:

> We had a long interview with Porter & Douglas today about the property at *Riversdale* which resulted in our buying out their interest. We have been dissatisfied with Porters management for some time. We have found that self-interest was uppermost, and that he looked more to his own profit than ours. And moreover that he has been selling *liquor* contrary to our positive and strongly expressed wishes. We determined to allow no one to open a rum shop on our lands there and that any one to whom we leased lands should come under a condition in the lease to forfeit it, should he sell liquor. And in the face of this Mr. Porter sells it in his own shop! (Journal, vol. 2, 29 January 1867)

They decided to buy out Porter and Douglas for $800 and $400 (their initial payments), as well as the same amounts as profits on their shares, and to purchase from Porter his house, barn, and several shanties. Porter was given until July to quit possession. In the meantime, he was to get 300,000 feet of logs sawn for flooring as well as a lot of timber cut. Rudolf admitted the firm's mistake: "Douglas is a very honest upright fellow, but no match for Porter. We relied upon him to keep Porter in check, but he said he could not do it." Fortunately they all parted on good terms. The firm now owned the entire Riversdale project and had added considerably to their initial payment of $10,000. Rudolf judged that they had paid Porter and Douglas liberally, but that they were glad to be rid of them and have complete control of the enterprise.

In March, they sent the planer from the Clarence Mills in Pictou to Riversdale to begin planing the flooring. Sandy McKimmie was appointed manager of the Howard Mills in July. Unfortunately, he suffered a fall of six feet from a pile of timber and became unconscious. Rudolf rushed over the new railway line to see him, and was relieved to report McKimmie nearly fully recovered. Clarence went to Boston in August to purchase a planing machine for the mills; he supervised its installation in October 1867. While they now had a more upright manager, the partners discovered he was not necessarily a good accountant. Rudolf spent all day in February 1868 trying to straighten out a year's work; he reported the next day, "Got the Riversdale accounts adjusted and balanced off this afternoon—a good job done" (Journal, vol. 2, 21 February 1868). That April they purchased Porter's eight hundred acres of leased Crown land for $400. They began to search for other enterprises to establish at Riversdale.

In June 1868, they had a long meeting with John Sullivan, an Englishman who had had a large mill constructed in England to manufacture paper from straw. He had spent all his capital in perfecting the process, but had lost the mill and his health while attempting to manage it for the company that had taken it over. After a year's rest, he now wanted to begin again with new partners and increased capitalization. Sullivan proposed either $110,000 for a two-machine mill, or $80,000 for one machine. He promised very large profits "on *paper*," Rudolf noted (Journal, vol. 2, 29 June 1868); he described Sullivan as "ardent, active and full of his scheme. We had not got much capital to invest in this, but could put the price of the land and timber etc. into it." Sullivan and Clarence visited Riversdale, and Rudolf reported that he was "very favorably impressed with the location and water, which is very soft, and suitable for paper making" (Journal, vol. 2, 30 June 1868). Rudolf, Clarence, and Sullivan returned to Riversdale two days later, wading upriver to further explore the site. They decided to hire a surveyor to measure the site, and Sullivan went over to Prince Edward Island to ascertain whether he could get enough straw for his mill; he concluded there would be no difficulty in obtaining what he required. Sullivan stayed for the rest of the month perfecting his plans. They prepared estimates of the paper mill and wrote a prospectus in order to attract capitalists in Halifax for their venture.

Rudolf and Sullivan travelled to Halifax at the end of the month. They had a subscription of $10,000 from Rudolf's brother-in-law, Alex Scott, in Scotland. John McLean, Rudolf's YMCA friend, also promised to subscribe and was anxious to see the mill started. The elder Primrose wrote a letter of introduction for them to Mather Almon, president of the BNS, but he declined to do anything for them. After five days of running about Halifax, Rudolf began to realize the defects of their prospectus: "Cannot get many of the Halifax people to take stock. They all want to be assured of a market for the paper we make and unless we shew them for certain that it can be sold at remunerative rates, they will not take hold of the thing" (Journal, vol. 2, 5 August 1868). After consultation with McLean and Howard (McLean's brother-in-law), they decided to return home and go to Boston later on to get reliable information on paper prices and on possible markets.

Their reputation and public character were at stake. Earlier that year, Rudolf had recorded a fierce newspaper attack by E.M. McDonald, owner and editor of the *Eastern Chronicle* and now an anti-Confederate, on their firm "and others, for obtaining a lease of a railway lot, and water privileges near the terminus at Fishers Grant [across the harbour from Pictou Town]. It accuses us by name of having been influenced by this to vote as we did at the Elections lately. We wrote to the Editors to stop [their] paper to us. It is a vile calumny, and will not injure us" (Journal, vol. 2, 13 January 1868). Fearful of the implications of Confederation for their economy, in the provincial elections of 1867 Nova Scotians voted in thirty-six Liberals (anti-Confederates) and only two Conservatives. As Unionists (pro-Confederation) and strong Liberals, the Primrose firm was an anomaly. Pro-Confederate Liberals shortly thereafter incorporated themselves into the federal Conservative party and became Liberal-Conservatives. In the meantime, the firm tried to keep a low profile in Pictou Town. On Dominion Day 1868, the partners "had agreed not to hoist [their flag] out of deference to the feelings of our Anti friends, but Archy [their office boy] put it up without asking any questions and of course once up, we could not haul it down. We do not care to exasperate them anymore than we can help" (Journal, vol. 2, 1 July 1868). Rudolf's previous family admiration for Joseph Howe, now leader of the anti-Confederate party, had greatly soured. At the opening of the Drummond Colliery, owned by the Intercolonial Coal Mining Co., in October 1868, Rudolf was disgusted with Howe's speech: "Mr. Howe in response to a call for him made a long rambling speech which from its coarseness, obscenity, and pointlessness, was a disgrace to him. He had the bad taste to introduce politics at this occasion, and made some very rude remarks about 'Canadians' forgetting or ignoring that we were all the guests [Mr. Drummond, president of ICM, was from Montreal] of Canadians, or largely so this day" (Journal, vol. 2, 1 October 1868).[13]

Meanwhile, the partners went ahead with their plans. They sent Rudolf and Sullivan to Saint John and Boston in August to investigate paper markets in New Brunswick and in the United States. After consulting J. and A. McMillan, large New Brunswick stationers, and their manager, Mr. Whitney, who said there could be a large market for paper in their province and promised to compile statistics as to quantity, they left for Portland and Boston. They began their inquiry at the office of the BNS agent, Mr. Odiorne. After meeting paper dealers and newspaper offices, they reported "various success— some said we could not sell paper readily, and one large House said they could dispose of 3 tons of such as we could make, per day. The sum of our investigations," Rudolf wrote, "is that we can sell the paper, but whether at the prices we can get 14 or 15 cents it will be profitable remains to be seen. *Rice Kendall & Co.*, who said they could sell any quantity of our paper said they supplied the New York markets with paper, and that Boston was *the* paper market, and that New York was supplied to a great extent from here" (Journal, vol. 2, 21 August 1868).

Armed with a more detailed prospectus, Rudolf, Howard, and Sullivan journeyed to Halifax in September. Now they were asking for capital of $100,000 on shares of $200 each, promising a profit of 41 per cent; they hoped "to make a final push for the stock, and if we don't succeed must abandon it for the present anyway" (Journal, vol. 2, 9 September 1868). By the end of October, they had only acquired a total of $79,000. They decided to settle up with Sullivan for his expenses to date, and he left by train for Canada. At the end of December, Rudolf wrote that their paper company was "in a doubtful position. We have been getting letters lately from McLean and by the last English mail from Scott expressing doubts respecting the paying prospects, and further that they had signed for their stock upon the faith they had in us as business men and that we had fully investigated the matter. Their inquiries however are not so satisfactory as they could wish, and they seem desirous of fastening upon us the responsibility of guaranteeing the profitableness of the Mill which we cannot, and therefore will not do" (Journal, vol. 2, 30 December 1868). The partners decided to leave further efforts to obtain shareholders to Sullivan and to the other shareholders, but they would not actively pursue the matter.

Rudolf revealed their vulnerability to character assassination at this stage: "It is made an objection that we being interested in the property at Riversdale are unduly influenced thereby, and are perhaps carried away by it to try to get the Mill erected at the risk of the stockholders. To this we reply, that we risk all we get for the site, and $6000 besides, and if it is a failure we lose all. We sen[t] a copy of the letter to McLean to Scott, so that he can see our views. Scott asked us to reduce his subscription one half if we could." On receipt of this letter, Scott became frightened about his liability and asked that his subscription be cancelled. McLean, who had lost a great deal of money because of the bankruptcy of his father-in-law, Archibald Campbell, on another matter wrote them "a most impertinent letter, evidently dictated when in a passion….We replied calmly, explaining that we had done nothing to call forth such a letter. He answered saying that he had been hasty…and that he felt so sore about losing such a large amount of money that that must be his excuse" (Journal, vol. 2, 11 January 1869).

Far from being deterred by this setback, which could be viewed as a chastening introduction to the world of financial capitalism, the partners embarked on another venture, albeit on a much smaller scale, to build a spool mill at Riversdale. C.H. Dunlop, manager of a New Brunswick spool mill that had burned down (his tools were in the bank's possession) arrived at Pictou with his family in September 1868. This time the partners decided to finance it like their ships, with limited ownership. The partners bought one-fourth of the speculation and the remaining three-fourths was bought by Scott, McLean, and J.W. Doull, a Halifax merchant and a director of the BNS. They took out a contract for the buildings at a cost of $2,700 and ordered Montgomery and Co. of Halifax to make the engines and machinery for driving the tools. Dunlop was to receive a salary of $1,000 while the works were being built and $1,200 thereafter, with 10 per cent of the profits.

The spool mill commenced operations in mid-January 1869. Dunlop brought them samples of the beech and birch spools. Rudolf reported on the eleventh that the "wood works very well and he is quite pleased with it. He is going to make up a case of them to go home [to Britain] by this weeks steamer (Friday she leaves) as a sample for Messrs. Brooks & Co. and Coats & Co. who have given us orders" (Journal, vol. 2, 11 January 1869).[14] Two days later, Clarence and Rudolf took the train over to the spool mill. Unfortunately, it was not in operation; the main shaft was out of order. Dunlop took the foot of the shaft to Montgomery in Halifax to be repaired. Once again, Rudolf reported that they were disappointed by their manager's performance: "Dunlops estimate of the cost of the Mill, and Machinery will be exceeded by the actual outlay 50 per cent. He has made a great miscalculation, and it shakes our confidence in his calculations as to profit, upon which we were induced to go into the speculation. We will have to exercise a very strict supervision over the outlay and management of the establishment" (Journal, vol. 2, 16 January 1869).

By the end of January, the mill had started again with six blocking machines at work. Rudolf went to Riversdale with James Primrose to get Dunlop's accounts in order preparatory to a meeting two days later with McLean and Doull, who came up from Halifax by special train to see the spool mill. On 2 February 1869, they all met at Pictou to go over the accounts, to decide on total capitalization, and to arrange a $10,000 line of credit with the BNS. They decided to apply for an act of incorporation for a total capital of $40,000 in 80 shares at $500 each. The Rudolf and Primrose firm were to be agents and would take over the management of the mill's business for a commission of 2½ per cent. They would employ a clerk at the mill and pay him out of the working capital.

Rudolf was to take on the financial management and accounting responsibilities. He settled the Montgomery engine repair bill for a reduced sum of $95. He expected to visit Riversdale every two weeks to pay the workers and to look after the accounts. Rudolf reported on 22 February 1869 that two cases of spools were sent to Coats & Co. of Paisley by steamer for Liverpool. This was their first shipment; one case contained 107 gross, the other 207 gross. Unfortunately, Coats and Co. rejected the shipment, and Rudolf reported that

> They are not made properly—badly finished and the wood too dark colored in some. We have written repeatedly and impressed verbally upon Mr. Dunlop the absolute necessity of making good work, especially our first samples. He has sent home [to England] spools with the *bark* on—rough ends where the block has been too short, and imperfect ones in other particulars. We are convinced that he is utterly incapable of managing the Mill efficiently. He is honest and well intentioned but with no head, or force [of character]. We have written to McLean telling him of the difficulties and asking whether we ought not to bring Mr. D's connection with the Mill to a close. Dunlop said he could find friends to buy [him] out, if the proprietors were dissatisfied. We also wrote Scott to the same effect. (Journal, vol. 2, 7 April 1869)

McLean and Doull replied by telegram urging them to dismiss Dunlop and to act promptly, which they apparently did by letter on 9 April. Rudolf revealed that they had spent $5,000 investing in the mill and that they were "in an undoubted mess" (Journal, vol. 2, 16 April 1869). One ray of consolation was that they managed to sell the Howard Mills (floorboard) property to the Reverend George Patterson[15] to set up his brother-in-law, John Miller, who had been thrown out of work by Archibald Campbell's failure. The Rudolf-Primrose firm took the stock of flooring on hand, which was what was owed them, "over $7000 and also $2200 for the property being a very great reduction on its cost. We are however glad to get rid of it," Rudolf wrote, "and it will give us the command of a large sum of money that was locked up there." He revealed that the elder Primrose was beginning to worry that they would all be ruined. To allay his anxiety, Howard offered to pay back half the money his father had lent them ($8,000) as soon as the flooring was sold, but his father declined the offer, with the exception of $2,400. With this added to his other investments, James Primrose considered that he had sufficient to live on and would leave the remainder of his investment in the Riversdale project. This would prove unfortunate. On 20 April Rudolf wrote an excited account about the demise of the spool mill:

> I little thought last evening that after paying the men at the Spool Mill, that it would be the *last* payment to them, and that my coming over yesterday out of the usual routine, should have been to see the *burning* down of the whole establishment....At 4 oclock we were alarmed by the cry of fire. McKimmie [at Howard Mills] heard the noise and called up the household. On hurrying out I saw the flames rising out of the top of the Mill at the end next the engine. On getting to the Mill I found it filled with a dense smoke which prevented any admission. I asked Mr. Dunlop if he had got out the papers from the office. He said no, that he had not even saved his boots or good clothes which were in the office. I got the windows broken in the office, and tried to reach the pay books off the table, as I had left the roll there the evening before. I seized hold of some papers and had to withdraw....(Journal, vol. 2, 20 April 1869)

They were able to rescue most of the papers and books on the desk. In two hours, the whole building had burned to the ground, and machinery and tools were lost. Apparently the fire had started in the wood shavings piled inside to fuel the furnaces. The watchman tried to douse it with buckets of water to no avail. Dunlop was sleeping in the mill office; he tried to open the steam valves but could not because of the smoke, and he himself barely escaped. Rudolf estimated their loss to be about $10,000; the mill was only partially insured and their expenditure had been over $20,000. As he noted, this was the second time Dunlop had been burnt out. The workmen, most of whom were from Scotland, were much worse off. They had large families and were wholly dependent on the mill work to support them.

Four days later Rudolf, Clarence, and Mr. D. Dickson, the insurance agent, went to Riversdale to inspect the ruins of the spool mill. Only the engine and boilers were retrievable: "We set the Scotch hands to work to gather up the fragments, and get a shed over the engine. These men are on pay being hired for 6 mos. We want to make some arrangements with them to get them home to the old country again," wrote Rudolf (Journal, vol. 2, 24 April 1869). On 3 May, Rudolf returned to Riversdale to pay off the Scottish labourers and to pay their passage home, as well as a fortnight's extra wages. In turn, they gave up their six-month's agreement but decided to move on to the United States rather than returning to Scotland. Despite the tragedy, the partners decided to move the spool factory beside the existing sawmill. Three or four of the original "blocker" and "finisher" spool machines could be reused. Instead of spools, they decided to manufacture blocks. In November they sent samples to Scotland, and in January 1870 Rudolf reported that four machines were in working order and that they had an order for 4,000 gross from the J. Clarke Co., Paisley. Once again, however, they found Dunlop's estimates to be unreliable. Rudolf reported that the "freight on the blocks is so great as they are so bulky that it eats up all they sell for" (Journal, vol. 2, 28 January 1870). The whole Riversdale experience had been a business lesson for Rudolf.

As Eric Sager observes, "The merchant capitalists of Atlantic Canada operated in conditions of pervasive uncertainty. Very often they were investing in industries with which they had no prior experience. Their prediction of future returns on capital was not based upon personal or local experience, but upon information transmitted from elsewhere."[16] These merchant capitalists were also beginning to experience other effects of economic transformation. For example, the Primrose-Rudolf firm's tobacco business, which had yielded profits of from £3,000–£5,000 in the period 1865–1867, began to face competition from new firms in New Glasgow and Cape Breton, and a five-cent federal government duty (total fifteen cents) on all their stock in bond.

Rudolf's assessment of their Riversdale financial disasters demonstrated his maturity of character by this time. He realized that the partners had been willing to risk a substantial amount of their capital in the several ventures there, but had not kept close control, as they had in the Pictou region, of the on-site business management or of the quality of product. While Rudolf himself had attracted large investments in the ventures from his friend McLean and brother-in-law, Alex Scott, their diatribes and threatened pull-out when downturns occurred made him also realize that even close associates would impugn his public character should they lose their money. MacDonald's political attack on them confirmed Rudolf's earlier low opinion of politicians. Above all, it demonstrated how, even with the best of intentions, businessmen who invested too hastily into schemes that they could not control were in danger of losing not only their public reputation but any future possibility of raising venture capital for other modern projects—their public character determined their business prospects. In this economic climate, shrewd judgments were even more necessary.

Rudolf was also experiencing doubts about his future relationship with his partners, particularly with the aging elder Primrose, whose judgment it had been to explore landward business ventures, and with Howard, whose personality he found difficult. Because the brothers and their father owned the majority of shares in their firm, they would retain the bulk of the assets (the building premises and even the good name of the firm) if there was a dissolution due to business failure. On the death of their father, however, they would realize their dependence on his business acumen. As Rudolf wrote, "I would merely have my character, my ability whatever that may be, and a little money to start anew wherever I could find an opening" (Journal, vol. 2, 19 May 1870).

In April 1870, therefore, Rudolf was at last open to Alex Scott's third attempt to have them form a business partnership in Scotland. Scott explained that his current partnership with Arthur and Co. would end in December. He argued that his business as a commission agent was a good one and had yielded him an average income of £2,500 per year. In May he elaborated: Scott planned to put capital ranging from £5,000 to £15,000 into the business and, after drawing interest on it of 5 per cent, he promised Rudolf that he would divide the business in half. In contrast to his minority position with Primrose and Rudolf, then, this new offer promised Rudolf increased decision-making power and opportunity for more independence based on his expected commission sales and half-ownership of the business. It would also enhance his public character.

Scott particularly dwelt on "the advantages that would accrue to Cassie & the children [if they were to move], and the happiness it would give to all" (Journal, vol. 2, 19 May 1870), especially when the three sisters and their mother would be together. Rudolf himself had noticed that whenever Cassie received her English and Scottish letters she felt "a pang of regret that she is so far away from them" (Journal, vol. 2, 22 April 1870). Mrs. Dawson had been causing considerable worry to Cassie and Norman because of her increasingly frail mental and physical state. Smith, who currently lived in the house with her, was planning to get married in the fall. From the Dawson family's perspective, the plan made a lot of sense. Rudolf's emotional attachment to his own family and friends in Pictou, however, presented him with a quandary: "the separation to me, with my Partners and above all my Mother and sister and James too, is what I can scarcely make up my mind to." He had to admit, however, that business was falling off, and he anticipated a time when a dissolution of their firm would be an inevitable necessity: "Should the business be so diminished that it would not yield a living to all of us, I should have to leave."

After consulting with Cassie, Rudolf decided to seek the advice of his mentor, James Primrose. He sent him Scott's second letter beforehand. On 21 May they held a private conversation together in the warehouse. The old gentleman opened by judging the offer "a most inviting proposition" but then asked for Rudolf's views. This third offer, Rudolf told him, was so good that he considered it a duty to his family to entertain it. Rudolf frankly outlined his assessment of their business and his future prognosis that, as the junior partner, he would have to leave the firm. Howard was promised the bank agency. As long as the elder Primrose remained, Rudolf had full confidence that he would be treated fairly. Then he revealed the ongoing difficulty he experienced working with Howard, "who I feared would not be so easy to manage with—I spoke of Howards dogged determination and peculiarities of temper and that I had to bear a great deal, which I endeavored to do patiently knowing his infirmities of body and disposition but it was a life of discipline which I felt I could hardly bind myself down to. He fully admitted all these things, and said he could not think of asking me to remain under the circumstances—that it was an offer which I ought not to refuse" (Journal, vol. 2, 21 May 1870). Primrose concluded by saying he did not know how they could do without Rudolf but supposed they would manage somehow. Howard, in contrast, was "terribly cast down at the news," and took some time to get over it. He admitted he leaned on Rudolf a great deal. Clarence remained non-committal—"seemed to be engrossed in thought." Howard's wife, Olly, "cried heartily, and does not try to hide her regret at the thought of our parting."

On the first of June, Rudolf wrote Scott accepting his offer and proposed that they would leave Pictou on the first of September. On the same day, he wrote his mother telling her about their proposed move. Anticipating her consternation at the news, Rudolf "besought her to look at it aright—that it was not happening by chance, but that it came about in the way of Providence" (Journal, vol. 2, 1 June 1870). In July they spent two weeks in Lunenburg saying their goodbyes to family, visiting his father's grave, and seeing old friends. Rudolf's mother begged him to let her keep their baby (Prim) for a year to comfort her. When Moyle left early to join his ship at Pictou, Rudolf noted that his mother "soon recovered her self possession, and baby took up her attention" (Journal, vol. 2, 25 July 1870). They decided to leave baby Prim with her: "it reconciled her to our going away, and we made the sacrifice for her sake" (Journal, vol. 2, 29 July 1870). Like his decision to leave, this was another instance of Rudolf's altruism and the influence of his ideal of char-

acter on his judgment. They said their farewells and many friends accompanied them down to the wharf to say goodbye. Rudolf's mother cried bitterly
and sat at her garret window watching as the steamer pulled away.

Arriving back in Pictou, Rudolf faced another test of his character, this
time in a more public domain. On the fourth and fifth of August, the St. James
Church bazaar was held to raise funds for the final payment of $1,000 on the
new parsonage. The Ladies' Committee raised over $1,200. The next day,
Mrs. Davies sent Rudolf the bazaar funds and asked him to pay the mortgage
and interest due to John McKinlay. He did so and then returned the rest of
the money to her. A week later he heard that the new minister, the Reverend
Henry Genever, was criticizing Rudolf for having paid off McKinlay's note
without consulting him or calling a vestry meeting. He wrote Rudolf's co-
warden, Richard Tanner, demanding that he call a vestry meeting to condemn
Rudolf and threatening to leave the parish if he did not do so. As a newly
arrived minister in Pictou's feuding cultural milieu, Genever was probably
using the issue to assert his authority over parish affairs; but he chose the
wrong adversary. Rudolf reacted with mature self-control: "I am quite willing to leave it to the congregation for I know that I have done nothing wrong,
and that Mr. G. will find that he has made a mistake. I am very sorry for his
sake for he is ruining himself in the eyes of the people. All I had to do with
the matter was simply to act as agent for the Ladies and pay the money according to their wishes—the money never was Parish funds, and the Vestry had
nothing to do with it" (Journal, vol. 2, 12 August 1870).

Several days later, Genever called on Rudolf at his house just before they
were starting off for a family picnic. He asked Rudolf to answer a few questions regarding the bazaar funds, in hopes of clearing up the misunderstand-
ing before the vestry meeting. Rudolf coolly replied that he "would not enter
into any private explanations with him whatever. That he had asked for a
meeting of the Vestry and Congregation, and that I would there answer all
questions—that the matter had now become a public scandal in that I would
be quite willing to submit my conduct to the Tribunal he had appealed to—
[t]hat I viewed his conduct as ungentlemanly, deceitful and unChristian-
like—that he had met me always with a smiling face, while at the same time
he was going about finding fault with me finally demanding a meeting of the
congregation to condemn my conduct on the eve of my departure" (Journal,
vol. 2, 19 August 1870). Rudolf continued in this vein, denying Genever's
right to question his duty as church warden to appropriate funds. When
Rudolf told him that he had acted as agent of the Ladies' Committee, Genever humbly apologized and asked for the letter to Tanner to be returned to
him, at which Rudolf replied, "No, Mr. Genever, this letter I will hand back

to Mr. Tanner, and you must withdraw it in the way it came. This is only a
private explanation and I want you to retract the charge in the same manner
it was made." Rudolf continued, "He demurred to this but I was firm in exact-
ing it, and as they were waiting for me to go to the Picnic, I rose and said I
must leave, and bowed him out." Genever wrote a letter to Tanner withdraw-
ing his previous one, and expressed his great regret for "having been under a
wrong impression, and acting on it"(Journal, vol. 2, 20 August 1870). Demonstrating now his mature self-confidence and firm grasp of moral principles,
Rudolf was able to mount a strong defence of his own public character. This
was to be recognized by the community.

Rudolf was fully applauded for his many contributions to St. James
Church. Genever presided at a meeting of the congregation a week later, at
which Rudolf was presented with a three-volume copy of Smith's Bible,
bound in calf, on behalf of the Sunday School teachers,

> a very valuable work costing over £6, with a suitable inscription printed on
> the inside cover. After this Mr. Hockin read an address from the Congrega-
> tion signed by every male member of it, to which I read a reply, and then went
> on to speak to the Teachers thanking them for their gift, and also address-
> ing the congregation urging upon them to not only be members of the con-
> gregation, but members of Christ, and of the Communion Roll. The meet-
> ing was very trying to me, and a great many tears were shed. Several of the
> members of the congregation spoke eulogizing me and regretting my loss.
> (Journal, vol. 2, 23 August 1870)

On Sunday, Rudolf received a large family Bible with coloured engravings
from the children of the Sunday School. He spoke "to the scholars for a little while thanking them for their kindness, and expressing the hope that they
would remain constant in their attendance at the School, and as they grew up
not to consider themselves too large to go [to Sunday School], but to stay in
it, and take the parts of Teachers when required" (Journal, vol. 2, 28 August
1870). The copy of the congregation's address to Rudolf in the Vestry Book
mentioned Rudolf's lengthy service as church warden; the "temporal prosperity of this Parish" was evidence of Rudolf's faithful discharge of his duties.
In Rudolf's reply, he noted that when he arrived the church was supported
almost entirely by aid from outside sources; now it was almost entirely self-
supporting.

Preoccupied with his Riversdale duties, he had not attended the Oriental Division for any meetings in the first quarter of 1869. On 22 March, he
attended a meeting to find the Reverend Leonard Gaetz, Wesleyan Methodist
minister, strongly promoting political action on behalf of prohibition. Rudolf

responded, "I took occasion to differ from the platform, and said I was in favor of Moral Suasion, and that I was something like Rip Van Winkle—having been absent from the meetings of the Division for some time I had returned to find everything changed—that a great step in advance had been taken, and I felt that I had been left behind. Our people are not prepared for such measures....I do not agree that *Temperance* is of such paramount concern as to make it above all questions at present....I think the question of Confederation and attachment to the British Throne, as opposed to Repeal and Annexation, is at this juncture, of infinitely more importance" (Journal, vol. 2, 22 March 1869). Rudolf's judgment on social issues now operated on a much broader plane than had been the case six years earlier. Not only was he more temperate, but he now perceived the complexity surrounding political and social issues. As James Moreira notes, "The most complex division in the [Temperance M]ovement arose from the different philosophical and tactical approaches to achieving abstinence. Some thought that through religious and/or social instruction drinkers would of their own volition swear off the bottle; this was 'moral suasion.' Others saw legislation as the only solution; prohibition. Some approached the matter from an evangelical standpoint; some tried to present statistical arguments....Some called for moderation, some for total abstinence....The positions and arguments were as multifaceted as there were advocates, and the divergent viewpoints brought constant cries of hypocrisy from opponents."[17] In May 1878, the Dunkin (or Scott) Act became a federal statute. It stipulated that if one-quarter of the electors of any municipal unit requested a vote by petition and if in the resulting election a simple majority favoured the Scott Act, then no liquor could be sold in that area except for medicinal, sacramental, or industrial purposes.[18]

While his ideal of character had become more sophisticated, Rudolf never lost his evangelical beliefs and emotional roots. This was particularly evident when the members of the YMCA paid their tribute to him. At one of the largest meetings ever held at Pictou in the Prince Street Hall, the president, Dr. Christie, opened the assembly with an address to Rudolf, after which he presented Rudolf with a pocket Bible and prayer book from the association. They asked also for Rudolf's portrait to hang in their new rooms. Numerous other speakers—Mr. Primrose, Jim and Abram Patterson, Clarence, and others—spoke in praise of Rudolf's work for the YMCA. John McLean, provincial chairman, praised both Norman and Cassie, after which he gave an excellent account of the Indianapolis convention. Prayers were offered by the reverends Gaetz, A.W. Herdman, and Alexander Ross, minister of Prince Street Church. Rudolf spoke for twenty minutes, thanking the people for their kind words and asking for their prayers to guide him in the future: "I said

I felt more than ever the responsibilities resting upon me, that I was like one set on a pinnacle and needed grace to keep me aright. Young men had been urged to follow my example but I said don't follow me—forget me, but take Christ for your example—follow in His footsteps. When the meeting was over a great many shook hands with me, among them Rev. Mr. Ross, who in his queer abrupt way said 'Ye'll need mair grace now, and ye'll get it too' and he gripped my hand with a grasp that made me feel that his prayers would not be wanting for it." (Journal, vol. 2, 25 August 1870). Jim Patterson gave him a copy of the new YMCA hymn book, saying that because of his poverty he could not afford much more, but felt very sorry about Rudolf's departure.

The evening after their move from their house, they had tea with Mrs. Primrose, Mrs. Dawson, and Smith. Rudolf excused himself at eight o'clock to attend a Town Mission Committee meeting at Miss Swan's rooms. He presided over the prayer meeting, after which he spoke to some of the mission beneficiaries, who gave Rudolf many good wishes as they parted. At the committee meeting that followed, they particularly asked for Rudolf's views as to their future direction. He suggested that they call the Ladies' Committee to a special meeting. On 5 September Rudolf and the committee met with the Ladies' Committee and Miss Swan. He urged the ladies to attend meetings, and they agreed immediately on the date of the next one. They also decided to invite younger women to participate in the committee work. That evening, Rudolf held his farewell meeting with the YMCA committee: "A number of prayers were offered for each others welfare and amid tears we sang that dear old hymn, 'Blest be the tie that binds.' It was a very sorrowful meeting to us. I felt bitterly parting with the tried Christian brethren on the Com[mittee] and that I should no more meet as one of them in the consecrated little [YMCA meeting] room—consecrated as being the place where many were brought to the Saviour during the past year. I can never forget the happy hours spent week after week in that small 'inner chamber'" (Journal, Vol. 2, 5 September 1870).

Within the short space of nine years, Rudolf's work, his family responsibilities, and the Pictou community itself had significantly influenced his own, as well as his ideal, of character. The manly public leadership roles he had had to play developed his facility in public speaking, improved his self-discipline, and greatly increased his feeling of self-confidence. His business responsibilities had helped to broaden his judgment; his evangelical experiences had deepened his compassion for the less fortunate members of his community and had strengthened his inner spirituality. Rudolf's Christian calling enabled him to weigh the conflict between his family responsibilities and his career goals; he was able to achieve a balanced sense of proportion in times

of crisis. While in Pictou, he had considerably improved the status and security of his family, and he had proven to be a nurturing father and a caring
husband and son. A major consideration in Cassie and Norman's decision to
move to Scotland was the future education and career opportunities for their
children. Rudolf had measured up to his evangelical ideal of responsible stewardship.

As to his own social and material progress over these years, Rudolf managed his public responsibilities very effectively; he improved his social status
from that of clerk to substantial property owner, philanthropic leader, and
merchant. At the dissolution of the firm of Primrose and Rudolf on 1 September 1870, he received a severance payment of $6,000, payable in four
installments. As well, each brother paid him interest of $1,500. Rudolf retained
his holdings in ships. After selling his house to Dr. Christie and most of his
family's furniture, Rudolf had $2,600 cash to pay for their ship's passage and
travel expenditures. He also took out a $5,000 life insurance policy.

Considering all the disasters that had occurred at Riversdale, Rudolf had
still improved his net worth. His foray into larger enterprises had taught him
that too much expansion, incorrect estimates of costs or future prices, or
extension of credit or trust in the wrong hands led to financial collapse and
jeopardized confidence in his character. More sophisticated expertise and perhaps a more extensive portfolio, such as those of McLean and the Primrose
brothers, were required in this transitional economic era; but Rudolf's major
difficulty, shared by many other small businessmen at this time, was that he
did not appreciate fully the limitations under which capital acted. Neither
their firm's business plans nor their supervision of their managers met the standards now demanded by international markets. Rudolf and the Primrose
brothers' experience with the Riversdale spool mill corroborates Kris Inwood's
conclusion that large Maritime wood processing mills in 1870 were seriously
inefficient in comparison with Ontario mills;[19] it would appear that poor
judgment regarding their choice of managers and their own inexperience
were the major source of inefficiency in the Riversdale case. Rudolf and the
Primroses were investing in industries in which they had no previous background, and they were using the traditional trading style of family-based merchants. In this new economic environment, they lacked the control of regional
prices and adequate information, as well as the authority that the elder Primrose previously had enjoyed. Government tariffs and ever-changing rail and
freight rates made it difficult for them to calculate their returns. The complex
problems associated with the realization of surplus value were not adequately
addressed by the Rudolf-Primrose firm during this period. Only in the tobacco
and shipping industries were the partners able to benefit from steady profits.

These industries were close at hand and were run by business associates and friends of long standing with the Primroses, as in earlier mercantile businesses. Larry McCann and Jill Burnett conclude that the New Glasgow entrepreneurs who established the Nova Scotia Steel Co. in 1882 succeeded because they sought outside capital "cautiously in a steady progression of market testing and prudent investment decisions." They also benefitted from "the factors of marriage, kinship, and length of family presence in the community." These factors, they considered were "of paramount importance for success."[20] Despite the promise of the railway, the Riversdale project had been too remote for adequate supervision by the Rudolf-Primrose firm; the partners were unable to overcome problems of distance, inexperienced managers, unstable economic conditions, and their own lack of background in this new financial milieu.

Perhaps Rudolf did not completely attain his goal of being a leading merchant in the Pictou region, but he did gain respect in his community for his responsible stewardship of his family, his Christian witness, and his business dealings. Both his private and his public ideals of character had played an important role in the formation of his own evangelical character. He had learned to balance competing responsibilities and had acquired the skill of making informed, humane judgments in his family and social milieus. He had also learned to function in a variety of roles and had developed a sense of security in his public speaking, as well as a new "soft-male" style of management. Rudolf had survived public scrutiny and was judged to be a disciplined human being with a mature Christian character by 1870. His ideal of character had been subjected to several serious reality checks; both business failures and the debates surrounding Canada's Confederation made him realize the importance of national issues. He resisted the temptation to retreat into an inner, private world and courageously led his family across the Atlantic to seek newer opportunities. His character would be his major asset in his future business travails in the United Kingdom.

CHAPTER 8

Later Life

I n Scotland, Rudolf began to experience the effects of structural change and the first non-commercial business cycle significantly affected by industrial development. Independent commercial agents, such as the Primroses, Rudolf, and Alex Scott, had developed a system of specialization in which they acted as intermediaries between manufacturer and retailer. This system began to be assaulted in the 1860s by new methods, originating in the United States and promoted by central Canadian manufacturers, that emphasized direct manufacturer/retailer connections. As well, a severe worldwide economic depression began in the late 1870s that would have a serious impact on export trade.

Although Rudolf worked hard, travelling frequently to Canada on behalf of Scott, Rudolf and Co., a general commission business associated with the textile firm of Messrs. Arthur and Co. in Glasgow, he found Scott a difficult partner. On 22 January 1872, Rudolf received an unpleasant letter from him accusing Rudolf of "greed." Family considerations disciplined Rudolf's response; a fourth son, Norman Scott, was born on 26 January 1872, and in July Louisa brought Prim back to them from Lunenburg. Two years later, Mrs. Dawson died. A month later, Cassie and Norman had a lengthy debate as to whether he would leave Arthur and Co. and his partnership with Scott and enter another with his brother-in-law, George Crow, who was married to Cassie's other sister, Jane. Crow wanted to break his existing partnership, and he offered one-quarter share in the business (mostly timber exports from

Florida and New Brunswick) to Rudolf. Crow was thirteen years older than Rudolf and was planning to retire in a few years, leaving his one-half share to his son, Arthur, and promising the other half to Rudolf. Once again, family connections and an opportunity to move to a more promising field prompted Rudolf, and on 28 January 1875 he went to Rock Ferry, outside Liverpool, to lease a house near George and Jane. Rudolf was startled the next day to hear George suggest that he *not* move his family from Scotland; Crow had just learned that one of his clients had defaulted owing the firm £10,000 the next month. By this time, however, Rudolf had made all the arrangements to leave, subletting their house and organizing his replacement, John Hockin of Pictou, in the partnership with Scott. When he arrived in Liverpool, Crow negotiated a less advantageous arrangement in which Rudolf would get no profits for 1875; this was hardly the "brilliant prospects" held out for him originally.

By mid-May there was a string of unpleasant correspondence between Rudolf and Scott regarding payment of outstanding debts and keeping of the firm's books. On 29 May, Rudolf decided not to take the matter to an arbitrator; he gave as his reasons Scott's temper and the possibility of bad relations between family members. Rudolf wrote that the whole affair "caused me much pain, and wounding of spirit, from the harsh, and ungenerous manner with which he treated me. I have borne with it in as quiet, and forgiving a way as I possibly could, and have restrained myself from any retaliating acts, for the sake of peace, and for preserving unbroken the happy intercourse of our families. He no doubt thinks he has acted aright, but I would not have acted so towards him, as I wrote him" (Journal, vol. 3, 1 January 1876). He reported that Liverpool business was "very dull"; there were few prospects and he regretted their move. Rudolf must have realized the degree to which he was being exploited by his more powerful, older brothers-in-law. He revealed the contradictions he felt in his concept of ideal character, between the external manly roles he was expected to perform and his inner evangelical instincts. He cited his insight into this dilemma, which he had gleaned from a Dr. Moren, staying at his hotel in Newfoundland: "we have two natures, or lives—one our natural one, which is not always allowed to develop or have fair play, and the other the worldly—the 'struggle-for-life'—the business hard-sided one" (Journal, vol. 3, 17 September 1875). He knew that his family responsibilities required him to soldier on. Cassie gave birth to a fifth son, George Rupert, on 12 October 1876.

As was his custom, Rudolf summarized the business trends of the previous year on New Year's Day. These entries reveal that for the next eleven years their business suffered from the severe worldwide economic depression. In January 1879, for instance, Rudolf noted the failures of the City Bank of

Glasgow and the winding down of the Caledonia Bank, leading to widespread misery and estimated losses in Scotland of forty million pounds sterling; he called it a "financial earthquake." Their own trade was "wretchedly bad....contending with overstocks, and great competition. Our profits are amounting to nothing and our incomes have not met our household expenses" (Journal, vol. 3, 1 January 1879); they were drawing on their capital to live. By October the partners wisely decided to purchase a steamship, believing that the carrying trade would shortly be run wholly by steam. Their first ship was called *Escambia*, bought for £26,000; her papers were signed on 16 October 1879, and she then set off on her first voyage to China and Japan. In November they arranged for Messrs. Leslie and Co., at Hepburn on Tyne, to build another steamship, the *Cascapedia* at a cost of £34,500; she was launched in January 1881. Two more steamships were purchased by the firm, the *Matapedia*, launched in February 1881, and the iron screw, *Cambodia*, whose first cargo was coal to the Far East on 6 July 1882. Rudolf recorded the loss of another of their ships, the *Acadia*, in September 1881; the captain and their firm were exonerated at a commission of inquiry. The next year, the *Escambia* floundered and sank off San Francisco. Rudolf had to hurry to Barcelona, Spain, to negotiate terms in the dispute with the cargo agents. The lawsuit that ensued eventually resulted in their receiving full payment from the insurance company for the vessel and partial settlement over the cargo.

Once again in Rudolf's career, ships had relieved his difficult financial situation. On the strength of the economic upturn, Crow had added Rudolf's name to the firm; Crow, Bogart and Rudolf was posted at 8B Rumford Place, Liverpool. In 1882, George Crow attempted to restructure the firm, easing out Bogart (£6,000 capital invested), retaining Rudolf (£8,500 in the firm), and adding the young son of their Florida partner, Will Keyser (£10,000 proposed); Crow himself had £25,000 invested in the firm (Journal, vol. 4, 16 February 1882). Crow wished his son, Arthur, to join but in 1881 they had lost £4,000 in their Pensacola, Florida, timber business and had to give up a previously lucrative New Brunswick account. Rudolf criticized the Crows for the expensive manner in which they were living. (In September 1883, Jane Crow held a dinner party for Dr. J.W. Dawson, their famous relative visiting from Montreal, but did not invite the Rudolfs.) Rudolf again regretted his move away from Nova Scotia, noting that his mother and sister and their many friends would be delighted if they returned, but by 1882 he was unwilling to make any more changes. He was forty-seven years of age and had a wife and six children to support. He felt he was too young to retire, and the interest from his capital was too limited to live on. In May 1882, Rudolf reported that the Primrose brothers' firm had been dissolved, and that Clarence and his son,

James, continued to run the wood business and mills at Riversdale, while Howard remained as agent of the Bank of Nova Scotia.

By 1883 Crow had succeeded in easing out Bogart, had agreed with Rudolf to a 10 per cent share of profits for their two young partners, Keyser and Arthur Crow, and had divided the remainder between himself (50 per cent) and Rudolf (30 per cent, which was a 5 per cent increase) for the next three to five years. The senior partners continued to travel extensively to solicit more business contracts: Rudolf to Quebec, New Brunswick, and Nova Scotia in 1884, and with his brother James to Northern Europe in 1886; and Crow to India with his daughters for four months in 1886. Rudolf reported that business in 1884 continued to be "very bad"; they made no money, freight revenue was very poor, their steamships were not paying their expenses, and the firm lost heavily on these investments. The next year was no better. Rudolf wrote that he was glad to see the last of 1885, which was a year "of unexampled dullness and depression in trade—a great deal of distress prevails" (Journal, vol. 5, 1 January 1886). The partners hoped for an improvement in trade, but the banks were hounding them to pay back their loan, and when Crow returned from India to the office in April 1886, Rudolf thought he looked very thin and careworn; he wrote, "Business is very dull—our steamers are a great drag on us, and we have had to get a large credit from our Bank, and all this presses very heavily upon us, and specially on him [Crow]. He hoped to get some of the Bombay people to take shares in the boats, and so relieve us of some of our holding, but so far he has not succeeded in doing so" (Journal, vol. 5, 19 April 1886). In May, Crow went to London to try to secure a loan. Again Rudolf noted, "The pressure of anxiety on us about this has been very great, and while George was away in India I had the weight of it, and had to see the manager Mr. Sharpe [at the Liverpool bank] about our money matters several times" (Journal, vol. 5, 18 May 1886). Sharpe had been very kind but admitted he had little power in the matter and had to defer to his directors.

Needless to say, with Rudolf's rigorous habits of self-discipline, attentiveness to duty, and repression of anxiety, his health began to suffer. As early as September 1877, he began to complain of severe dyspepsia with weight loss and pain in his chest and right shoulder. On an extended trip to the United States and Canada between November 1877 and the end of January 1878, Rudolf reported that he had contracted dysentery in Florida and was unwell there and on the journey home from Halifax to Liverpool. In March 1882, he noted that he stayed home from work with an attack of bilious cholera. The next year he again had a bowel complaint in February and was ill with diarrhea in August. He complained of being very tired in February 1884, and again suffered from bowel complaint in September of that year. Even so, he embarked on his trip to Canada. In December he had such a sharp bilious attack that he lost consciousness. By the fall of 1885, Rudolf's continuing indigestion led him to take a short sea voyage in October in an attempt to relieve it. Rudolf admitted in December that he had not been feeling well for six months and had had another severe attack of dyspepsia (indigestion) during the summer; he was worried about their business and the continuing economic depression. Even an address he was preparing to give for his Congregational mission at nearby Bebington caused him anxiety.[1] Up to this time Rudolf was not sick enough either to call a doctor or to stay home from work.

As he explained at the time of his move from Pictou, a major reason for doing so was to improve opportunities for his children; but their needs added to his expenses. In 1880, the family moved to a larger house, two doors away, at an increased yearly rent of £80. The older children began to benefit from the opportunities offered at nearby schools. In 1878, Will and Rob began to attend Birkendale School at a cost of £60 and £50 per year. Edith attended Misses Laurie's School in the same year and won first prize in English and French. In October 1880, Will spent a year in Switzerland studying French. Robbie was persuaded by Dr. Dawson's son, George Mercer Dawson, who told him tales of his adventures in western Canada, to spend a year at his family's ranch there. He proceeded via Pictou. Rudolf's journal includes a clipping from the *Pictou News* in which Mr. Robert Rudolf, of Liverpool, England, is described as the son of "Norman Rudolf, Esq., formerly one of our most prominent Pictonians" (Journal, vol. 4, 15 May 1883). Robbie went on to Lunenburg and then to the "ranch" of Rankine Dawson in Medicine Hat. He found neither cattle nor adequate shelter and led a rough life with extremes of temperature and many mosquitoes. By the end of July, he wrote home saying that he wanted to be a doctor and asked for the Edinburgh University calendar and his books on Euclid. Rudolf's first advice was that he should not give up on the West, but should either go on a farm for a year or get something else to do. If at the end of a year he was still determined to return "to this over-stocked country and draw on me for the necessary funds, and come home," Rudolf continued, his mother would be very pleased. "But as I have told Robbie *men* must not consult their feelings but do what *duty* calls" (Journal, vol. 4, 4 September 1883). Appropriate gender and middle-class roles continued to be an important aspect of what Rudolf deemed to be ideal character.

Robbie at first obeyed his father's injunction about the manly role expected of him. At the end of October, he found work as a surveyor for the railway line at $40 a month; but in January he returned home. His father hired a tutor to coach him; Robbie wrote and passed his medical entrance exams in October 1884. He passed his first year at Edinburgh University and was appointed a demonstrator in botany. In January 1886, Rudolf wrote congratulating his son on passing his anatomy exam with first-class honours. By the end of the year, Robbie passed his first professional exams. Aleck Primrose, Howard's son who had initially inspired Robbie, meanwhile passed his final medical exams at Edinburgh University, as well; he eventually became Dean of Medicine at the University of Toronto. Prim had enrolled at Liverpool University in 1885 and passed his senior Cambridge exams in March. In June he began work at the Standard Insurance Company. Willie, meanwhile, was a clerk at Mr. Smith's office in 1881. He took his first business trip to Birmingham in July 1884. Rudolf wrote that, on his twenty-second birthday on 26 March 1886, Will was working at the dockyard measuring timber. In September 1886, he was appointed manager of the Smith firm's dock office with four or five clerks working under him. Before dying, Rudolf saw the fruits of his sacrifice at least with respect to the three older boys, with whom he had maintained a very close, loving relationship. He was assured that they would continue the character ideal and lineage of the Rudolfs.

Above all, he was pleased that their three eldest children had converted to Christianity. After the Rendle Street Mission on 8 March 1883, Willie expressed a "concern for his soul" and asked for membership in their church (Journal, vol. 4, 4 March 1884). Robbie converted several days later, just as Edie was leaving on a trip to Egypt with the Crow family. Rudolf proudly recorded the boys' first communion on 1 April 1883. Five days later, Robbie left for Nova Scotia and the West. After several interviews, Willie was admitted to full church membership at the end of May 1883. On his return home in April 1884, Robbie was also admitted to church membership. The more independent-minded Edith converted while visiting her aunt, Maggie Scott, at Towie, Scotland, in June 1884. In mid-March of that year, Rudolf took Norrie and George, their two youngest boys, to one of his services at Bebington; they told him they understood everything in his sermon, and believed the working people in attendance also would have comprehended it. In December 1884, Rudolf was elected a deacon. Edie was admitted to full church membership in January 1885. Rudolf took Edie to a prayer meeting with him in March 1886. Willie was secretary of the Sunday School picnic in June of the same year. His children, then, had committed themselves to their parents' evangelical Christian values.

The closely knit family also supported their father when he became president of the Young Men's Literary Society in 1884. In April 1886 at the United Conversazione (soiree) of the Rock Ferry Literary and Municipal Societies

(Rudolf serving as president), the exhibitors included Mrs. Rudolf, Miss Rudolf, and Robert D. Rudolf (who exhibited a microscope). Rudolf reported that the receipts from the large number of people in attendance would defray their expenses. In May Rudolf resigned, however, stating that not enough young men were taking interest in the society and in its public lectures: "I therefore considered that the Society was not deemed of any use in the community" (Journal, vol. 5, 3 May 1886). He pinpointed the reasons: "I have felt for some time that the Church people have looked upon our Society as associated with Dissent, and have kept aloof from it" (Journal, vol. 5, 17 May 1886). He therefore recommended that J.H. Kenion, who was president of the Microscopical Society, be appointed president of the Literary Society. Rudolf noted the large and influential attendance of members thereafter.

Rudolf wanted his children to adopt his liberal principles. In 1880, he was elected member of the Liverpool Reform Club and used its reading room and the dining room for noon meals. He appreciated the business contacts he made here, and he wanted to identify himself with the Liberal Party in England. Six years later, Rudolf took a stand in support of Prime Minister William Ewart Gladstone's proposal to grant Home Rule to Ireland. He noted that the Liverpool elections on the second of July would be difficult to call as

> There is great diversity of opinion on the subject, and no one can tell what the issue will be. Many of the leaders, and rank & file of the Liberal party disagree with the proposed bill, and they are opposing the Gladstone candidates They call themselves Unionists....The split up in party reminds me of the one that took place in Nova Scotia on the Confederation question. There a large number of Liberals voted for Union, and thereby alienated themselves from their party. I was among them, believing that the union of the Provinces was a great and useful act which would solidify the interests of the various sections, and create a Kingdom, or Dominion as it is now called, which would be worthy of respect at home and abroad. (Journal, vol. 5, 28 June 1886)

Rudolf was lucky to win a ballot at the Reform Club to attend a very large rally at Heughers Circus, Liverpool, at which Gladstone was to speak. In his description of Gladstone's address, Rudolf emphasized the "grand old man's" magnificent peroration, in which he appealed to Englishmen to use *love* rather than coercion in their treatment of Ireland. The reaction of the audience resembled an evangelical revival meeting: people "rose to their feet with one impulse, and hundreds wiped the tears that rolled down their cheeks, and cheered like those whose souls had been stirred to their very bottom." This experience was profoundly moving for Rudolf, drawing together as it did his moral beliefs in Christian love and his liberal principles. As he concluded,

"Though I never hear him again, I am thoroughly satisfied and 'I die content' as Genl. Wolfe said at the capture of Quebec."

As with his Christian faith, Rudolf effectively passed on his liberal character ideals to his younger children. He recounted the journey Cassie and their youngest son, Georgie, made to get a good view of Gladstone as he left Birkenhead. Norrie also went and got "a capital sight of him. These little boys," Rudolf wrote, "are as full of enthusiasm about the great Liberal leader, as their father is. I must say that one of the great desires of my life has been thoroughly gratified today viz to see Gladstone, and hear him speak" (Journal, vol. 5, 28 June 1886). Rudolf's loving relationship with his children helped him instill in them not only his liberal values but also the gendered qualities of Christian character he considered important. An insight into the process can be gleaned by a diary entry written when Rudolf received a letter from Cassie, who was vacationing with the children in Wales in 1876. With regard to Rob, who was apparently "Papa sick," Rudolf wrote that he hoped "he may always feel a desire to see me, and trust me as his best earthly friend and companion. I play a great deal with them all, and try to enter into all their pursuits and pleasures. I feel that in this way I can maintain my influence over them, and keep them united to me and so I hope and pray from evil" (Journal, vol. 3, 14 July 1876). When Will and Edith reacted with terror to thunder and lightning, Rudolf regretted this "unmanly" behaviour for the former, "but one don't mind it at all in a girl" (Journal, vol. 3, 1 August 1876). By participating with their children in birthday parties, musical evenings, and picnics, and by constantly praising them for their good endeavours, Rudolf and his wife developed a positive, encouraging family atmosphere. Even when he was feeling so ill in the summer of 1886, Rudolf played tennis with Willie at a nearby tennis club and helped the two younger boys cut the grass to mark off their family tennis court. At their silver wedding anniversary (twenty-fifth), on 15 November 1884, Cassie and Norman agreed that goodness and mercy, as well as happiness and comfort, had been granted them. Rudolf emphasized how important their children were and how proud they were of them: "Cares and responsibilities have been given us with our children, but in them we have great reason to rejoice so far, as parents. Three of them have given themselves to the Lord, and *all* give promise of future usefulness. May God bless and keep them & guide & direct us still in training them" (Journal, vol. 4, 15 November 1884). His children embodied Rudolf's character ideal and promised to continue the traditions and obligations expected of members of his family.

A final mark of the depth of Rudolf's Christian character was the way in which he faced his impending death. At the beginning of October 1886, he felt so terrible that they summoned a doctor. After diagnosing dyspepsia, Dr. Robson ordered complete rest and a bland diet. After a month, Rudolf returned for a week of work, but still felt very tired and "very much deranged" (Journal, vol. 5, 30 October 1886). The doctor advised him not to return to work and to stick to simple foods. At last on 5 November, Rudolf heard the terrible news; he was diagnosed with cancer of the stomach. In his diary, he wrote first about Cassie's bitter sobbing, her arms around his neck: "I tried to comfort her, and to say 'Gods will be done'" (Journal, vol. 5, 5 November 1886). She had known the verdict for a week but kept it from Norman, fearing it would distress him. Rudolf continued, "So my days are numbered! The summons has come, and I must obey. Yet it is very hard to leave the dear ones I love so much on earth. But I must not murmur, or rebel. I desire to bow to my Heavenly Fathers will in this thing. Something may yet be done by medical skill to save me, and we must just wait to hear what Dr. Cameron will say. I tried to speak calmly to Edie about it. My feelings overcame me, and I could not control my voice or tears for a few minutes. She, poor girl, tried to console me, by expressing her confidence, that if I were taken away, God would raise up friends to take care of them all."

A second doctor confirmed that Rudolf had terminal stomach cancer. He accepted this verdict with resignation and a prayer that he could continue to be guided and comforted by God: "He has led & guided me in the past, and He will sustain me for what yet He has in store for me. I pray that my faith may not fail, but that I may be able to trust Him to the end. What a comfort His promises are to me now, and oh how I thank Him that I have learned to know something of his love & tenderness. Simply to the Cross I cling & in the forgiveness of sins through Christ my Saviour. He has said 'let not your heart be troubled, neither let it be afraid. Ye believe in God, believe in Me also—Lord I believe—help Thou mine unbelief'" (Journal, vol. 5, 9 November 1886). Before closing his diary, he noted that he had written a long letter to James, explaining the prognosis and asking him to break the news gently to their mother (who was suffering from stomach problems and was shortly to die), and to his sister, Louisa, who had recently given birth to a baby girl. He also wrote Howard and knew that all the people in Pictou would be sorry to hear the news. He found it "a relief to get these letters off." On their last wedding anniversary, Norman Rudolf made his final diary entry, sorry that for the first time he could not give Cassie a little present to mark the occasion. He died on 17 December 1886, aged fifty-one.

CONCLUSION

The Victorian ideal of character was a complex notion. On one level, it was part of the mid-nineteenth-century rise of the middle-class to cultural power and economic and political influence. For males, respectability—meaning attitude and behaviour—became a major hallmark of this new culture and of their public character. Young men such as Norman Rudolf strove to improve their lowly station as clerks, to realize a measure of economic independence, and to achieve recognition as community leaders. A new Reform/Liberal political ideal, stressing merit and talent over traditional patronage policies, gave many of these young men further incentive to strive for positions of authority. Disciplined work habits and a strong will to succeed became attributes of this new character ideal.

A major influence on the midcentury character ideal was the state of the western world's economy during the 1860s. Promises of job opportunities in urban centres provided incentives for young men to move away from the authority of their family patriarchs and to eschew traditional styles of work. With the rise of responsible government and expansion of the franchise, young men felt that their views would be heard in this new political climate. Free trade gave rise to a more volatile economic scene, and young merchants realized that to meet the competitive challenges of other trading nations they had to cultivate an aggressive, more sophisticated manly character. As Rudolf knew, if they failed in their business ventures, their public character could be badly stained, their credit rating would plummet, and future business prospects would be seriously at risk.

To moderate this materialistic aspect of the character ideal, evangelicals created a more humane ideal, based on Christian concepts of morality, the affirmation of ordinary life, stewardship, and the sanctity of the family, daily prayer, and worship. A Christian with an ideal character was a person who viewed life as a calling and, instead of merely seeking material wealth and power, sought to find meaning in his own life and to improve the everyday lives of others in his community. Numerous voluntary organizations, such as the Young Men's Christian Association, the Masonic Order, literary societies, and mechanics institutes, were organized to foster these values. By means of their Christian activism and their newly acquired persuasive strategies, these Christian leaders, working in a variety of community associations and church groups, hoped to transform the will, values, and personal piety of individuals and to improve their communities.

Ideal effects were envisaged. A Christian, companionate relationship in marriage would lead to the veneration of motherhood, to more humane child-rearing practices, and to a new view of homes as private retreats. What was not fully realized was the degree to which this private world of the family would conflict with the independent public character considered the ideal for the middle-class male businessman. As the cult of domesticity became more prominent, the father's identity and his ideal role in the upbringing of his children came into question. In his evangelical work in the community, the middle-class male leader, using strategies of emotional persuasion rather than authoritarian coercion, would in time find himself accused of immoral, manipulative practices. Religious beliefs and character ideals would become ensnared by social and political moral causes. The mid-nineteenth-century ontological concept of ideal character, based on the belief that human beings are creatures of God and made in His image, and that they have immortal souls and are agents of rational choice, would become clouded by serious world crises, such as economic depression and war. Structural solutions as well as individual transformation, as many came to realize, were required to solve these problems and establish a more secure, orderly world.

The study of Norman Rudolf was undertaken to give insight not only into the society in which he lived and worked, but also to draw attention to the important role ideals and character played in this culture. Rudolf's diary gives the modern historian an archive of the way in which his ideal of character was constructed—by means of character analyses of individuals in his society, through discussion with elderly mentors, and above all, as a result of reflection on his everyday experiences with his family and in his community.

The Scottish Pictou context was important. Because of its long history of evangelical activism, its role in bringing modernity to the region, and its professional leadership trained in the principles of the Scottish Enlightenment, the Town of Pictou provided a seminal venue for developing Rudolf's concept of ideal character. As has been discussed, in Rudolf's evangelical version were embedded many Victorian concepts such as gender identification, the cult of domesticity, and the rise of a respectable middle class, as well as political issues, such as freer trade, Liberal political ideals, support for activist benevolent societies, and evangelical moral reform. He himself had only a limited understanding of these deeper concepts, but he participated actively in many of these causes. Rudolf was aware of some of the contradictions inherent in his Victorian idealistic goals, for instance, the fear of effeminacy in masculine gender identity, or the danger of increasing the democratic vote, which would give more power to non-property owners. Above all, he recognized the balancing act involved in attending to his various responsibilities to his family, to his work, and to community service, not to mention the cultivation of his inner spirit versus the need to compete aggressively in the world.

Rudolf was fortunate to be developing his ideal of character and to be working and living during an era of economic expansion in the 1860s in Nova Scotia, when there was ample opportunity for careers open to merit. His family heritage, evangelical upbringing, and disciplined tutelage under James Primrose instilled in the young man the necessary incentives for manly success. Rudolf's personality, his close association with female friends, and the new evangelical theology allowed him to develop a new "soft-male" style of leadership, which proved particularly effective in the upbringing of his children, and for his militia work and YMCA leadership. His unusually frank journal uses a wealth of images, symbols, and narrative strategies to reflect as well as to create optimistic ideals of political reform and of bourgeois, evangelical character. Rudolf and his peers believed it possible to transform their community and to inculcate a new set of moral values. When he left Pictou in 1870, he believed that substantial progress had been made in this area and the community recognized Rudolf's leadership, particularly in his church work and with the YMCA. In this respect, then, Rudolf's record of evangelical stewardship mirrored his ideal of public character.

Although he stated publicly that his aim was to be successful in his occupation as a merchant, and he willingly participated in a variety of risk-taking ventures with the Primrose firm, Rudolf began to understand some of the complex economic factors limiting their success, particularly with the Riversdale projects. He realized that he was living in turbulent times, and when he moved to the United Kingdom he experienced even more dire economic conditions. All too aware of his responsibilities as principal provider for his large family, Rudolf maintained a courageous outlook and stoically carried on with the necessary duties of his firm. Even when seriously ill, he did not shirk the required travel or daily office work. Unlike his father, he remained solvent and lived long enough to see at least three of his boys enter "useful" careers.

It was in Rudolf's close engagement in the lives of his children that he revealed his true character and deep humanity. He was concerned for their immortal souls, for their moral integrity, and for their future usefulness as stewards of their families and communities. By means of his nurturing behaviour, his full support of his wife, his participation in his children's play and later sports, and the involvement of his children in his church work, Rudolf cultivated Christian values and close emotional family ties that would endure after his death. He epitomized in his family relations the Christian goal of sanctification, a sharing of God's love (agape) for the world and for other human beings. His daily prayers and frequent scrutiny of his life, as well as constant praise and gratitude to God, sustained him at the end of his life. Rudolf accepted his fate and was primarily concerned about the effect of his death on his loved ones. Even as he was dying, then, Rudolf demonstrated the altruistic, evangelical character he held as his ideal, and he acknowledged its source in his daily Bible readings and in his belief in God's guidance and love. While Rudolf, like many other Victorians, could be faulted for his concept of ideal character, which was tentative and full of contradictions, his life and journal nevertheless demonstrate how this ideal motivated individuals to try to make sense of their lives and to achieve a degree of dignity by becoming responsible stewards of their families, their community, and their work environment.

Robert Dawson Rudolf with his wife, Rosa, and two children,
Bobby (Robert) and Catherine. Photo by J. Kennedy, Toronto (n.d.).
Courtesy of Margo (Rudolf) Coleman, Toronto

NOTES

INTRODUCTION

1 Norman Rudolf, Journal, vol. 2, 22 April 1870, Nova Scotia Archives and Records Management, Halifax. Rudolf was a highly literate writer, with only a few idiosyncrasies; he rarely uses apostrophes for possessive cases, for example. Quotations from the journal have for the most part been reproduced as in the original; where changes are necessary to avoid confusion, corrections to spelling are indicated in square brackets, while punctuation is corrected silently.

2 Stefan Collini, "The Idea of 'Character' in Victorian Political Thought," *Transactions of the Royal Historical Society*, 5th ser., 35 (1985): 31.

3 Andrew C. Holman, *A Sense of Their Duty: Middle-Class Formation in Victorian Ontario Towns* (Montreal and Kingston: McGill-Queen's University Press, 2000), 99, 106.

4 In the British context, the term "gentry" meant the people ranked below the nobility in position and birth.

5 J. Murray Beck, "William Rudolf," in *Dictionary of Canadian Biography*, vol. 8, *1851–1860*, ed. Francess G. Halpenny (Toronto: University of Toronto Press, 1985), 782–83.

6 Judith Fingard, "How 'foreign Protestants' Came to Nova Scotia," *Canadian Geographical Journal* 93 (1976): 54–59. As Fingard explains, over 2,400 immigrants from the German and French states of the Holy Roman Empire and from Switzerland, as well as a small number from the Netherlands, came to Nova Scotia in the 1750s. They were primarily German-speaking people who were recruited by the British government, through the Boards of Trade, to fill up seaboard colonies from Georgia to Nova Scotia. The settlers were suffering religious persecution, severe economic problems, and/or the ravages of war in Europe (the Seven Years' War). More than half of the immigrants were described as farmers; a good number had mechanical and military skills. Christopher Rudolf was born at Illesheim, Franconia (part of the Holy Roman Empire), and had the advantages of schooling and of military and clerical experience as private secretary of the Duke of Wurtemberg between 1746 and 1751.

7   Stefan Collini, *Political Thought and Intellectual Life in Britain, 1850–1930* (Oxford: Clarendon, 1991), 111.
8   See Judith Fingard, *The Anglican Design in Loyalist Nova Scotia, 1783–1816* (London: Society for the Propagation of Christian Knowledge, 1972). In 1815, there were only seventeen college students and twenty-four pupils in the grammar school at King's.
9   See, B. Anne Wood, "Schooling/Credentials for Professional Advancement: A Case Study of Pictou Presbyterians," in *The Contribution of Presbyterianism to the Maritime Provinces of Canada*, ed. Charles H.H. Scobie and G.A. Rawlyk, 54–69 (Montreal and Kingston: McGill-Queen's University Press, 1997). Unfortunately, their application for degree-granting status was defeated by the Nova Scotia Council; it would have broken the King's College monopoly on higher education and control of character training by Anglican clerics. In 1817 there were fifty-three boys enrolled in the Pictou Grammar School, as against seventy-eight students in the rest of the province's grammar schools and twenty-three students at Pictou Academy. The following year, sixteen students matriculated from the academy and fifteen students graduated from King's.
10 R.D. Gidney and W.P.J. Millar, *Professional Gentlemen: The Professions in Nineteenth-Century Ontario* (Toronto: University of Toronto Press, 1994), 10.
11 David Alexander Sutherland, "The Merchants of Halifax 1815–1850: A Commercial Class in Pursuit of Metropolitan Status" (PhD diss., University of Toronto, 1975), 29.
12 J. Murray Beck, *Joseph Howe*, vol. 2, *The Briton Becomes Canadian, 1848–1873* (Kingston and Montreal: McGill-Queen's University Press, 1983), 8, 19. For an insight into William Rudolf's powerful control of county politics, see Brian Cuthbertson, *Johnny Bluenose at the Polls: Epic Nova Scotian Election Battles, 1758–1848* (Halifax, NS: Formac, 1994), 170–75.
13 See T.W. Acheson, *Saint John: The Making of a Colonial Urban Community* (Toronto: University of Toronto Press, 1985), 55.
14 Judith Fingard, "The Emergence of the Saint John Middle Class in the 1840s," *Acadiensis* 17, no. 1 (Autumn 1987): 163–69.
15 Acheson, *Saint John*, 159.
16 William Rudolf's first wife, Catherine Stevens of Halifax, died of consumption in 1825, a year after their marriage, leaving no children.
17 This church suffered a terrible fire on Hallowe'en eve 2001. It is now being restored. There were numerous Rudolf family memorabilia, including a large wooden family crest, at the rear of the church.
18 See Lorraine Cole, "Feminist Theory," in *Changing Patterns: Women in Canada*, ed. Sandra Burt, Lorraine Cole, and Lindsay Dorney, 19–58 (Toronto: McClelland and Stewart, 1988), 32; gender, they write, "refers to the social and psychological creation of masculine and feminine beings, who are socialized to fulfil a complex set of requirements and expectations about what it is to be a woman...or a man." As T.W. Acheson comments, a boy's coming of age could begin as early as eleven years of age and was well under way at age sixteen. It was a process influenced by the sex of the child as well as by the status and ethnicity of the parents. Acheson, *Saint John*, 238.
19 John Tosh, *A Man's Place: Masculinity and the Middle-Class Home in Victorian England* (New Haven and London: Yale University Press, 1999), 3–4.
20 Robert Dawson was the brother of James Dawson, father of Sir William Dawson, principal of McGill College. As well as his trading activities, Robert Dawson led the establishment of the Pictou Sabbath School Society, which in 1829 had twenty-nine schools and over one thousand students. The society imported books and operated a circulat-

ing religious library. James Dawson, when his trading business failed, opened a stationery bookselling business. B. Anne Wood, *God, Science, and Schooling: John William Dawson's Pictou Years (1820–1855)* (Truro, NS: Nova Scotia Teachers College, 1991), 6.

21 A new meritocratic, competitive school policy was introduced at this time in an effort to attract male students from across the province and to win increased grants from the provincial government. Female students reacted by trying to form their own department. Shortly thereafter Pictou Academy returned to its previous co-educational policy, and prize-giving was dropped for several years. B. Anne Wood, "Schooling/Credentials for Professional Advancement"; and B. Anne Wood, "Constructing Nova Scotia's 'Scotchness': The Centenary Celebrations of Pictou Academy in 1916," *Historical Studies in Education / Revue d'histoire de l'éducation* 6, no. 2 (1994): 281–302.

22 As Jane Errington notes, while many middle-class couples enjoyed a companionate relationship, deeply caring for one another and attempting to accommodate the wishes and needs of their partners, both felt their mutual obligations extended to other family members, such as caring for aged parents. Elizabeth Jane Errington, *Wives and Mothers, Schoolmistresses and Scullery Maids: Working Women in Upper Canada, 1790–1840* (Montreal and Kingston: McGill-Queen's University Press, 1995), 37.

23 Donald Yacovone describes this ideal in his analysis of the American Christian abolitionists during this era. Donald Yacovone, "Abolitionists and the 'Language of Fraternal Love,'" in *Meanings for Manhood: Constructions of Masculinity in Victorian America*, ed. Mark C. Carnes and Clyde Griffen, 91 (Chicago and London: University of Chicago Press, 1990).

24 Charles Taylor, *Sources of the Self: The Making of the Modern Identity* (Cambridge: Harvard University Press, 1989), 10.

25 Ibid., 69.

26 Ibid., 184.

27 Robert Fothergill, *Private Chronicles: A Study of English Diaries* (London: Oxford University Press, 1974), 44. As he suggests, the effect of keeping a diary helped generate patterns and these, in turn, became a source of themes, such as "character," that would give the work a design.

28 George Herbert (1593–1633) wrote *The Country Parson, his Character, and Rule of Holy Life*, which was first published in 1652 as part of *Herbert's Remains: or, Sundry Pieces of that Sweet Singer of the Temple, Mr. George Herbert.* As John R. Gillis writes, the "conception of a lifetime as a continuous spiritual journey was consistent with the worldly orientation of the emerging merchant classes. It complemented the rise of the patriarchal household as a spiritual as well as economic center." John R. Gillis, *A World of Their Own Making: Myth, Ritual, and the Quest for Family Values* (New York: Harper Collins, 1996), 52.

29 Patrick Joyce, *Democratic Subjects: The Self and the Social in Nineteenth-Century England* (Cambridge: Cambridge University Press, 1994), 51.

30 Samuel Smiles's book *Self-Help* was published in 1859. While there is no evidence that Rudolf read this work, he did borrow books regularly from the Bible Society's reading room and he read the British newspapers where Smiles's ideas would have been broadcast. In 1871 *Character* was published, and in 1880 *Duty.* In his first book Smiles insisted that elevation of character was more important than "getting-on," and that character, not wealth, was the end of human existence. George Watson, *The English Ideology: Studies in the Language of Victorian Politics* (1973), cited in Stefan Collini, "The Idea of 'Character,'" 38.

31 Collini, "The Idea of 'Character,'" 38.

32 See Frank M. Turner, *Contesting Cultural Authority: Essays in Victorian Intellectual Life* (Cambridge: Cambridge University Press, 1993), 74; and Cecilia Morgan, *Public Men and Virtuous Women: The Gendered Languages of Religion and Politics in Upper Canada, 1791–1850* (Toronto: University of Toronto Press, 1996), 22. Nineteenth-century diaries should not be read without paying some attention to the use of narrative strategies or rhetorical devices available to the author.

33 Avrom Fleishman, *Figures of Autobiography: The Language of Self-Writing in Victorian and Modern England* (Berkeley and Los Angeles: University of California Press, 1983), 10.

34 Linda H. Peterson, *Victorian Autobiography: The Tradition of Self-Interpretation* (New Haven and London: Yale University Press, 1986), 128–30, 150.

35 Mark C. Carnes, "Middle-Class Men and the Solace of Fraternal Ritual," in *Meanings for Manhood: Constructions of Masculinity in Victorian America*, ed. Mark C. Carnes and Clyde Griffen, 38 (Chicago and London: University of Chicago Press, 1990).

36 Vol. 1, 20 February 1862–30 November 1864; Vol. 2, December 1864–31 May 1874; Vol. 3, 20 July 1874–6 December 1879; Vol. 4, 1 January 1880–12 November 1885; and Vol. 5, 14 November 1885–15 November 1886.

37 Tosh, *A Man's Place*, 199.

CHAPTER ONE

1 J.M. Bumsted estimates that over fifteen thousand Highland Scots came to British North America between 1770 and 1850, most settling in Nova Scotia, Prince Edward Island, and Upper Canada. J.M. Bumsted, "Scots," in *The Canadian Encyclopedia*, ed. James H. Martin (Edmonton, AB: Hurtig, 1988), vol. 3; and Bumsted, "Scottish Emigration to the Maritimes, 1770–1850: A New Look at an Old Theme," *Acadiensis* 10, no. 2 (spring 1981): 65–85.

2 See B. Anne Wood, "The Significance of Evangelical Presbyterian Politics in the Construction of State Schooling: A Case Study of the Pictou District, 1817–1866," *Acadiensis* 20, no. 2 (spring 1991): 66–68.

3 James W. Dawson, *A Handbook of the Geography and Natural History of the Province of Nova Scotia for the Use of Schools, Families and Travellers* (Pictou, NS: James Dawson, 1857), 35.

4 Graeme Wynn, "Exciting a Spirit of Emulation among the 'Plodholes': Agricultural Reform in Pre-Confederation Nova Scotia," *Acadiensis* 20, no. 1 (autumn 1999): 5–51; and Alan R. MacNeil, "A Reconstruction of the State of Agriculture in Eastern Nova Scotia," (MA thesis, Queen's University, 1985). As MacNeil observes, the paternalistic attitude and the unfeasibility of many of their plans alienated many local farmers (47). See also Alan R. MacNeil, "Cultural Stereotypes and Highland Farming in Eastern Nova Scotia, 1827–1861," *Histoire Sociale / Social History* 19, no. 37 (May 1986): 39–56.

5 See J.S. Martell, "Early Coal Mining in Nova Scotia," in *Cape Breton Historical Essays*, ed. Don MacGillivray and Brian Tennyson, 50 (Sydney, NS: College of Cape Breton, 1980).

6 Coal production increased from 148,000 to 326,000 tons between 1851 and 1860. Average net exports of coal between British North America and the United States (in thousands $) increased from 19 to 51, an increase in the share of trade from 27 per cent to 72 per cent. Marilyn Gerriets and Julian Gwyn, "Tariffs, Trade and Reciprocity: Nova Scotia, 1830–1866," *Acadiensis* 25, no. 2 (spring 1996), table 8: 75. See also Julian Gwyn, *Excessive Expectations: Maritime Commerce and the Economic Development of Nova Scotia, 1780–1870* (Montreal and Kingston: McGill-Queen's University Press, 1998), chapter 7.

7   See *Norway House*, sketch in L.B. Jensen, *Wood and Stone: Pictou, Nova Scotia* (Halifax, NS: Petheric Press, 1972), n.p. As the text cites, the walls were a foot and a half thick, and the oval-shaped entrance hall was elegant with four marble-backed alcoves. Doors were imported from Scotland. The house still exists, now serving as a retirement home. Brick additions have altered the original appearance.

8   The United Secessionists were a breakaway branch of the Presbyterian Church whose members rejected church establishment, including the appointment and support of ministers by the state, in any form. In the 1851 census returns for Pictou County the following numbers were recorded for each denomination: Church of Scotland, 9,886; Presbyterian Church of Nova Scotia (previously Secessionists), 7,665; Free Church, 3,588; Roman Catholic, 2,031; Church of England, 1,105; Methodist, 334; Baptist 197; Quaker, 37; Universalist, 4; Congregationalist, 1; other denominations, 56; cited in Pictou Academy fonds, Annual Report to Lieutenant-Governor, Pictou, 27 November 1854, 8, mfm at Places, Pictou Academy, Reel 4, Nova Scotia Archives and Records Management (NSARM).

9   R.D. Anderson, *Education and Opportunity in Victorian Scotland* (Oxford: Clarendon, 1983), 15.

10 The Reverend Charles Elliott was the Anglican member of the Pictou Board of School Commissioners. In 1838, he intervened on behalf of George Christie to establish a second grammar school, competing with Pictou Academy, in the town. As Elliott wrote, "this is the only local department in which the Antiburgher [Secessionist] party are [*sic*] unable to carry everything before them." Charles Elliott to Rupert D. George, Pictou, 5 July 1838, RG14, vol. 49–50, item 317:1–2, Education general records collection, NSARM.

11 See B. Anne Wood, "Schooling/Credentials for Professional Advancement: A Case Study of Pictou Presbyterians," in *The Contribution of Presbyterianism to the Maritime Provinces of Canda*, ed. Charles H.H. Scobie and G.A. Rawlyk, 54–69 (Montreal and Kingston: McGill-Queen's University Press, 1997).

12 See B. Anne Wood, *God, Science, and Schooling: John William Dawson's Pictou Years, 1820–1855* (Truro: Nova Scotia Teachers College, 1991); Robert Nicholas Bérard, *Character Education and Nation Building in the Maritimes, 1880–1920* (Truro: Nova Scotia Teachers College, 1993); Janet Guildford, *Family Strategies and Professional Careers: The Experience of Women Teachers in Nineteenth-Century Nova Scotia* (Truro: Nova Scotia Teachers College, 1994); and Donald Soucy, *For the Hand or For the Mind? Dawson's and Forrester's Advocacy of Education in Art* (Truro: Nova Scotia Teachers College, 1992).

13 This house is now a Pictou restaurant. Numerous sketches of other beautiful Victorian homes, many still occupied, can be found in Jensen, *Wood and Stone*.

14 Robert Stacey, ed., *William G.R. Hind: The Pictou Sketchbook Le Carnet Pictou* (Windsor, ON: Art Gallery of Windsor, 1990), 44–46.

15 See L.D. McCann, "'Living a double life': Town and Country in the Industrialization of the Maritimes," in *Geographical Perspectives*, ed. Douglas Day, 106 (Halifax, NS: Saint Mary's University, 1988). McCann describes Pictou Town as a "traditional mercantile wholesale trading complex."

16 Brian Cuthbertson, *Johnny Bluenose at the Polls: Epic Nova Scotian Election Battles 1758–1848* (Halifax, NS: Formac, 1994), 298. See also J. Murray Beck, *Politics of Nova Scotia*, vol. 1, *Nicolson–Fielding, 1710–1896* (Tantallon, NS: Four East Publications, 1985), 133.

17 Jeffrey McNairn, *The Capacity to Judge: Public Opinion and Deliberative Democracy in Upper Canada, 1791–1854* (Toronto: University of Toronto Press, 2000), 6, 7.

18 Patrick Joyce, *Democratic Subjects: The Self and the Social in Nineteenth-Century England* (Cambridge: Cambridge University Press, 1994), 174–75, 166, 216. See also Stefan Collini, *Public Moralists: Political Thought and Intellectual Life in Britain, 1850–1930* (Oxford: Clarendon, 1991), 113.

19 Clyde Griffen, "Reconstructing Masculinity from the Evangelical Revival to the Waning of Progressivism: A Speculative Synthesis," in *Meanings for Manhood: Constructions of Masculinity in Victorian America*, ed. Mark C. Carnes and Clyde Griffen, 187 (Chicago and London: University of Chicago Press, 1990).

20 See B. Anne Wood, "Thomas McCulloch's Use of Science in Promoting a Liberal Education," *Acadiensis* 17, no. 1 (autumn 1987): 56–73.

21 See Andrew Hook and Richard B. Sher, eds., *The Glasgow Enlightenment* (East Linton, Scotland: Tuckwell Press, 1995); Paul Wood, *The Aberdeen Enlightenment and the Arts Curriculum in the Eighteenth Century* (Aberdeen: Aberdeen University Press, 1993); and B. Anne Wood, "Thomas McCulloch's Use of Science."

22 Joyce, *Democratic Subjects*, 170–71.

23 George Combe was the leading popularizer of phrenology through his book *Constitution of Man*, which by 1860 had sold one hundred thousand copies in Britain and two hundred thousand in the United States.

24 Joyce, *Democratic Subjects*, 171–72.

25 There is no mention of the Rudolf children attending Sunday School in Pictou. In Britain, however, one of the main reasons the Rudolfs left the Anglican Church and joined the Rock Ferry Independent Church in 1877 was that the local Church of England had no Sunday School, whereas the latter Congregational church had.

26 Dr. John Waddell was educated at Pictou Academy and then studied medicine in Nova Scotia, Glasgow and London. In 1839, he received a diploma from the Royal College of Surgeons and in 1840 began medical practice in Truro. He was appointed superintendent of the New Brunswick Lunatic Asylum in 1849 and remained there until 1876. He visited hospitals in Canada and in the United States, and attempted to introduce the latest and most humane methods of treatment, including occupational therapy—gardening and handwork. He was greatly respected throughout the province. W.A. Spray, "John Waddell," in *Dictionary of Canadian Biography*, vol. 10, *1871–1880*, ed. Francess Halpenny, 695 (Toronto: University of Toronto Press, 1972); and S.D. Clark, *The Developing Canadian Community* (Toronto: University of Toronto Press, 1968), 155. The large number of evangelical preachers suffered mental breakdowns, Clark suggests, because "the highly emotional religious appeal was mentally disturbing."

27 Joyce, *Democratic Subjects*, 189.

28 Collini, *Public Moralists*, 96.

29 This was an expression of Rudolf's evangelical social activism. It reflected his optimistic belief, shared by other evangelicals, that environmental factors, such as control of liquor distribution and consumption, and of gambling, would lead to behavioural changes (see chapter 5).

30 John R. Gillis, *A World of Their Own Making: Myth, Ritual, and the Quest for Family Values* (New York: Harper Collins, 1996), 52, 53.

CHAPTER TWO

1 See James Cameron, *Political Pictonians: The Men in the Legislative Council, Senate, House of Commons, House of Assembly, 1767–1967* (Ottawa: n.p., n.d.), 3–6, 170. In 1843, George Smith resigned to contest the Pictou Township seat, which he won and retained until 1845. He was judge of probate for Pictou from 1849 until his death in 1850. For Smith's

bankruptcy, due mainly to his political debts, see Brian Cuthbertson, *Johnny Bluenose at the Polls: Epic Nova Scotian Election Battles, 1758–1848* (Halifax, NS: Formac, 1994), 251–53, 256.

2 Patrick Joyce, *Democratic Subjects: The Self and the Social in Nineteenth-Century England* (Cambridge: Cambridge University Press, 1994), 118; and Leonore Davidoff and Catherine Hall, *Family Fortunes: Men and Women of the English Middle Class, 1780–1850* (London: Hutchinson, 1987), 110–11.

3 Ida Rudolf was buried in the churchyard of St. James Church, Pictou, where her gravestone can still be seen.

4 John B. Gillis, *A World of Their Own Making: Myth, Ritual, and the Quest for Family Values* (New York: Harper Collins, 1996), 210. With the invention of daguerreotype in the 1840s, miniatures of children and memorial photography became possible (207).

5 See Neil Sutherland, *Children in English-Canadian Society: Framing the Twentieth-Century Consensus* (Toronto: University of Toronto Press, 1976), 56–57.

6 Joyce, *Democratic Subjects*, 174, 196; see also Davidoff and Hall, *Family Fortunes*, 329–43.

7 Bret E. Carroll describes the religious and psychological functions that many American men of the period associated with home and family life. He suggests that there were "new and softer paternal ideals" beginning to affect fatherhood by mid-century. Carroll, "'I must have my house in order': The Victorian Fatherhood of John Shoebridge Williams," *Journal of Family History* 24, no. 3 (July 1999): 282.

8 See Henry P. Wood, *David Stow and the Glasgow Normal School* (Glasgow: Jordanhill College of Education, 1987); Alexander Forrester, *The Teacher's Text-Book* (Halifax, NS: n.p., 1867), and his education reports, as well as the *Journal of Education* (Nova Scotia) from 1855–1864. See also B. Anne Wood, "The Significance of Evangelical Presbyterian Politics in the Construction of State Schooling: A Case Study of the Pictou District, 1817–1866," *Acadiensis* 20, no. 2 (spring 1991): 79–85; and B. Anne Wood, *God, Science, and Schooling: John William Dawson's Pictou Years, 1820–1855* (Truro: Nova Scotia Teachers College, 1991).

9 See David Hogan, "Modes of Discipline: Affective Individualism and Pedagogical Reform in New England, 1820–1850," *American Journal of Education* 99 (November 1990): 3; and George Perry, "'The Grand Regulator': State Schooling and the Normal-School Idea in Nova Scotia, 1838–1855," *Acadiensis* 32, no. 2 (spring 2003): 60–83.

10 John Tosh, *A Man's Place: Masculinity and the Middle-Class Home in Victorian England* (New Haven and London: Yale University Press, 1999), 91.

11 Davidoff and Hall, *Family Fortunes*, 179.

12 The ancient notion of primogeniture, being the right or principle of inheritance or succession to the first-born, especially the inheritance of a family estate by the eldest son, was a central feature of Scottish-Canadian culture. Fathers expected their daughters' husbands would care for them. Sons were expected to look after their mother financially, and daughters to care for her emotional, medical, and social needs. This system placed considerable power over the family in the hands of the eldest son, whose character, it was assumed, had been properly cultivated to take on this responsibility.

13 As Stefan Collini suggests, altruism and character "constitute the animating dynamic of much of the political thought of the period [mid-nineteenth century] in ways neglected by concentrating on the history of the more familiar theoretical 'isms.'" See Collini, *Public Moralists: Political Thought and Intellectual Life in Britain, 1850–1930* (Oxford: Clarendon Press, 1991), 7.

14 Helen Primrose left for Halifax in February 1864. She apparently tried living at the cottage but couldn't get along with the ladies. Rudolf last reported her moving in Sep-

tember 1866 to New York to work as a milliner. Neither Primrose nor her friends could dissuade her.

15 Tosh, *A Man's Place*, 2–3.

16 Cynthia R. Comacchio, *The Infinite Bonds of Family: Domesticity in Canada, 1850–1940* (Toronto: University of Toronto Press, 1999), 40, 41; and Davidoff and Hall, *Family Fortunes*, 368.

17 Undulant fever, or brucellosis, is an infectious disease transmitted to humans by bacteria in the milk of infected cattle. It brings on fever, spleen, and bowel disorders, and pain in the joints.

18 Margaret Marsh, *Suburban Lives* (New Brunswick, NJ: Rutgers University Press, 1990), 76. She places the period at which masculine domesticity begins in North America as the beginning of the twentieth century with the rise of suburbia.

19 Davidoff and Hall, *Family Fortunes*, 113. See also, Tosh, *A Man's Place*, 112–13; and Gillis, *A World of Their Own Making*, 165.

20 Davidoff and Hall, *Family Fortunes*, 113.

21 As John Gillis remarks, "paying too much attention to children earned a man the label of 'mollicot' and challenged his masculinity" in that era. Gillis, *A World of Their Own Making*, 192.

22 Anna Mathilda Oxner (1811–1886), like her husband, was a descendant of "foreign Protestants." Her father, John Nicholas Oxner, was of Swiss origin. Anna Rudolf had six children, four of whom survived.

23 E. Anthony Rotundo, "Boy Culture: Middle-Class Boyhood in Nineteenth-Century America," in *Meanings for Manhood: Constructions of Masculinity in Victorian America*, ed. Mark C. Carnes and Clyde Griffen, 21, 29 (Chicago and London: University of Chicago Press, 1990).

24 One of the sons, James Eisenhauer, who sat in the provincial Assembly from 1867 to 1878, ran in Lunenburg as a Liberal in the 1887 national election and defeated the Conservatives by 122 votes. By this time his family's fish export business was among the largest in the Maritimes. Eisenhauer strongly opposed the National Policy of Sir John A. Macdonald, which protected home industry, and campaigned for free trade with the United States. Brian Cuthbertson, *Lunenburg Then and Now* (Halifax, NS: Formac, 2002), 54.

25 As Davidoff and Hall remark, "Family prayers were a way of signifying the place of religion at home." Davidoff and Hall, *Family Fortunes*, 109.

26 Tosh, *A Man's Place*, 93.

27 Ibid., 115.

28 Errington stresses the mutual obligations that cemented ties of kinship within the Victorian family; see Elizabeth Jane Errington, *Wives and Mothers, Schoolmistresses and Scullery Maids: Working Women in Upper Canada, 1790–1840* (Montreal and Kingston: McGill-Queen's University Press, 1995), 37. Both Louisa and Anna Rudolf came frequently to Pictou to help care for the children when Cassie gave birth. Cassie continued to bear major responsibility for her own mother. Mrs. Dawson's adopted daughter, Minnie Harris, was given over to the care of Cassie's sister, Maggie Scott, in Scotland when she became disillusioned by her schooling in Pictou. The Rudolfs took Mrs. Dawson with them to Scotland when they left in 1870. Anna Rudolf, meanwhile, was given the care of Prim, the Rudolfs' youngest child, to assuage her loneliness at the departure of Norman and Cassie.

29 As Wendy Mitchinson notes, married women without children in the nineteenth century were believed to be prone to uterine (womb) disease. Physicians considered the "natural" role of women to be maternal. Wendy Mitchinson, "The Medical Treatment

of Women," in *Changing Patterns: Women in Canada*, ed. Sandra Burt, Lorraine Cole, and Lindsay Dorney, 244 (Toronto: McClelland and Stewart, 1988). In turn, as John Tosh observes, "Husbands without children suffered a loss of masculine status." See Tosh, *A Man's Place*, 80.

30 Steven Mintz, *A Prison of Expectations: The Family in Victorian Culture* (New York: New York University Press, 1983), 63.

31 Charles Taylor, *Sources of the Self: The Making of the Modern Identity* (Cambridge: Harvard University Press, 1989), 22.

32 Ibid., 292.

33 Ibid., 294.

34 Mintz, *A Prison of Expectations*, 101.

35 Catherine Hall, *White, Male and Middle-Class: Explorations in Feminism and History* (New York: Routledge, 1992), 60.

CHAPTER THREE

1 See James Frost, "The History of the Bank of Nova Scotia," MG1, vol. 3198, #12, James Frost fonds, NSARM; Joseph Schull and J. Douglas Gibson, *The Scotiabank Story: A History of the Bank of Nova Scotia, 1832–1918* (Toronto: Macmillan, 1982), 37; and Leonore Davidoff and Catherine Hall, *Family Fortunes: Men and Women of the English Middle-Class, 1780–1850* (London: Hutchinson, 1987), 207. The first agent's responsibility for bad debt became more common after a number of bank failures in the United Kingdom in 1825–26, which led to the instability of country banks.

2 David G. Burley, *A Particular Condition in Life: Self-Employment and Social Mobility in Mid-Victorian Brantford, Ontario* (Montreal: McGill-Queen's University Press, 1994), 103–104.

3 Stefan Collini, "The Idea of 'Character' in Victorian Political Thought," *Transactions of the Royal Historical Society*, 5th ser., 35 (1985): 32–33.

4 Ibid., 39.

5 Ibid., 44.

6 Stefan Collini, Donald Winch, and John Burrow, *That Noble Science of Politics: A Study in Nineteenth-Century Intellectual History* (Cambridge: Cambridge University Press, 1983), 28.

7 Davidoff and Hall, *Family Fortunes*, 246.

8 Andrew C. Holman, *A Sense of Their Duty: Middle-Class Formation in Victorian Ontario Towns* (Montreal and Kingston: McGill-Queen's University Press, 2000), 41. As Davidoff and Hall remark, "Solid respectability was also demonstrated in [bankers'] lifestyle and homes." Davidoff and Hall, *Family Fortunes*, 245.

9 See T.W. Acheson, "The 1840s: Decade of Tribulation," in *The Atlantic Region to Confederation: A History*, ed. Phillip A. Buckner and John G. Reid, 309–11 (Toronto: University of Toronto Press and Acadiensis Press, 1994). Presumably, the Bank of Nova Scotia took up the role of creditor in the Pictou district previously undertaken by the British commercial firms.

10 See Cecilia Morgan, "'When Bad Men Conspire, Good Men Must Unite': Gender and Political Discourses in Upper Canada, 1820s–1830s," in *Gendered Pasts: Historical Essays in Femininity and Masculinity in Canada*, ed. Kathryn McPherson, Cecilia Morgan, and Nancy M. Forrestal, 19 (Don Mills, ON: Oxford University Press, 1999).

11 See Collini, Winch, and Burrow, *That Noble Science of Politics*, 164. Like the first writers for the *Edinburgh Review*, Bagehot believed that "Whiggism is not a creed, it is a

character. Perhaps as long as there has been a political history in this country there have been certain men of a cool, moderate, resolute firmness, not gifted with high imagination, little prone to enthusiastic sentiment, heedless of large theories and speculations, careless of dreamy scepticism, with a clear view of the next step, and a wise intention to take it, a strong conviction that the elements of knowledge are true, and a steady belief that the present world can, and should, be quietly improved" (168).

12 Clarence Primrose (born 1830) was listed as a merchant in 1871. He and his wife, Rachel (née Carré), had five children. He was educated at Pictou Academy and the University of Edinburgh.

13 Howard Primrose was born in 1833. He married Olidia (Olly, née Campbell) and they had three children. Their son, later Colonel Alexander Primrose, became dean of Medicine at the University of Toronto and a prominent citizen of Toronto. At the retirement of his father, in 1872, Howard became the Pictou agent of the Bank of Nova Scotia.

14 Daniel T. Rodgers, *The Work Ethic in Industrial America, 1850–1920* (Chicago: University of Chicago Press, 1978), 101, 39.

15 See Phillip A. Buckner, "The 1860s: An End and a Beginning," in *The Atlantic Region to Confederation: A History*, ed. Phillip A. Buckner and John G. Reid, 363 (Toronto: University of Toronto Press and Acadiensis Press, 1994).

16 John G. Reid, *Six Crucial Decades: Times of Change in the History of the Maritimes* (Halifax, NS: Nimbus, 1987), 117–18, 113.

17 Douglas McCalla, "An Introduction to the Nineteenth-Century Business World," in *Essays in Canadian Business History*, ed. Tom Traves, 18 (Toronto: McClelland and Stewart, 1984). I would agree with McCalla's criticism (16) of T.W. Acheson and David Sutherland, who condemned Atlantic Canadian entrepreneurs because they did not, in their view, invest in secondary industries in their regions, thus retarding the development of a viable industrial base in the region. As will be argued in chapter 7, while the Primrose firm did invest extensively in their region, other factors accounted for the failure of some of their enterprises.

18 See E. Anthony Rotundo, *American Manhood: Transformations in Masculinity from the Revolution to the Modern Era* (New York: Harper-Collins, 1993), 204.

19 A game played by drawing numbered disks from a bag which were then used to cover the corresponding numbers on cards.

20 Lynne Marks calls this "social fathering." It was designed to groom the young man for political leadership in the community. See Lynne Marks, *Revivals and Roller Rinks: Religion, Leisure and Identity in Late-Nineteenth Century Small-Town Ontario* (Toronto: University of Toronto Press, 1996), 54. Marks argues that small-town amateur sports clubs, led by middle-class community leaders and designed to build character, were undermined by the desire of later town teams to win games (because paid, professional, working-class players manned them).

21 For exclusivist accounts of masculinity, correctly criticized by feminist historians, see Rotundo, *American Manhood*, 200–205; David Leverenz, *Manhood and the American Renaissance* (Ithaca, NY: Cornell University Press, 1989); Jock Phillips, *A Man's Country: The Image of the Pakeha Male* (Auckland, NZ: Penguin Books, 1987); and especially J.A. Mangan and James Walvin, eds., *Manliness and Morality: Middle-Class Masculinity in Britain and America, 1800–1840* (Manchester: Manchester University Press, 1987).

22 Collini, "The Idea of 'Character,'" 49.

23 Ibid., 50.

CHAPTER FOUR

1 See Kenneth C. Dewar, *Charles Clarke, Pen and Ink Warrior* (Montreal and Kingston: McGill-Queen's University Press, 2002), 132–37.

2 Joseph Plimsoll Edwards, "The Militia of Nova Scotia, 1749–1867," *Collections of the Nova Scotia Historical Society*, 17 (1913): 48–99; David R. Fawcey-Crowther, "Militiamen and Volunteers: The New Brunswick Militia 1787–1871," *Acadiensis* 20, no. 1 (autumn 1990): 148–73; and R.H. Roy, "The Canadian Military Tradition," in *The Canadian Military: A Profile*, ed. H.J. Massey, 6–48 (Toronto: Copp, 1972).

3 J.K. Johnson, *Becoming Prominent: Regional Leadership in Upper Canada, 1791–1841* (Kingston and Montreal: McGill-Queens University Press, 1989), 71, 79.

4 Edwards, "The Militia of Nova Scotia," 103.

5 John Keegan, *A History of Warfare* (New York: Vintage/Random House, 1994), 270.

6 See Jock Phillips, *A Man's Country: The Image of the Pakeha Male* (Auckland, NZ: Penguin Books, 1987); and E. Anthony Rotundo, *American Manhood: Transformations in Masculinity from the Revolution to the Modern Era* (New York: Harper-Collins, 1993), and Rotundo., "Body and Soul: Changing Ideals of American Manhood, 1770–1920," *Journal of Social History* 16, no. 4 (summer 1983): 23–38.

7 See David G.Burley, *A Particular Condition in Life: Self-Employment and Social Mobility in Mid-Victorian Brantford, Ontario* (Montreal: McGill-Queen's University Press, 1994), 173. The discrepancy between the myth of self-made success and the bargaining discourse that concealed or denied differences in class and the possibility of success in business prospects, Burley claims, meant that the successful independent business people denied that they were greatly different from others and implicitly obligated them to respect the efforts of others in pursuit of success.

8 Phillips, *A Man's Country*, 103.

9 Charles Taylor, *Sources of the Self: The Making of the Modern Identity* (Cambridge, MA: Harvard University Press, 1989), 20, 22, 153–55, 214–15 and 285–86.

CHAPTER FIVE

1 The Pictou Sabbath School Society was established by Robert Dawson, father of Cassie, and by his brother, James Dawson, father of J. William Dawson, who became principal of McGill University. In 1829, there were twenty-nine schools and one thousand students in the district. The society imported books and operated a circulating religious library.

2 See Allan Dunlop, "The Pictou Literature and Scientific Society," *Nova Scotia Historical Quarterly* 3, no. 2 (June 1973): 99–116.

3 For further details, see B. Anne Wood, "Schooling for Presbyterian Leaders: The College Years of Pictou Academy, 1816–1838," in *The Burning Bush and a Few Acres of Snow: The Presbyterian Contribution to Canadian Life and Culture*, ed. William Klempa, 19–37 (Ottawa: Carleton University Press, 1994); and, B. Anne Wood, "Promoting 'Schooled Subjectivities' in 19th c. Nova Scotia," *Acadiensis* 28, no. 2 (spring 1999): 41–57.

4 See B. Anne Wood, "The Significance of Evangelical Presbyterian Politics in the Construction of State Schooling: A Case Study of the Pictou District, 1817–1866," *Acadiensis* 20, no. 2 (spring 1991): 62–85.

5 See B. Anne Wood, *God, Science, and Schooling: John William Dawson's Pictou Years, 1820–1855* (Truro: Nova Scotia Teachers College, 1991).

6   See Allan C. Dunlop, "Pharmacist and Entrepreneur: Pictou's J.D.B. Fraser," *Nova Scotia Historical Quarterly* 4, no. 1 (March 1974): 1–21.

7   Dunlop, "The Pictou Literature and Scientific Society," 109.

8   As Cecilia Morgan notes, parades were significant for the process of shaping middle-class culture. Because women as well as children and people of the lower orders would have been present as spectators along the parade route, they played an important role "in the spectacle's hegemonic effects." Cecilia Morgan, *Public Men and Virtuous Women: The Gendered Languages of Religion and Politics in Upper Canada, 1791–1850* (Toronto: University of Toronto Press, 1996), 200. Rudolf's confrontation reveals that hegemony had not yet been achieved; there was a contest between middle-class status seekers and evangelical moralists.

9   See T.W. Acheson, *Saint John: The Making of a Colonial Urban Community* (Toronto: University of Toronto Press, 1985), 150; and E.R. Forbes, "Prohibition and the Social Gospel," *Acadiensis* 1, no. 1 (autumn 1971): 12. The American fraternal order Sons of Temperance was introduced to Nova Scotia in 1847.

10 Sharon Anne Cook notes that the early temperance lodges in Ontario drew members from the upper stratum as well as those from the working class who were bent on self-improvement. They attempted to turn themselves into an elite group, setting and enforcing moral standards in an often intemperate community, and thereby establishing a new community standard led by this new moral elite. See, Sharon Anne Cook, *"Through Sunshine and Shadow": The Women's Christian Temperance Union, Evangelicalism, and Reform in Ontario, 1874–1930* (Montreal and Kingston: McGill-Queen's University Press, 1995), 21.

11 Morgan, *Public Men and Virtuous Women*, 16.

12 For further development of this theme, see John Webster Grant, *A Profusion of Spires: Religion in Nineteenth-Century Ontario* (Toronto: University of Toronto Press, 1988), 190.

13 Acheson, *Saint John*, 152. See also John S. Gilkeson Jr., *Middle-Class Providence, 1820–1940* (Princeton, NJ: Princeton University Press, 1986), 52–55.

14 John MacLeod, "The Dryness of the Liquor Dealer," in *Tempered by Rum: Rum in the History of the Maritime Provinces*, ed. James H. Morrison and James Moreira, 83 (Porter Lake, NS: Pottersfield Press, 1988).

15 The identification of reform or liberal policies with individual character was a common element of discourse in Scottish and Upper Canadian political culture; see Morgan, *Public Men and Virtuous Women*, 66–68.

16 Premier Joseph Howe was worried about what he considered Nova Scotia's downward spiral towards democracy and republicanism since the adoption in 1854 of universal suffrage; he judged that a small minority could easily be bought to carry the election for the opposition. He therefore put forward a bill to restrict the franchise to those holding real estate worth $150 or personal property worth $300. Unfortunately for Howe, H.G. Pineo, a legislative councillor, defeated the bill by one vote and prevented the property qualifications from coming into effect until after the next election. Needless to say, the bill would have had a negative effect on the vote of non-property owners, whose voting privileges in future would be curtailed. See J. Murray Beck, *Joseph Howe*, vol. 2, *The Briton Becomes Canadian, 1848–1873* (Kingston and Montreal: McGill-Queen's University Press, 1983), 169–70.

17 See James Cameron, *Political Pictonians: The Men in the Legislative Council, Senate, House of Commons, House of Assembly, 1767–1967* (Ottawa: n.p., n.d.), 48–49. McDonald was elected member of Parliament in the spring of 1873. In 1878, he was appointed minister of Justice and attorney general by Sir John A. Macdonald.

18 There were 108 names on the list paying £17 3s 7½ p in 1857.
19 Vestry Book, Parish of St. James, vol. 1, Pictou, 17 April 1865.
20 Jesus Hominum Salvator (Saviour of Men), or In Hoc Signo (vinces), meaning "In this sign (thou shalt conquer)."
21 See Leonore Davidoff and Catherine Hall, *Family Fortunes: Men and Women of the English Middle Class 1780–1850* (London: Hutchinson, 1987), 118.
22 Grant, *A Profusion of Spires*, 129.

CHAPTER SIX

1 Murray G. Ross, *The Y.M.C.A. in Canada: The Chronicle of a Century* (Toronto: Ryerson Press, 1951), 27.
2 Steven Mintz, *A Prison of Expectations: The Family in Victorian Culture* (New York: New York University Press, 1983), 104.
3 T.W. Acheson, *Saint John: The Making of a Colonial Urban Community* (Toronto: University of Toronto Press, 1985), 116. See also Lewis Saum, *The Popular Mood of Pre–Civil War America* (Westport, CT: Greenwood Press, 1980), 57–67, 110.
4 Michael Gauvreau, "Beyond the Half-Way House: Evangelicalism and the Shaping of English Canadian Culture," *Acadiensis* 20, no. 2 (spring 1991): 166.
5 Michael Gauvreau, "Protestantism Transformed: Personal Piety and the Evangelical Social Vision, 1815–1867," in *The Canadian Protestant Experience, 1760–1940*, ed. George A. Rawlyk, 50 (Montreal and Kingston: McGill-Queen's University Press, 1990).
6 Marguerite Van Die, "'The Marks of a Genuine Revival': Religion, Social Change, Gender, and Community in Mid-Victorian Brantford Ontario," *Canadian Historical Review* 79, no. 3 (September 1998): 541, 547.
7 See Gordon Darroch, "Domestic Revolution and Cultural Formation in Nineteenth-Century Ontario, Canada," *History of the Family* 4, no. 4 (1999): 439. Following Michel Foucault, Darroch terms this process of "turning specific social practices and ideas into taken-for-granted understandings of what was appropriate and respectable, and rendering alternatives as marginal, deviant or even unimaginable…a new form of subjectivity, a sense of private, individualized responsibility, identified…as disciplinary individualism."
8 John Geddie was born in Banff, Scotland, on 10 April 1815. His family emigrated to Pictou in 1816. Geddie attended Pictou Academy and Divinity Hall. He was ordained and inducted in Cavendish and New London, PEI, on 13 March 1838. See E.A. Betts, *Our Fathers in the Faith: Being an Account of Presbyterian Ministers Ordained Before 1875* (Halifax, NS: Oxford Street Press, 1983), 43–44.
9 His brother, George N. Gordon, was killed by the natives in Erromango, another island in the New Hebrides, on 20 May 1861. James D. also was later martyred in Erromango. Betts, *Our Fathers in the Faith*, 46, 47.
10 Born in Cape Breton and educated at Free Church College, Halifax, Donald Morrison was inducted in Strathalbyn, PEI, in 1860. He and his bride left Halifax in October 1863 to go as missionaries to the New Hebrides. They arrived in 1864 and were posted on Fati, but he became ill and went to Australia to recover. He died in New Zealand on 23 October 1869. Betts, *Our Fathers in the Faith*, 97.
11 Reverend William McCullagh was posted to Aneityum while the Reverend John Geddie was on furlough. He then left for Australia and took charge of a school at Deloraine in 1868. Betts, *Our Fathers in the Faith*, 65.

12 See Mark C. Carnes, *Secret Ritual and Manhood in Victorian America* (New York: Yale University Press, 1989); Carnes, "Middle-Class Men and the Solace of Fraternal Ritual," in *Meanings for Manhood: Constructions of Masculinity in Victorian America*, ed. Mark C. Carnes and Clyde Griffen, 37–52 (Chicago and London: University of Chicago Press, 1990); and John Tosh, *A Man's Place: Masculinity and the Middle-Class Home in Victorian England* (New Haven and London: Yale University Press, 1999), 132–42.

13 Struggles between groups of men openly competing for power and the middle-class construction of architectural space are rarely referred to in the scholarly literature on masculinity; see Cecilia Morgan, "'When Bad Men Conspire, Good Men Must Unite': Gender and Political Discourses in Upper Canada, 1820s–1830s," in *Gendered Pasts: Historical Essays in Femininity and Masculinity in Canada*, ed. Kathryn McPherson, Cecilia Morgan, and Nancy M. Forrestal, 12–28 (Don Mills, ON: Oxford University Press, 1999); and Andrew Holman, *A Sense of Their Duty: Middle-Class Formation in Victorian Ontario Towns* (Montreal and Kingston: McGill-Queen's University Press, 2000), 107.

14 Tosh, *A Man's Place*, 4.

15 Holman, *A Sense of Their Duty*, 167.

16 Richard L. Bushman, *The Refinement of America: Persons, Houses, Cities* (New York: Knopf, 1992), 406.

17 Tosh, *A Man's Place*, 29.

18 John Crerar was a shipbuilder. In 1874, he was chosen as president of the newly incorporated Pictou Bank. As James Cameron writes, "The Crerar name in Pictou was a commanding one in the time the Pictou Bank was founded. Crerar was a synonym for business acumen. For public relations, if nothing else, John Crerar's choice as president was a wise one." James M. Cameron, *About Pictonians* (Hantsport, NS: Lancelot Press, 1979), 92.

19 As Elizabeth Jane Errington notes, while wives had considerable moral strength and influence over their husbands, especially with respect to appropriate ethical actions, in family decisions there were usually clear bounds; husbands bore the ultimate responsibility while wives were expected to bear primary responsibility for peace and harmony within the home. This was the Victorian division of spheres. Elizabeth Jane Errington, *Wives and Mothers: Schoolmasters and Scullery Maids: Working Women in Upper Canada, 1790–1840* (Montreal and Kingston: McGill-Queen's University Press, 1995), 36–37.

20 Robert Doull was a Pictou merchant who was treasurer of the County of Pictou, as well as lieutenant colonel in the Nova Scotia Militia (see chapter 4). He held high office in the Independent Order of Odd Fellows (IOOF), representing the Maritime provinces at the IOOF's Grand Lodge meeting in San Francisco, California, in 1869. He was a Conservative and was twice elected to Parliament, in 1872–1874, and again in 1878–1882. He was also on the Board of Directors of the Pictou Bank in 1874, when he was "at the peak of his local power and influence," according to James Cameron. Cameron, *About Pictonians*, 93.

21 See Cecilia Morgan, *Public Men and Virtuous Women: The Gendered Languages of Religion and Politics in Upper Canada, 1791–1850* (Toronto: University of Toronto Press, 1996), 12–21.

22 Errington emphasizes the importance of symbols and rituals that middle-class women (in this case, Anna Rudolf and later her son) established, which set standards of behaviour and patterns of continuity for the family. Errington, *Wives and Mothers*, 18.

23 In England, the donning of breeches or trousers marked the beginning of a male child's gender identity. See Tosh, *A Man's Place*, 104.

24 Errington asserts that most colonial householders lacked the time, energy, and inclination to "play" with their children. Errington, *Wives and Mothers*, 73. One wonders
whether Norman and Cassie Rudolf were exceptional in this respect.

25 Tosh, *A Man's Place*, 83.

26 As Margaret Conrad, Toni Laidlaw, and Donna Smyth write, "It is impossible to discuss Nova Scotia women and their society without discussing the colossal influence
of the sea. The pre-eminence of provincial fleets in the world-wide carrying trade
meant that the lives of most people in the coastal towns were defined by the ocean
trades." Margaret Conrad, Toni Laidlaw, and Donna Smyth, eds., *No Place Like Home:
Diaries and Letters of Nova Scotia Women, 1771–1938*, 17 (Halifax, NS: Formac, 1988).

27 See John A. Gillis, *A World of Their Own Making: Myth, Ritual, and the Quest for Family
Values* (New York: Harper Collins, 1996), 85, 42–43.

28 Tosh, *A Man's Place*, 86.

29 Ibid., 93.

30 Ross, *The Y.M.C.A. in Canada*, 63, 64.

31 George Munro Grant (1835–1902) was born in Stellarton, and educated at Pictou
Academy and at Glasgow University. In 1861, he returned from Scotland, was ordained,
and did missionary work at River John, NS, and in Prince Edward Island. In May
1863, he was inducted in St. Matthew's Church, Halifax, and served an outstanding
pastorate. In 1877, he was appointed principal at Queen's University, Kingston, Ontario.
He belonged to the Kirk and to the Presbyterian Church in Canada. E. Arthur Betts,
Maritime Presbyterian Ministers (Halifax, NS: Oxford Street Press, 1983), 49.

32 Michael Gauvreau describes a true "gentleman" for the evangelical at this time as "a pious
Christian and a practical man, bent on applying his talents to the improvement of self
and society." Gauvreau, "Protestantism Transformed," 73.

33 As Mary Ryan observes, many of these men's associations identified themselves in
domestic terms to serve as halfway homes for young men uprooted from their parental
families. Mary Ryan, *Cradle of the Middle Class: The Family in Oneida County, New York,
1790–1865* (Cambridge: Cambridge University Press, 1981), 176–77.

34 Kenneth C. Dewar, *Charles Clarke, Pen and Ink Warrior* (Montreal and Kingston: McGill-
Queen's University Press, 2002), 85.

35 See Aubrey Lippincott, "Dalhousie College in the 'Sixties,'" *Dalhousie Review* 16
(1936–1937): 289. As he writes, "we took a great deal of interest in public questions,
and most of us attended the closing oratorical efforts by pro-Confederation leaders....A
large proportion of us also listened to Joseph Howe's Shakespeare Tercentenary address
which the London Athenaeum pronounced the finest heard on that occasion by any
English-speaking audience."

36 Andrew Holman describes the myriad of subtle ways in which the middle class cultivated a sense of the self—through personal conduct, daily face-to-face relationships,
personal dress, and deportment and speech in society. He concludes that "these aspects,
rather than inherited wealth and paraded foppery....[were] evidence of true gentility."
He adds that cultivated speech was "to be at all times sincere, natural, unaffected, tact-
ful, and unselfish." Public speaking had to have an elevated tone, which Rudolf's topic
of the YMCA and its evangelical work would have epitomized. Holman, *A Sense of
Their Duty*, 159, 160,163–64.

37 This would appear to contradict the contention of Marguerite Van Die that "women
were able to draw on evangelical religion to create bonds of intimacy and to form community in ways that were more difficult for the majority of men." Van Die, "'A Women's
Awakening': Evangelical Belief and Female spirituality in Mid Nineteenth-Century

Canada," paper presented to the 70th annual meeting of the Canadian Historical Association, Kingston, Ontario, 1991.

38 David MacLeod, *Building Character in the American Boy: The Boy Scouts, YMCA and Their Forerunners, 1870–1920* (Madison, WI: University of Wisconsin Press, 1983), 32.

CHAPTER SEVEN

1 See D.A. Muise, "The 1860s: Forging the Bonds of Union," in *The Atlantic Provinces in Confederation*, ed. E.R. Forbes and D.A. Muise, 13–47 (Toronto: University of Toronto Press, 1993); and John G. Reid, *Six Crucial Decades: Times of Change in the History of the Maritimes* (Halifax, NS: Nimbus Publishing, 1987), 93–121.

2 See Douglas McCalla, "An Introduction to the Nineteenth-Century Business World," in *Essays in Canadian Business History*, ed. Tom Traves, 18 (Toronto: McClelland and Stewart, 1984).

3 As Ray Guy notes, during the forties, fifties, and sixties, J.W. Dawson and Abraham Gesner conducted a detailed geological survey of Pictou County, indicating that there was good mineral potential in the area. They predicted that there would be considerable exploitation of red hematite, limestone, fire clay, and moulding sand. R.M. Guy, "Industrial Development and Urbanization of Pictou County, N.S. to 1900" (MA thesis, Acadia University, 1962), 115.

4 Ibid., 118.

5 Ibid., 101–106.

6 See L.D. McCann, "The Mercantile-Industrial Transition in the Metal Towns of Pictou County, 1857–1931," *Acadiensis* 10, no. 2 (spring 1981): 29–64. And Guy, "Industrial Development," 101.

7 McCann, "The Mercantile-Industrial Transition," Figure 6, 43. Four other contemporaries of Rudolf were listed as in the $20,000–$40,000 category: John A. Dawson (Rudolf's brother-in-law), Robert Doull, James Ives, and [James?] Paterson.

8 In 1866, the firm tried to change the name of *Henquist* to *Rothiemay*, but this was disallowed by the government.

9 Rosemary E. Ommer, "Anticipating the Trend: the Pictou Ship Register, 1840–1889," *Acadiensis* 10, no. 1 (autumn 1980): 85.

10 See Eric W. Sager and Gerald E. Panting, *Maritime Capital: The Shipping Industry in Atlantic Canada, 1820–1914* (Kingston and Montreal: McGill-Queen's University Press, 1990), 164.

11 As Ray Guy observes, almost all the roads that appeared in the Meacham's Pictou County Atlas of that era and many others not existing today were built during the 1860 boom period, which resulted in new mining operations and new towns growing rapidly. Guy, "Industrial Development," 54.

12 It opened on 30 June 1867 at a cost of $2,321,567. Guy, "Industrial Development," 68.

13 Nova Scotian anti-Confederates won eighteen of nineteen seats for the federal House of Commons in September 1867. The federal members of Parliament introduced a resolution demanding Nova Scotia's release from union. Joseph Howe and Charles Tupper, representing the Anti-Confederate and the Confederate positions respectively, travelled to London to gain support for their side, but Howe failed to make any headway with British officialdom. In the autumn, at a meeting in Portland, Maine, with Canada's Finance minister, John Rose, Howe agreed to an offer of better terms, an additional subsidy of $80,000 to the province for a ten-year period to maintain its existing levels of service without additional taxation or borrowing. At issue also was the

anti-Confederate belief that the previous Reciprocity Treaty with the Americans would be restored if the region could remain free from Canadians. Muise, "Forging the Bonds of Union," 42–44.

14 James Coats (1774–1857) was the founder of a cotton-thread business in Paisley, Scotland. Sir Peter (1808–1890) and Thomas Coats (1809–1883), his sons, continued the thread manufacturing business. The company name was later changed to J. and P. Coats Limited.

15 George Patterson (1824–1897) was educated at Pictou Academy, at Dalhousie College, and at the University of Edinburgh, Scotland. He was ordained and inducted at Green Hill, Pictou County, on 31 October 1849. He took a great interest in local history, publishing *A History of the County of Pictou, Nova Scotia* (Montreal: Dawson Brothers; 1877, rpt. Belleville, ON: Mika Studio, 1972). See Allan Dunlop, "George Patterson," in *Dictionary of Canadian Biography*, vol. 12, *1891–1900*, ed. Francess G. Halpenny, 828–30 (Toronto: University of Toronto Press, 1990).

16 Eric W. Sager, "'Buying Cheap and Selling Dear': Merchant Shipowners and the Decline of the Shipping Industry in Atlantic Canada," in *Canadian Papers in Business History*, ed. Peter Baskerville, 63 (Victoria, BC: University of Victoria, 1989).

17 James Moreira, "Rum in the Atlantic Provinces," in *Tempered by Rum: Rum in the History of the Maritime Provinces*, ed. James H. Morrison and James Moreira, 24 (Porters Lake, NS: Pottersfield Press, 1988).

18 C. Mark Davis, "Rum and the Law: The Maritime Experience," in *Tempered by Rum: Rum in the History of the Maritime Provinces*, ed. James H. Morrison and James Moreira, 46 (Porters Lake, NS: Pottersfield Press, 1988).

19 Kris E. Inwood, "Maritime Industrialization from 1870 to 1910: A Review of the Evidence and Its Interpretation," *Acadiensis* 21, no. 1 (autumn 1991): 134.

20 Larry McCann and Jill Burnett, "Social Mobility and the Ironmasters of Late Nineteenth Century New Glasgow," in *People and Place: Studies of Small Town Life in the Maritimes*, ed. Larry McCann, 76, 77 (Fredericton, NB: Acadiensis Press, 1987).

CHAPTER EIGHT

1 In September 1877 Rudolf and his wife and children had begun to attend the local Rock Ferry Independent Church, under Mr. Mines. He regretted leaving the Church of England, but found it too High Church for their evangelical tastes and lacking in any Sunday schools for their children. The Rock Ferry Church had a mission at Bebington, which Rudolf was to lead beginning in December 1883.

BIBLIOGRAPHY

Acheson, T.W. "The 1840s: Decade of Tribulations." In Buckner and Reid, *The Atlantic Region to Confederation: A History*, 307–32.

———. "Evangelicals and Public Life in Southern New Brunswick, 1830–1880." In *Religion and Public Life in Canada*, ed. Marguerite Van Die, 50–68. Toronto: University of Toronto Press, 2001.

———. *Saint John: The Making of a Colonial Urban Community.* Toronto: University of Toronto Press, 1985.

Anderson, R.D. *Education and Opportunity in Victorian Scotland.* Oxford: Clarendon Press, 1983.

Bebbington, D.W. *Evangelicalism in Modern Britain: A History from the 1730s to the 1950s.* Boston: Unwin, 1989.

Beck, J. Murray. *Joseph Howe.* vol. 2, *The Briton Becomes Canadian, 1848–1873.* Kingston and Montreal: McGill-Queen's University Press, 1983.

———. *Politics of Nova Scotia*, vol. 1, *Nicholson–Fielding, 1710–1896.* Tantallon, NS: Four East Publications, 1985.

———. "William Rudolf." In *Dictionary of Canadian Biography*, vol. 8, *1851–1860*, ed. Francess G. Halpenny, 782–83. Toronto: University of Toronto Press, 1985.

Bérard, Robert Nicholas. *Character Education and Nation Building in the Maritimes, 1880–1920.* Truro: Nova Scotia Teachers College, 1993.

Betts, E. Arthur. *Maritime Presbyterian Ministers.* Halifax, NS: Oxford Street Press, 1983.

———. *Our Fathers in the Faith: Being an Account of Presbyterian Ministers Ordained Before 1875.* Halifax, NS: Oxford Street Press, 1983.

Bliss, Michael. *Northern Enterprise: Five Centuries of Canadian Business.* Toronto: McClelland and Stewart, 1987.

Buckner, Phillip A. "The 1860s: An End and a Beginning." In Buckner and Reid, *The Atlantic Region to Confederation*, 360–86.

Buckner, Phillip A., and John G. Reid, ed. *The Atlantic Region to Confederation: A History*. Toronto: University of Toronto Press and Acadiensis Press, 1994.

Bumsted, J.M "Scottish Emigration to the Maritimes, 1770–1850: A New Look at an Old Theme." *Acadiensis* 10, no. 2 (spring 1981): 65–85.

———. "Scots." In *The Canadian Encyclopedia* vol. 3, ed. James H. Marsh, 1959–1960. Edmonton, AB: Hurtig, 1988.

Burley, David G. *A Particular Condition in Life: Self-Employment and Social Mobility in Mid-Victorian Brantford, Ontario*. Montreal and Kingston: McGill-Queen's University Press, 1994.

Burt, Sandra, Lorraine Cole, and Lindsay Dorney, eds. *Changing Patterns: Women in Canada*. Toronto: McClelland and Stewart, 1988.

Bushman, Richard L. *The Refinement of America: Persons, Houses, Cities*. New York: Knopf, 1992.

Buss, Helen M. *Mapping Our Selves: Canadian Women's Autobiography in English*. Montreal and Kingston: McGill-Queen's University Press, 1993.

Cameron, James M. *About Pictonians*. Hantsport, NS: Lancelot Press, 1979.

———. *Political Pictonians: The Men in the Legislative Council, Senate, House of Commons, House of Assembly, 1767–1967*. Ottawa: n.p.,. n.d.

Carnes, Mark C. "Middle-Class Men and the Solace of Fraternal Ritual." In Carnes and Griffen, *Meanings for Manhood*, 37–52.

———. *Secret Ritual and Manhood in Victorian America*. New Haven: Yale University Press, 1989.

Carnes, Mark C., and Clyde Griffen, eds. *Meanings for Manhood: Constructions of Masculinity in Victorian America*. Chicago and London: University of Chicago Press, 1990.

Carroll, Bret E., "'I must have my house in order': The Victorian Fatherhood of John Shoebridge Williams." *Journal of Family History* 24, no. 3 (July 1999): 275–304.

Chatfield, Michael. *A History of Accounting Thought*. New York: Robert E. Krieger Publishing, 1977.

Clark, S.D. *The Developing Canadian Community*. Toronto: University of Toronto Press, 1968.

Cole, Lorraine, "Feminist Theory." In Burt, Cole, and Dorney, *Changing Patterns*, 19–58.

Collini, Stefan. *English Pasts: Essays in History and Culture*. Oxford: Oxford University Press, 1999.

———. "The Idea of 'Character' in Victorian Political Thought." *Transactions of the Royal Historical Society*, 5th ser., 35 (1985): 29–50.

———. *Public Moralists: Political Thought and Intellectual Life in Britain, 1850–1930*. Oxford: Clarendon Press, 1991.

Collini, Stefan, Donald Winch, and John Burrow. *That Noble Science of Politics: A Study in Nineteenth-Century Intellectual History*. Cambridge: Cambridge University Press, 1983.

Comacchio, Cynthia R. "Beneath the Sentimental Veil: Families and Family History in Canada." *Labour/Le Travail* 33, 1994: 279–302.

———. *The Infinite Bonds of Family: Domesticity in Canada, 1850–1940*. Toronto: University of Toronto Press, 1999.

Conrad, Margaret, Toni Laidlaw, and Donna Smyth. *No Place Like Home: Diaries and Letters of Nova Scotia Women, 1771–1938*. Halifax, NS: Formac, 1988.

Cook, Sharon Anne. *"Through Sunshine and Shadow": The Women's Christian Temperance Union, Evangelicalism, and Reform in Ontario, 1874–1930.* Montreal and Kingston: McGill-Queen's University Press, 1995.

Cuthbertson, Brian. *Johnny Bluenose at the Polls: Epic Nova Scotian Election Battles, 1758–1848.* Halifax, NS: Formac, 1994.

———. *Lunenburg: Then and Now.* Halifax, NS: Formac, 2002.

Darroch, Gordon. "Domestic Revolution and Cultural Formation in Nineteenth-Century Ontario, Canada." *History of the Family* 4, no. 4 (1999): 427–45.

Davidoff, Leonore, and Catherine Hall. *Family Fortunes: Men and Women of the English Middle Class, 1780–1850.* London: Hutchinson, 1987.

Davis, C. Mark. "Rum and the Law: The Maritime Experience." In Morrison and Moreira, 40–52.

Davis, Philip. *Memory and Writing from Wordsworth to Lawrence.* Liverpool: Liverpool University Press, 1983.

Dawson, James W. *A Handbook of the Geography and Natural History of the Province of Nova Scotia for the Use of Schools, Families and Travellers.* Pictou, NS: James Dawson, 1857.

Demos, John. *Past, Present, and Personal: The Family and the Life Course in American History.* New York: Oxford University Press, 1986.

DesBrisay, Mather Byles. *History of the County of Lunenburg.* Bridgewater, NS: Bridgewater Bulletin, 1870. Rpt. Belleville, ON: Mika Studio, 1967.

Dewar, Kenneth C. *Charles Clarke, Pen and Ink Warrior.* Montreal and Kingston: McGill-Queen's University Press, 2002.

Dunlop, Allan C. "George Patterson." In *Dictionary of Canadian Biography*, vol. 12, *1891 to 1900*, ed. Francess G. Halpenny, 828–30. Toronto: University of Toronto Press, 1990.

———. "Pharmacist and Entrepreneur: Pictou's J.D.B. Fraser." *Nova Scotia Historical Quarterly* 4, no. 1 (March 1974):1–21.

———. "The Pictou Literary and Scientific Society." *Nova Scotia Historical Quarterly* 3, no. 2 (June 1973): 99–116.

Edwards, Joseph Plimsoll, "The Militia of Nova Scotia, 1749–1867." *Collections of the Nova Scotia Historical Society* 17 (1913): 63–110.

Errington, Elizabeth Jane. *Wives and Mothers, Schoolmistresses and Scullery Maids: Working Women in Upper Canada, 1790–1840.* Montreal and Kingston: McGill-Queen's University Press, 1995.

Fawcey-Crowther, David R., "Militiamen and Volunteers: The New Brunswick Militia 1787–1871." *Acadiensis* 20, no. 1 (Autumn 1990): 148–73.

Fingard, Judith. *The Anglican Design in Loyalist Nova Scotia, 1783–1816.* London: Society for the Propagation of Christian Knowledge, 1972.

———. "The Emergence of the Saint John Middle Class in the 1840s." *Acadiensis* 17, no. 1 (Autumn 1987): 163–69.

———. "How 'foreign Protestants' Came to Nova Scotia," *Canadian Geographical Journal* 93 (1976): 54–59.

Fleishman, Avrom. *Figures of Autobiography: The Language of Self-Writing in Victorian and Modern England.* Berkeley and Los Angeles: University of California Press, 1983.

Forbes, E.R. "Prohibition and the Social Gospel." *Acadiensis* 1, no. 1 (autumn 1971): 11–36.

Forrester, Alexander. *The Teacher's Text-Book*. Halifax, NS: n.p., 1867.

Fothergill, Robert. *Private Chronicles: A Study of English Diaries*. London: Oxford University Press, 1974.

Frost, James. "The History of the Bank of Nova Scotia." MG1, Vol. 3198, #12, James Frost fonds. Nova Scotia Archives and Records Management.

Gauvreau, Michael. "Beyond the Half-Way House: Evangelicalism and the Shaping of English Canadian Culture." *Acadiensis* 20, no. 2 (spring 1991): 158–77.

———. "Protestantism Transformed: Personal Piety and the Evangelical Vision." In *The Canadian Protestant Experience, 1760–1990*, ed. George A. Rawlyk, 48–97. Montreal and Kingston: McGill-Queen's University Press, 1990.

Gerriets, Marilyn, and Julian Gwyn. "Tariffs, Trade and Reciprocity: Nova Scotia, 1830–1866." *Acadiensis* 25, no. 2 (spring 1996): 62–81.

Gidney, R.D., and W.P.J. Millar. *Professional Gentlemen: The Professions in Nineteenth-Century Ontario*. Toronto: University of Toronto Press, 1994.

Gifford, Don. *The Farther Shore: A Natural History of Perception, 1798–1984*. New York: Atlantic Monthly Press, 1990.

Gilkeson, John S., Jr. *Middle Class Providence, 1820–1940*. Princeton: Princeton University Press, 1986.

Gillis, John R. *A World of Their Own Making: Myth, Ritual, and the Quest for Family Values*. New York: Harper Collins, 1996.

Grant, John Webster. *A Profusion of Spires: Religion in Nineteenth-Century Ontario*. Toronto: University of Toronto Press, 1988.

Griffen, Clyde. "Reconstructing Masculinity from the Evangelical Revival to the Waning of Progressivism: A Speculative Synthesis." In Carnes and Griffen, *Meanings for Manhood*, 183–204.

Guildford, Janet. "Creating the Ideal Man: Middle-Class Women's Constructions of Masculinity in Nova Scotia, 1840–1880." *Acadiensis* 24, no. 2 (spring 1995): 5–23.

———. *Family Strategies and Professional Careers: The Experience of Women Teachers in Nineteenth-Century Nova Scotia*. Truro: Nova Scotia Teachers College, 1994.

Guildford, Janet, and Suzanne Morton, eds. *Separate Spheres: Women's World in the Nineteenth Century Maritimes*. Fredericton, NB: Acadiensis Press, 1994.

Gusdorf, Georges. "Conditions and Limits of Autobiography." In Olney, *Autobiography*, 28–48.

Guy, R.M. "Industrial Development and Urbanization of Pictou County, N.S., to 1900." MA thesis, Acadia University, 1962.

Gwyn, Julian. *Excessive Expectations: Maritime Commerce and the Economic Development of Nova Scotia, 1740–1870*. Montreal and Kingston: McGill-Queen's University Press, 1998.

Hacking, Ian. *Rewriting the Soul: Multiple Personality and the Sciences of Memory*. Princeton, NJ: Princeton University Press, 1995.

Hall, Catherine. "The Sweet Delights of Home." In *A History of Private Life*, vol. 4, *From the Fires of Revolution to the Great War*, ed. Michelle Perrot, 47–93. London: Belknap Press, 1990.

———. *White, Male and Middle-Class: Explorations in Feminism and History*. New York: Routledge, 1992.

Hardin, James, ed. *Reflection and Action: Essays on the Bildungsroman*. Columbia, SC: University of South Carolina Press, 1991.

Hareven, Tamara K., ed. *Family and Kin in Urban Communities, 1700–1930*. New York: New Viewpoints, 1977.

Himmelfarb, Gertrude. *The De-Moralization of Society: From Victorian Virtues to Modern Values*. New York: Vintage, 1996.

Hogan, David J. "Modes of Discipline: Affective Individualism and Pedagogical Reform in New England, 1820–1850." *American Journal of Education* 99 (November 1990): 1–56.

Holman, Andrew. "'Cultivation' and the Middle-Class Self in Nineteenth-Century America." *Canadian Review of American Studies* 23, no. 2 (Winter 1993): 183–93.

———. *A Sense of Their Duty: Middle-Class Formation in Victorian Ontario Towns*. Montreal and Kingston: McGill-Queen's University Press, 2000.

Hook, Andrew, and Richard B. Sher, eds. *The Glasgow Enlightenment*. East Linton, Scotland: Tuckwell Press, 1995.

Howarth, William. "Some Principles of Autobiography." In Olney, *Autobiography*, 84–114.

Inwood, Kris E. "Maritime Industrialization from 1870 to 1910: A Review of the Evidence and Its Interpretation." *Acadiensis* 21, no. 1 (autumn 1991): 132–55.

Jensen, L.B. *Wood and Stone: Pictou, Nova Scotia*. Halifax, NS: Petheric Press, 1972.

Johnson, J.K. *Becoming Prominent: Regional Leadership in Upper Canada, 1791–1841*. Kingston and Montreal: McGill-Queen's University Press, 1989.

Joyce, Patrick. *Democratic Subjects: The Self and the Social in Nineteenth-Century England*. Cambridge: Cambridge University Press, 1994.

Keegan, John. *A History of Warfare*. New York: Vintage / Random House, 1994.

Leverenz, David. *Manhood and the American Renaissance*. Ithaca, NY: Cornell University Press, 1989.

Lippincott, J. Aubrey. "Dalhousie College in 'The Sixties.'" *Dalhousie Review* 16 · (1936–1937): 285–90.

MacIntosh, Robert. *Different Drummers: Banking and Politics in Canada*. Toronto: Macmillan, 1991.

MacLeod, David. *Building Character in the American Boy: The Boy Scouts, YMCA and Their Forerunners 1870–1920*. Madison, WI: University of Wisconsin Press, 1983.

MacLeod, John. "The Dryness of the Liquor Dealer." In Morrison and Moreira, *Tempered by Rum*, 76–88.

MacNeil, Alan R. "Cultural Stereotypes and Highland Farming in Eastern Nova Scotia, 1827–1861." *Histoire Sociale / Social History* 19, no. 37 (May 1986): 39–56.

———. "A Reconstruction of the State of Agriculture in Eastern Nova Scotia." MA thesis, Queen's University, 1985.

Mangan, J.A., and James Walvin, eds. *Manliness and Morality: Middle-Class Masculinity in Britain and America 1800–1840*. Manchester: Manchester University Press, 1987.

Marks, Lynne. *Revivals and Roller Rinks: Religion, Leisure and Identity in Late-Nineteenth-Century Small-Town Ontario*. Toronto: University of Toronto Press, 1996.

Marsh, Margaret S. *Suburban Lives*. New Brunswick, NJ: Rutgers University Press, 1990.

Martell, J.S. "Early Coal Mining in Nova Scotia." In *Cape Breton Historical Essays*, ed. Don Macgillivray and Brian Tennyson, 41–53. Sydney, NS: College of Cape Breton Press, 1980.

McCalla, Douglas. "An Introduction to the Nineteenth-Century Business World." In *Essays in Canadian Business History*, ed. Tom Traves, 13–23. Toronto: McClelland and Stewart, 1984.

McCann, L.D. "'Living a double life': Town and Country in the Industrialization of the Maritimes." In *Geographical Perspectives*, ed. Douglas Day, 93–113. Halifax, NS: Saint Mary's University, 1988.

———. "The Mercantile-Industrial Transition in the Metal Towns of Pictou County, 1857–1931." *Acadiensis* 10, no. 2 (spring 1981): 29–64.

McCann, L.D., and Jill Burnett. "Social Mobility and the Ironmasters of Late Nineteenth Century New Glasgow." In *People and Place: Studies of Small Town Life in the Maritimes*, ed. Larry McCann, 59–77. Fredericton, NB: Acadiensis Press, 1987.

McDannell, Colleen. *The Christian Home in Victorian America, 1840–1900*. Bloomington, IN: Indiana University Press, 1986.

McLaren, Angus. *The Trials of Masculinity: Policing Sexual Boundaries 1870–1930*. Chicago and London: University of Chicago Press, 1997.

McNairn, Jeffrey L. *The Capacity to Judge: Public Opinion and Deliberative Democracy in Upper Canada, 1791–1854*. Toronto: University of Toronto Press, 2000.

Millman, Thomas R., and A.R. Kelley. *Atlantic Canada to 1900: A History of the Anglican Church*. Toronto: Anglican Book Centre, 1983.

Mintz, Steven. *A Prison of Expectations: The Family in Victorian Culture*. New York: New York University Press, 1983.

Mintz, Steven, and Susan Kellog. *Domestic Revolutions: A Social History of American Family Life*. New York: Free Press, 1988.

Mitchinson, Wendy. "The Medical Treatment of Women." In Burt, Cole, and Dorney. *Changing Patterns*, 237–63.

———. *The Nature of Their Bodies: Women and Their Doctors in Victorian Canada*. Toronto: University of Toronto Press, 1991.

Moreira, James. "Rum in the Atlantic Provinces." In Morrison and Moreira, *Tempered by Rum*, 15–30.

Moretti, Franco. *The Way of the World: The Bildungsroman in European Culture*. London: Verso, 1987.

Morgan, Cecilia. *Public Men and Virtuous Women: The Gendered Languages of Religion and Politics in Upper Canada, 1791–1850*. Toronto: University of Toronto Press, 1996.

———. "'When Bad Men Conspire, Good Men Must Unite' Gender and Political Discourses in Upper Canada, 1820s–1830s." In *Gendered Pasts: Historical Essays in Femininity and Masculinity*, ed. Kathryn McPherson, Cecilia Morgan, and Nancy M. Forrestal, 12–28. Don Mills, ON: Oxford University Press, 1999.

Morgan, Henry James, ed. *The Canadian Men and Women of the Times: A Handbook of Canadian Biography of Living Characters*. Toronto: Briggs, 1912.

Morrison, James H., and James Moreira, eds. *Tempered by Rum: Rum in the History of the Maritime Provinces*. Porters Lake, NS: Pottersfield Press, 1988.

Mrozek, Donald J. "The Habit of Victory: The American Military and the Cult of Manliness." In Mangan and Walvin, *Manliness and Morality*, 220–41.

Muise, Delphin Andrew. "The 1860s: Forging the Bonds of Union." In *The Atlantic Provinces in Confederation*, ed. E.R. Forbes and D.A. Muise, 13–47. Toronto: University of Toronto Press, 1993.

————"Elections and Constituencies: Federal Politics in Nova Scotia, 1867–1878." PhD diss., University of Western Ontario, 1971.

————. "The Federal Election of 1867 in Nova Scotia: An Economic Interpretation." *Nova Scotia Historical Society Collections* 36 (1967–1968): 327–51.

Murphy, Terence. "The Religious History of Atlantic Canada: The State of the Art." *Acadiensis* 15, no. 1 (autumn 1985): 152–74.

Noll, Jan. *Canada Dry: Temperance Crusades before Confederation.* Toronto: University of Toronto Press, 1995.

Olney, James, ed. *Autobiography: Essays Theoretical and Critical.* Princeton, NJ: Princeton University Press, 1980.

Ommer, Rosemary E. "Anticipating the Trend: The Pictou Ship Register, 1840–1889." *Acadiensis* 10, no. 1 (autumn 1980): 67–89.

Patterson, George. *A History of the County of Pictou, Nova Scotia.* Montreal: Dawson Brothers, 1877; rpt. Belleville, ON: Mika Studio, 1972.

Perry, George D. "'The Grand Regulator': State Schooling and the Normal-School Idea in Nova Scotia, 1838–1855." *Acadiensis* 32, no. 2 (spring 2003): 60–83.

Peterson, Linda H. *Victorian Autobiography: The Tradition of Self-Interpretation.* New Haven and London: Yale University Press, 1986.

Phillips, Jock. *A Man's Country: The Image of the Pakeha Male.* Auckland, NZ: Penguin Books, 1987.

Prentice, Alison, Paula Bourne, Gail Cuthbert Brandt, Beth Light, Wendy Mitchinson, and Naomi Black. *Canadian Women: A History.* Toronto: Harcourt Brace Jovanovich, 1988.

Preston, Richard. "Military Influence on the Development of Canada." In *The Canadian Military: A Profile,* ed. by Hector J. Massey, 49–85. Toronto: Copp, 1972.

Reid, John G. *Six Crucial Decades: Times of Change in the History of the Maritimes.* Halifax, NS: Nimbus, 1987.

Rodgers, Daniel T. *The Work Ethic in Industrial America, 1850–1920.* Chicago: University of Chicago Press, 1978.

Ross, Murray George. *The Y.M.C.A. in Canada: The Chronicle of a Century.* Toronto: Ryerson Press, 1951.

Rotundo, E. Anthony. *American Manhood: Transformations in Masculinity from the Revolution to the Modern Era.* New York: Harper-Collins, 1993.

————. "Body and Soul: Changing Ideals of American Manhood, 1770–1920." *Journal of Social History* 16, no. 4 (summer 1983): 23–38.

————. "Boy Culture: Middle-Class Boyhood in Nineteenth-Century America." In Carnes and Griffen, *Meanings for Manhood,* 15–36.

————. "Learning about Manhood: Gender Ideals and the Middle-Class Family in Nineteenth-Century America." In Mangan and Walvin, *Manliness and Morality,* 35–51.

Roy, R.H. "The Canadian Military Tradition." In *The Canadian Military: A Profile,* ed. H. J. Massey, 6–48. Toronto: Copp, 1972.

Ryan, Mary. *Cradle of the Middle Class: The Family in Oneida County, New York, 1790–1865.* Cambridge: Cambridge University Press, 1981.

Sager, Eric W. "'Buying Cheap and Selling Dear': Merchant Shipowners and the Decline of the Shipping Industry in Atlantic Canada." In *Canadian Papers in Business History,* ed. Peter Baskerville, 59–74. Victoria, BC: University of Victoria, 1989.

Sager, Eric W., and Gerald E. Panting. *Maritime Capital: The Shipping Industry in Atlantic Canada, 1820–1914*. Kingston and Montreal: McGill-Queen's University Press, 1990.

Samson, Daniel, ed. *Contested Countryside: Rural Workers and Modern Society in Atlantic Canada, 1800–1950*. Fredericton, NB: Acadiensis Press, 1994.

Saum, Lewis. *The Popular Mood of Pre–Civil War America*. Westport, CT: Greenwood Press, 1980.

Schull, Joseph, and J. Douglas Gibson. *The Scotiabank Story: A History of the Bank of Nova Scotia, 1832–1918*. Toronto: Macmillan, 1982.

Shaffner, Randolph P. *The Apprenticeship Novel: A Study of "Bildungsroman" as a Regulative Type in Western Literature with a Focus on Three Classic Representatives by Goethe, Maughan, and Mann*. New York: Peter Lang, 1984.

Simons, Judy. *Journals of Literary Women from Fanny Burney to Virginia Woolf*. Iowa City: University of Iowa Press, 1990.

Smith, Paul. *Discerning the Subject*. Minneapolis, MN: University of Minnesota Press, 1988.

Soucy, Donald. *For the Hand or For the Mind? Dawson's and Forrester's Advocacy of Education in Art*. Truro: Nova Scotia Teachers College, 1992.

Spender, Stephen. "Confessions and Autobiography." In Olney, *Autobiography*, 115–122.

Spray, W.A. "John Waddell." In *Dictionary of Canadian Biography*, vol. 10, *1871–1880*, ed. Francess G. Halpenny, 695. Toronto: University of Toronto Press, 1972.

Springhill, John. "Building Character in the British Boy: The Attempt to Extend Christian Manliness to Working-Class Adolescents, 1880–1914." In Mangan and Walvin, *Manliness and Morality*, 52–74.

Stacey, Robert, ed. *William G.R. Hind: The Pictou Sketchbook Le Carnet Pictou*. Windsor, NS: Art Gallery of Windsor, 1990.

Sutherland, David. "Halifax Merchants and the Pursuit of Development, 1783–1850." *Canadian Historical Review* 59, no. 1 (March 1978): 1–17.

———. "The Merchants of Halifax 1815–1850: A Commercial Class in Pursuit of Metropolitan Status." PhD diss., University of Toronto, 1975.

Sutherland, Neil. *Children in English-Canadian Society: Framing the Twentieth Century Consensus*. Toronto: University of Toronto Press, 1976.

Taylor, Charles. *Sources of the Self: The Making of the Modern Identity*. Cambridge: Harvard University Press, 1989.

Thompson, F.M.L. *The Rise of Respectable Society: A Social History of Victorian Britain, 1830–1900*. London: Fontana, 1988.

Tosh, John. *A Man's Place: Masculinity and the Middle-Class Home in Victorian England*. New Haven and London: Yale University Press, 1999.

———. "What Should Historians Do with Masculinity? Reflections on Nineteenth-Century Britain." *History Workshop* 38 (autumn 1994): 179–202.

Turner, Frank M. *Contesting Cultural Authority: Essays in Victorian Intellectual Life*. Cambridge: Cambridge University Press, 1993.

Van Die, Marguerite. *An Evangelical Mind: Nathaniel Burwash and the Methodist Tradition in Canada, 1839–1918*. Kingston and Montreal: McGill-Queen's University Press, 1989.

———. "'The Marks of a Genuine Revival': Religion, Social Change, Gender, and Community in Mid-Victorian Brantford, Ontario." *Canadian Historical Review* 79, no. 3 (September 1998): 524–63.

————, ed. *Religion and Public Life in Canada: Historical and Comparative Perspectives.* Toronto: University of Toronto Press, 2001.

————. "'A Women's Awakening': Evangelical Belief and Female Spirituality in Mid Nineteenth-Century Canada." Paper presented to the 70th annual meeting of the Canadian Historical Association, Kingston, Ontario, 1991.

Vance, Norman. *The Sinews of the Spirit: The Ideal of Christian Manliness in Victorian Literature and Religious Thought.* Cambridge: Cambridge University Press, 1985.

Wand, J.W.C. *Anglicanism in History and Today.* London: Readers Union, 1964.

Ward, Peter W., ed. *A Love Story from 19th c. Quebec: The Diary of George Stephen Jones.* Peterborough, ON: Broadview Press, 1989.

Westfall, William. "Constructing Public Religions at Private Sites: The Anglican Church in the Shadow of Disestablishment." In Van Die, *Religion and Public Life in Canada,* 23–49.

————. *Two Worlds: The Protestant Culture of Nineteenth-Century Ontario.* Kingston and Montreal: McGill-Queen's University Press, 1989.

Willett, T.C. *A Heritage at Risk: The Canadian Militia as a Social Institution.* Boulder, CO and London: Westview Press, 1987.

Wohl, Anthony, ed. *The Victorian Family: Structure and Stresses.* London: Croom Helm, 1978.

Wood, B. Anne. "Constructing Nova Scotia's 'Scotchness': The Centenary Celebrations of Pictou Academy in 1916." *Historical Studies in Education / Revue d'histoire de l'éducation* 6, no. 2 (1994): 281–302.

————. *God, Science, and Schooling: John William Dawson's Pictou Years, 1820–1855.* Truro: Nova Scotia Teachers College, 1991.

————. "Promoting 'Schooled Subjectivities' in 19th c. Nova Scotia." *Acadiensis* 38, no. 2 (spring 1999): 41–57.

————. "Schooling/Credentials for Professional Advancement: A Case Study of Pictou Presbyterians." In *The Contribution of Presbyterianism to the Maritime Provinces of Canada,* ed. Charles H.H. Scobie and G.A. Rawlyk, 54–69. Montreal and Kingston: McGill-Queen's University Press, 1997.

————. "Schooling for Presbyterian Leaders: The College Years of Pictou Academy, 1816–1832." In *The Burning Bush and a Few Acres of Snow: The Presbyterian Contribution to Canadian Life and Culture,* ed. William Klempa, 19–37. Ottawa: Carleton University Press, 1994.

————. "The Significance of Evangelical Presbyterian Politics in the Construction of State Schooling: A Case Study of the Pictou District, 1817–1866." *Acadiensis* 20, no. 2 (spring 1991): 62–85.

————. "Thomas McCulloch's Use of Science in Promoting a Liberal Education." *Acadiensis* 17, no. 1 (autumn 1987): 56–73.

Wood, Henry P. *David Stow and the Glasgow Normal School.* Glasgow: Jordanhill College of Education, 1987.

Wood, Paul. *The Aberdeen Enlightenment and the Arts Curriculum in the Eighteenth Century.* Aberdeen: Aberdeen University Press, 1993.

Wynn, Graeme. "Cultural Stereotypes and Highland Farming in Eastern Nova Scotia 1827–1861." *Histoire Sociale / Social History* 19, no. 37 (May 1986): 39–56.

————"Exciting a Spirit of Emulation among the 'Plodholes': Agricultural Reform in Pre-Confederation Nova Scotia." *Acadiensis* 20, no. 1 (autumn 1990): 5–51.

INDEX

Books in the Studies in Childhood and Family in Canada Series
Published by Wilfrid Laurier University Press

Making Do: Women, Family, and Home in Montreal during the Great Depression by
Denyse Baillargeon, translated by Yvonne Klein • 1999 / xii + 232 /
ISBN: 0-88920-326-1 / ISBN-13: 978-0-88920-326-6

Children in English-Canadian Society: Framing the Twentieth-Century Consensus by
Neil Sutherland with a new foreword by Cynthia Comacchio • 2000 /
xxiv + 336 pp. / illus. / ISBN: 0-88920-351-2 / ISBN-13: 978-0-88920-351-8

Love Strong as Death: Lucy Peel's Canadian Journal, 1833–1836 edited by J.I. Little •
2001 / x + 229 pp. / illus. / ISBN: 0-88920-389-X / ISBN-13: 978-0-88920-389-1

The Challenge of Children's Rights for Canada by Katherine Covell and R. Brian
Howe • 2001 / x + 244 pp. / ISBN: 0-88920-380-6 / ISBN-13: 978-0-88920-380-8

NFB Kids: Portrayals of Children by the National Film Board of Canada, 1939–1989
by Brian J. Low • 2002 / 288 pp. / illus. / ISBN: 0-88920-386-5 /
ISBN-13: 978-0-88920-386-0

Something to Cry About: An Argument against Corporal Punishment of Children in Canada
by Susan M. Turner • 2002 / xix + 317 pp. / ISBN: 0-88920-382-2 /
ISBN-13: 978-0-88920-382-2

Freedom to Play: We Made Our Own Fun edited by Norah L. Lewis • 2002 /
xiv + 210 pp. / ISBN: 0-88920-406-3 / ISBN-13: 978-0-88920-406-5

The Dominion of Youth: Adolescence and the Making of Modern Canada, 1920–1950
by Cynthia Comacchio • 2006 / x + 302 / illus. / ISBN: 0-88920-488-8 /
ISBN-13: 978-0-88920-488-1

Evangelical Balance Sheet: Character, Family, and Business in Mid-Victorian Nova Scotia
by B. Anne Wood • 2006 / xxx + 198 / illus. / ISBN: 0-88920-500-0 /
ISBN-13: 978-0-88920-500-0

Yacovone, Donald. "Abolitionists and the 'Language of Fraternal Love.'" In Carnes and Griffen, *Meanings for Manhood*, 85–95.